# THE SPECTRUM OF ENGLISH MURDER

# THE SPECTRUM OF ENGLISH MURDER

*The Detective Fiction of
Henry Lancelot Aubrey-Fletcher
and G. D. H. and Margaret Cole*

## CURTIS EVANS

**COACHWHIP PUBLICATIONS**
Greenville, Ohio

*The Spectrum of English Murder*, by Curtis Evans
Copyright © 2015 Curtis Evans
All rights reserved.

Front cover: W. L. F. Wastell, Lord Mayor (Royal Photographic Society Collection / National Media Museum); Jarrow marchers (National Media Museum); Flintlock (Konstantin Kirillov); Dagger (Ermess)

ISBN 1-61646-297-3
ISBN-13 978-1-61646-297-0

CoachwhipBooks.com

## CONTENTS

INTRODUCTION — 7
Death on the Right, Death on the Left: Ideology and Aesthetics in Golden Age Detective Fiction

CHAPTER ONE — 13
Death on the Right: Henry Lancelot Aubrey-Fletcher (1887-1969)

CHAPTER TWO — 115
Death on the Left: G. D. H. and Margaret Cole (1889-1959/1893-1980)

APPENDIX I — 223
Crime Genre Works by Henry Lancelot Aubrey-Fletcher

APPENDIX II — 225
Crime Genre Works by G. D. H. and Margaret Cole

BIBLIOGRAPHY — 229

INDEX — 237

DEDICATED

to Edward Aubrey-Fletcher with best wishes,
on the happy occasion of his 85th birthday

*and*

in memory of those who died 75 years ago
in the *Arandora Star* tragedy.

# INTRODUCTION

## Death on the Right, Death on the Left: Ideology and Aesthetics in Golden Age Detective Fiction

THAT THE BRITISH GOLDEN AGE of detective fiction was politically and socially conservative is a verity of many mystery genre histories, from the influential popular early-1970s studies by Colin Watson (*Snobbery with Violence: English Crime Stories and Their Audience*, 1971) and Julian Symons (*Bloody Murder: From the Detective Story to the Crime Novel*, 1972) to more recent popular studies by P. D. James (*Talking about Detective Fiction*, 2009) and Lucy Worsley (*A Very British Murder: The Story of a National Obsession*, 2013). While some academic works have challenged aspects of this view, many others have simply echoed it.[1]

In my book *Masters of the "Humdrum" Mystery: Cecil John Charles Street, Freeman Wills Crofts, Alfred Walter Stewart and the British Detective Novel, 1920-1961* (2012), one of my goals was to show how these three Golden Age British "Humdrums"—so dubbed by Julian Symons because in their mysteries they emphasized puzzles over purely literary features—were not actually the pillars of political and social orthodoxy they have been assumed to be but were, rather, much more varied in their thought, as they expressed it in their genre writing. My book manuscript originally included two additional chapters, one on Sir Henry Lancelot

---

[1] For a discussion of the historiography of Golden Age detective fiction, see my book *Masters of the "Humdrum" Mystery: Cecil John Charles Street, Freeman Wills Crofts, Alfred Walter Stewart and the British Detective Novel, 1920-1961* (Jefferson, NC: McFarland, 2012), 5-44.

Aubrey-Fletcher (1887-1969), an English baronet who wrote detective fiction as "Henry Wade," and one on G. D. H. and Margaret Cole (1889-1959/1893-1980), a prominent English socialist intellectual couple who dabbled in detective fiction. My publisher cut these two chapters on length grounds (even without them the manuscript numbered something over 150,000 words) and because I classified Wade and the Coles as "false Humdrums," i.e., writers customarily labeled Humdrums who in fact were not such. I have decided to publish these two long chapters as a separate book, *The Spectrum of English Murder: The Detective Fiction of Henry Lancelot Aubrey-Fletcher and G. D. H. and Margaret Cole*. Both Aubrey-Fletcher, a conservative landed baronet, and the Coles, academic socialist intellectuals, are unjustly neglected mystery writers from the English Golden Age whose works challenge the traditional view of English Golden Age detective fiction as both aesthetically and politically reactionary.[2]

In his Henry Wade mysteries Henry Lancelot Aubrey-Fletcher grew increasingly restive with the Golden Age puzzle form, and he helped pioneer key new developments in the genre, namely the police procedural novel, where emphasis is placed on the realistic depiction of police investigations of crime, and the crime novel, where the puzzle is subordinated to deeper treatments of purely literary elements, such as theme, character and setting. As early as 1931, in the middle of the Golden Age of classical detective fiction, a Henry Wade detective novel, *No Friendly Drop*, was enthusiastically praised in the British journal *Truth* for precisely the literary qualities that so often are assumed to be absent from the work of the writers styled "Humdrum." While the *Truth* reviewer found the novel's mystery plot "ingenious and well thought-out," s/he was most impressed with the human story. "The people with whom [the novel] deals are just the sort you might easily meet in everyday life," the reviewer declared. The novel was "no mere

---

[2] Like Cecil John Charles Street, Freeman Wills Crofts and Alfred Walter Stewart, not to mention such luminaries as Agatha Christie, Dorothy L. Sayers and G. K. Chesterton, Aubrey-Fletcher and the Coles were charter members of Britain's Detection Club, an organization, founded in 1930, of the country's leading detective novelists.

mechanical jig-saw puzzle but a really good story with a latent undercurrent of genuine human tragedy that, even apart from its detective interest, would make it worth reading."[3]

The *Truth* reviewer's insights are penetrating ones. While "Henry Wade" produced some of the most finely crafted puzzle-oriented detective novels of the Golden Age, even in his earlier years as a writer he also included more purely literary elements in his genre tales. Over the 1930s Wade began experimenting with the mystery form, much in the way Dorothy L. Sayers was doing (though Wade in my view actually was more of an innovator). By 1940, he had added to his puzzle masterworks significant examples of police procedural and crime novels. Far from being a traditionalist "Humdrum," Henry Wade was one of the most committed and talented innovators of the Golden Age generation of crime writers, and he today remains a figure of significance in the history of the genre, for those who are truly familiar with his work.

Additionally, in his fiction Wade was a thoughtful observer of the English scene from the mid-1920s to the mid-1950s, one who incisively chronicled over this period the decline of his country's landed gentry class and the baneful impact on society of two world wars. Wade laments the landed gentry's decline, but he recognizes at the same time that this group's own flaws facilitated the process. Moreover, in his books Wade forthrightly examines such social ills as English civic corruption (including in the police force) and anti-Semitism. With the ascendance to power of the Labour party in 1945, Wade's works became more predictably "conservative," but even these books offer much keen analysis of social ills.

Although G. D. H. and Margaret Cole never had the genre ambitions of Henry Wade, their classification as Humdrums is a similarly faulty one. With the Coles, husband-and-wife academic socialists, overt political writing always came first, their mysteries being composed, as Margaret Cole stated, for relaxation and relatively modest monetary remuneration. Unlike the true Humdrums, the Coles in their mysteries evinced less interest in technical,

---

[3] The quotations from the *Truth* review are drawn from a quoted excerpt found in the back matter of Henry Wade, *The Hanging Captain* (London: Constable, 1932).

material detail; and, with a few notable exceptions like G. D. H. Cole's first (and solo) detective novel, *The Brooklyn Murders* (1923), a Freeman Wills Crofts pastiche, and a later Cole work from 1940, *Counterpoint Murder*, they rarely structured their works around highly complex plots.[4] The two writers are more accurately seen, along with Michael Innes and Ronald Knox, as Golden Age academic "farceurs" (to use another of Julian Symons' categorizations), because, on the purely literary level, their novels are most distinguishable today for their light satire and humor. In this vein the pair produced some fine mystery tales.

Significantly, much of the Coles' satire in their detective fiction is political in nature. G. D. H. and Margaret Cole were two of the most committed and prominent socialist intellectuals in twentieth-century England, and one should hardly have expected that they would have completely set aside their politics when writing their mysteries. Though the Coles were part of England's cultural elite and reflected some of the flaws characteristic of many in that class (including, in Margaret Cole's case, an offputtingly condescending attitude to servants), they nevertheless consciously made their detective fiction a rich repository of socialist sentiment, mocking titans of industry, lords of land, conservative politicians, militant military officers, establishment ecclesiastics and xenophobes of all stripes. In the third edition of Julian Symons' *Bloody Murder*, Symons states that the Coles' mystery tales "never treated seriously the social realities with which in life they were so much concerned" (a revision of Symons' claim in the first edition that the Coles "ignored" these social realities), but the fact is that the Coles in their detective fiction frequently used satire and humor to make points about social inequities and injustices; and it is high time that they received due credit for their having done so.[5]

---

[4] *Counterpoint Murder* is the only detective novel by the Coles that really bears comparison, in terms of inspired, highly complex plotting ingenuity, with the best "Humdrum" works.

[5] Julian Symons, *Bloody Murder: From the Detective Story to the Crime Novel* (1972; rpnt, New York: Mysterious Press, 1993), 118.

With a single exception—Henry Wade's fine novel *Lonely Magdalen*—the detective fiction of Henry Wade and G. D. H. and Margaret Cole remains out-of-print today, even as books by inferior writers from the Golden Age are being reprinted and even lauded. I hope that this situation will soon be rectified and that Henry Wade and the Coles, like the writers I discuss in *Masters of the "Humdrum" Mystery*, will fully see the light again, long after the closing of detective fiction's Golden Age.

                                        Curtis Evans
                                        Germantown, TN
                                        August 17, 2014

NOTE ON SPOILERS

Occasionally in the text I discuss elements of mystery solutions. When this is done, these discussions are signposted *SPOILERS* and *END SPOILERS*, in order to give readers the opportunity to avoid these sections of the text if so desired.

# CHAPTER 1 // DEATH ON THE RIGHT

## Henry Lancelot Aubrey-Fletcher
## (1887-1969)

### Introduction
### The Baronet Who Wrote Detective Fiction

That country houses are a favored setting of Golden Age British detective novels has long been a critical truism. Although the country house paradigm exaggerates the significance of a setting that had already become clichéd in Britain by the 1930s, it nevertheless is true that country houses saw a sizable share of fictional British murder in the Golden Age period, particularly in the 1920s. Very few of the British writers of Golden Age mystery fiction, however, sprang from country houses and the landed aristocracy and gentry traditionally associated with them. Perhaps the most conspicuous exception to this historical fact is Henry Lancelot Aubrey-Fletcher, sixth Baronet of Clea, who under the pseudonym Henry Wade wrote twenty crime novels between 1926 and 1957, including some half-dozen genre masterpieces. During a crime-writing career lasting three decades, "Henry Wade" was enthusiastically praised as "one of the best and soundest detective writers" and Wade's novels were confidently placed "at the top of the [detective story class]."[1]

After Aubrey-Fletcher retired from fiction writing in his seventieth year, the Henry Wade books enjoyed two brief printing revivals, one in the early seventies in Britain and another in the

---

[1] The critical praise is drawn from the front matter in Henry Wade, *Here Comes the Copper* (1938; rpnt., London: Hutchinson, 1972). Two other titled Golden Age British

United States in the mid-eighties (the latter as part of Harper Collins' HarperPerennial series). Yet neither these short-lived resurrections in print nor the esteem in which Henry Wade has been held over the decades by collectors and such discriminating genre writers and critics as Dorothy L. Sayers, Francis Iles, Anthony Boucher, Michael Gilbert, Jacques Barzun and (more recently) Martin Edwards has managed to secure the author a sure place in the Golden Age firmament, either in the estimation of academic critics or of the larger lay reading public. This failure in perception on the part of the former group is particularly odd, as Henry Wade novels illustrate as well as any of the period the transition in the mystery genre from, as Julian Symons put it, the detective story to the crime novel—a transition typically celebrated by the academic critics who have followed in Symons' wake. Symons himself dismissively classified Wade as a "Humdrum" detective novelist (and not even the best of them—that title went to Freeman Wills Crofts), while a more recent academic synthesizer afforded the author only an ill-informed and grudging acknowledgement of the role he played in developing the "police procedural" mystery

(cont.) detective novelists that come to mind are Ronald Gorell Barnes, 3rd Baron Gorell (1884-1963), and Nigel Amyas Orde-Powlett, 6th Baron Bolton (1900-1963). Both men were, like Aubrey-Fletcher, greatly impacted by the First World War, in their own cases succeeding to their titles through the deaths in battle of elder brothers. Barnes served in the Great War as well, while Orde-Powlett was a military cadet. Both wrote war poetry in addition to detective novels. Orde-Powlett's two detective novels, *Driven to Death* (1931) and *The Cast to Death* (1932) are forgotten today, as are the dozen by Lord Gorell, though in fact two of Gorell's mystery tales, *In the Night* (1917) and *The Devouring Fire* (1928), made strong impressions in England in their day and Gorell became a founding member of the Detection Club in 1930, later serving as co-president of the Club between 1958 and his death in 1963. (This was because he assisted his immeasurably better known but shy co-president, Agatha Christie, with public speaking and demanded co-presidential status.) For a dismissive description of Gorell's involvement with the Detection Club, see the introduction by Christianna Brand (1907-1988), a prominent mystery writer and Detection Club member, to the 1979 Gregg reprint of the Detection Club joint novel *The Floating Admiral* (1932). Brand derisively dubbed the Baron "Lord Sheep" (p. vii). Beyond doubt, neither Gorell nor Orde-Powlett had anywhere near the sort of influence on the genre that Aubrey-Fletcher had.

subgenre. In truth, Aubrey-Fletcher's achievement as a mystery writer is three-fold: first, he fashioned several brilliant puzzle novels, jewels in the Golden Age crown; second, he significantly contributed to the development of the crime novel with realistic tales of police procedure and of character; and third, he powerfully chronicled in both his detective and crime fiction the decline and fall of England's traditional power elite, its landed aristocracy and gentry. Any one of these accomplishments would justly compel critical praise for "Henry Wade"; three grouped together in the hands of one British writer necessarily make that writer one of the most accomplished figures in Britain's Golden Age of mystery fiction.

Henry Lancelot Aubrey-Fletcher's ancestry was a distinguished one, as a cursory perusal of the Aubrey-Fletcher entry in *Burke's Peerage and Baronetage* will reveal. The family title was created in 1782 for Henry Fletcher, one of the directors of the East India Company and a Member of Parliament from Cumberland for thirty-four years. The name Henry afterwards was given to the next six generations of eldest sons in the family, making a potentially confusing genealogy. The author's uncle and the fourth Baronet, Henry Aubrey-Fletcher (the family took the additional surname Aubrey upon inheriting Aubrey estates in 1903), like the original Sir Henry was a longtime parliamentarian, serving in the Commons from 1880 until his death in 1910.[2]

Upon the fourth Baronet's dying without issue, the family title descended to his younger brother, Lancelot. Lancelot Aubrey-Fletcher, as he was now known, as a younger man would have had no great expectation of inheriting his married brother's title. He became an attorney and resided at Hookwood House in Limpsfield, Surrey and later Westfield Lodge in Bracknell, Berkshire. His first wife died after only three years of marriage, leaving him no offspring. His second wife, Emily Harriet Wade, whom he married in

---

[2] For genealogical information on Henry Lancelot Aubrey Fletcher and the Aubrey-Fletcher family, see *thePeerage.com, a Genealogical Survey of the Peerage of Britain as well as the Royal Families of Europe* (http://www.thepeerage.com).

1882, gave him two children, Kathleen Margaret (1884) and Henry Lancelot (1887). Emily Wade was one of fourteen children of Reverend Nugent Wade, rector of St. Anne's, Soho and canon of Bristol and a prominent member of the Anglo-Catholic Oxford Movement. Reverend Wade, it is noted, "founded the St. Barnabas' House of Charity in Soho, which ministered to prostitutes, and St. Mary's Crown Street, an Anglo-Catholic centre in a slum district within the parish of Soho. He made St. Anne's Soho a gathering place for the new generation of Anglo-Catholics in London." Although it would seem unlikely that young Henry Lancelot knew his maternal grandfather well, he would later take the name "Wade" for his pseudonymous surname. A younger brother of Emily's was George Edward Wade, a prominent painter and sculptor whose last work, addressing the theme of World War One, was the Stourbridge War Memorial (1931).[3] Influence from his uncle George Wade perhaps may be seen in the Henry Wade novels *Mist on the Saltings*, where the central character is a painter, and the story "These Artists!", which concerns a sculptor.

At Hookwood, the family home for at least half the decade of the 1890s, Lancelot Fletcher and his family would appear to have lived comfortable lives. Hookwood, described in 1889 as a "modest country-house," was a Georgian brick mansion that stood in its own grounds behind the Norman church in Limpsfield, a lovely Surrey village. Here Scottish-born statesman and historian Mountstuart Elphinstone had lived while he wrote his highly-regarded two-volume *History of India*. In 1891, seven servants staffed the house for the Fletchers, including a cook, kitchen maid, parlourmaid, housemaid, ladies maid, nurse and, living over the stables, a coachman. Still, there is no question but that the family moved up in the world after Lancelot became Baronet in 1910 and

---

[3] On Nugent Wade, see *R. C. Singleton's Diary (1847): Diary of a Victorian Education Reformer*, http://singletonsdiary.wordpress.com/2009/03/04/nugent-wade. On George Edward Wade, see "George Wade," http://www.drawpaintsculpt.com/artist-biographies/george-wade.

moved to Buckinghamshire to reside in a majestic Palladian mansion, Chilton House, which Sir Henry had inherited, along with the surname Aubrey, from Charles Aubrey in 1903. Despite assuming the title at the relatively advanced age of sixty-four, Lancelot Aubrey-Fletcher held it for twenty-seven years, until his own death, at the venerable age of ninety, in 1937; whereupon it passed to his forty-nine year old son, Major (as he was known by this time) Henry Lancelot Aubrey-Fletcher.[4]

As it did with so many members of his generation, the Great War proved a momentous event in Henry Lancelot Aubrey-Fletcher's life. The effect of the First World War on English society is a recurring theme throughout the Henry Wade novels of the Twenties and Thirties. Before war came, Aubrey-Fletcher received the Eton and Oxford badge of learning customary to his social class. Concerning his Oxford education, the author later wrote regretfully to the scholarly Dorothy L. Sayers, mystery author and translator of Dante, that he had not taken scholarship sufficiently seriously at the time. One college activity in which he participated enthusiastically, however, was the Oxford University Dramatic Society (OUDS). Still in existence today is a photograph of Aubrey-Fletcher as Bottom, the rustic transformed into an ass in Shakespeare's *A Midsummer Night's Dream*, in which the future baronet's head indeed is covered with a prop ass's head.[5]

---

[4] J. W. Kaye, *Lives of Indian Officers*, Vol. I (London: W. H. Allen, 1889), 445; 1891 English Census, Class RG12, Piece 583, Folio 80, Page 13, GSU roll 6095693. For photos of Chilton House, see *Buckinghamshire Town & Village Photos*, http://www.countyviews.com/bucks/index.htm and http://www.chiltonhouse.co.uk.

[5] On Henry Lancelot Aubrey-Fletcher's performance as Bottom, see Edward Aubrey-Fletcher to Curtis J. Evans, 28 November 2004, letter in possession of author. Although Oxford does not play a great role in Henry Wade's crime fiction, the institution figures centrally in one of his better John Poole short stories, "The Missing Undergraduate," which reads rather like a Dorothy L. Sayers or Michael Innes tale. It is found in Wade's 1933 short story collection, *Policeman's Lot*.

After leaving Oxford in 1908, Henry Lancelot joined the 1st Battalion of the elite Grenadier Guards, the most senior regiment in the infantry. Three years later, he wed Mary Augusta Chilton, a daughter of the Reverend Robert William Chilton, Rector at Great Horkesley, Essex (village settings in coastal, eastern England would be memorably evoked by the author in his novels *Mist on the Saltings* and *New Graves at Great Norne*). When war came in 1914, Aubrey-Fletcher left for France with his battalion, leaving behind his wife and two little sons. During the war he rose to become, as his fellow author of detective fiction John Street had in the Royal Artillery, a Major. He served with distinction in the conflict, suffering two wounds and receiving the French Croix de Guerre and the Distinguished Service Order. After the war's conclusion Major Aubrey-Fletcher returned to the life of a landed gentleman at Chilton House. However, the life the heir presumptive led by no means was one of idleness. Although nearly twenty years were to pass before he succeeded to the Baronetcy, Aubrey-Fletcher was extensively involved in county affairs throughout this period, serving at various times as a County Alderman (experience he used in *The Dying Alderman*), the High Sheriff of Buckinghamshire (experience he used in *The High Sheriff*) and a member of the Buckinghamshire County Council. As Chairman of the Finance Committee of the latter organization, Aubrey-Fletcher earned yet another distinction: hostile editorial commentary from *Land and Liberty*, the land reform journal published by single tax advocate John Paul.[6] Opposition to what he viewed as confiscatory taxes aimed at the landed aristocracy was another concern to which the author gave voice in his Henry Wade tales, particularly in the novel *Too Soon to Die*, written after the Labour Party assumed control of the government in 1945 and pushed through social legislation deemed ruinous by British conservatives.

---

[6] Buckinghamshire Lieutenancy, Permanent Lieutenants for Buckinghamshire, Major Sir Henry Lancelot Aubrey-Fletcher Bt. CVO DSO (1887-1969), Lieutenant 1954-1961, http://www.buckscc.gov.uk/lieutenancy/permanent_lieuten-ants/major_sir_henry_lancelot.htm; *Land & Liberty* 44 (February 1937): 21.

Among Aubrey-Fletcher's non-civic organizations at this time was the First Editions Club, which had been founded in 1922, one of the co-founders being A. J. A. Symons, the elder brother of Julian Symons. Aubrey-Fletcher was a member of this club and a keen book collector. Sprinkled throughout Henry Wade novels are literary references, including some favorable ones to then modern-day authors, rather a rarity among Golden Age mystery writers. A Sotheby catalogue of books Aubrey-Fletcher offered for sale in 1935 reveals a heavy concentration in the Elizabethan, Jacobean and Georgian periods.[7] Whether these books were ones collected by Aubrey-Fletcher himself or whether he simply was clearing out, with permission from his elderly father, collections of family forebears is not clear, but, in any event, they are suggestive of the family's large holdings at this time.

Aubrey-Fletcher was as keen a huntsman as a book collector. He relished the pursuit of foxes in the famed Bicester Hunt (a fifty-mile area of country stretching from Aylesbury to Daventry and encompassing parts of Buckinghamshire, Oxfordshire, Warwickshire and Northamptonshire) and of stags in Scotland, more experience which found its way into his novels. *The High Sheriff* deals extensively with horse and hound country society, while the horrific murder that takes place during the stag "gralloching" (disemboweling) in *Heir Presumptive* was drawn by the author from an actual fatal hunting accident of which he was aware. "[My father] always taught me to approach a stag which had been shot with great care in case it kicked out," recalls Edward Aubrey-Fletcher, the author's youngest (and sole surviving) child. Edward also remembers the

---

7 *The Book Collector's Quarterly* 5 (Jan.-Mar. 1935): 47. Included in the Sotheby sale were works by Aphra Behn, Francis Beaumont, James Boswell, Edmund Burke, Cervantes, Colley Cibber, William Congreve, Daniel Defoe, John Dennis, Henry Fielding, John Gay, William Godwin, Thomas Hutchinson (a colonial governor of Massachusetts), Samuel Johnson, John Milton, Montaigne, David Ramsay (an early American historian), Shakespeare, Thomas Shadwell, Thomas Southerne, Richard Steele, John Vanbrugh and George Whitefield. Sotheby & Co., *Catalogue of Printed Books and a Few Manuscripts* (1935), 25-33.

moving two minutes silences held "when the Bicester Hounds used to meet in front of Chilton House on Armistice Day."[8]

After his father's death Sir Henry Lancelot Aubrey-Fletcher and his family resided at Chilton House for only a short time. The Manor of Chilton had been granted by William the Conqueror to Walter Gifford in 1066—it is listed in the *Domesday Book*—and structural evidence suggests that parts of the house date back to the twelfth century. However, Chilton underwent from 1740-51 a complete remodeling in the Palladian style, making it into a great symmetrical mansion in the classical manner, with a pilastered central block and pedimented doorway and great matching wings on either side—the sort of ultra-rational country house beloved by Golden Age detective novelists. With the onset of a second World War, however, the family retired from Chilton House to Townhill, a former farmhouse "just over the garden wall," in the words of Edward Aubrey-Fletcher, that had been restored in the Thirties. During the war, Chilton House was occupied by an order of Irish nuns, who used the church as a school. The family never returned to reside in their home of over forty years, instead renting it to tenants (decades later the house would be restored by Sir Henry Lancelot's grandson and the eighth Baronet, Sir Henry Egerton Aubrey-Fletcher, who currently with his wife manages the grand mansion as a nursing home). Two of the best Henry Wade novels from the 1950s, *Diplomat's Folly* (1951, but set in 1947) and *Too Soon to Die* (1953, but set in 1949-50) chronicle the impending collapse of the country house regime under the burdens of post-war austerity and taxation. The former novel opens with a description of an elegant dinner for eight in the oak-paneled dining-room of Shackley Manor:

> Silver and fine glass glittered in the light of candles on the long refectory table. In the shadows an elderly butler moved silently and efficiently about his duties, helped by a young maid; in the large open

---

[8] Edward Aubrey-Fletcher to Curtis J. Evans, 28 November 2004.

fire-place logs of generous size threw up tongues of blue and yellow flame, adding cheerfulness to the scene.

At first glance one might have thought that this was England in 1937 or thereabouts—pre-Munich. But it was not; it was facade—the brave face presented by Major-General Vane Tabbard to a dirty and disappointing world.[9]

Despite the pessimistic view of the modern world that the author voiced in his post-World War Two novels (and, for that matter, his pre-World War Two novels), the Aubrey-Fletchers maintained themselves better than many other members of their social class. Chilton House was no longer family-occupied, but Aubrey-Fletcher's sons all graduated Eton and Oxford, like their father, and the three eldest sons, again like their father, served in and survived *their* World War, two in the Grenadier Guards, one in the Royal Air Force (the youngest son, Edward Aubrey-Fletcher, having been born in 1930 of course was not involved in World War Two, but he too served in the Grenadier Guards after graduating from Oxford). Aubrey-Fletcher himself served as Lord-Lieutenant of Buckinghamshire from 1954 to 1961, a crowning achievement in his list of civil honors.[10] Moreover, unlike his "Humdrum" contemporaries, John Street and Freeman Wills Crofts, Aubrey-Fletcher's literary work enjoyed a post-war critical revival. Indeed, in the United States, a country where "Henry Wade" had enjoyed only indifferent success, Macmillan in the 1950s published five of his six newest novels; and two of his 1930s classics, *Heir Presumptive* and *No Friendly Drop*, were championed by the influential American critic Anthony Boucher and reprinted in Macmillan's Murder Revisited series. This revived acclaim notwithstanding,

---

[9] "Parishes, Chilton," in William Page, ed., *A History of the County of Buckinghamshire*, Vol. 4 (London: St. Catherine Press, 1927), 22-27; Edward Aubrey-Fletcher to Curtis Evans, 28 November 2004; Henry Wade, *Diplomat's Folly* (London: Constable, 1951), 1.
[10] Edward Aubrey-Fletcher to Curtis J. Evans, 28 November 2004.

Aubrey-Fletcher ceased writing mystery fiction with *The Litmore Snatch* in 1957, authoring no works from that point until his death in 1969.

Henry Wade's fame faded quickly in the 1960s, yet several keen critics of the genre kept his name alive among connoisseurs. In his introduction to a 1965 reprinting of *Lonely Magdalen* (part of the Classics of Detection and Adventure series), Michael Gilbert, himself a respected Silver-Age mystery fiction writer, praised the author's impressive knowledge and handling of police procedure. Three years later, critic Charles Shibuk acknowledged Wade as "a pioneer of historical significance" and also "a writer of extreme merit." Finally, in 1971, Jacques Barzun and Wendell Hertig Taylor in their *Catalogue of Crime* ringingly proclaimed "Wade one of the great figures of the classical period," asserting that his "plots, characters, situations and means rank with the best, while his prose has elegance and force."[11] Influenced by the latter's advocacy, HarperCollins reprinted seven of Henry Wade's titles in attractive paperback editions in the 1980s (unfortunately, the publisher omitted several of his best novels, including *The Dying Alderman*, *No Friendly Drop*, *The High Sheriff* and *Lonely Magdalen*), but the author had, until very recently, with the publication by a small press of a lone Wade novel, *Lonely Magdalen*, remained entirely out of print since.

### The Detective Fiction of Henry Wade

Henry Wade's very first detective novel, *The Verdict of You All* (1926), announced the arrival in the mystery genre of an original voice, one that would gain in strength with each published book over the next several years, until the author attained master status. The dedication of *The Verdict of You All*, made "in all sympathy to the innocent and still more to the guilty," strikes an unusual

---

[11] Charles Shibuk, "Henry Wade," in Francis M. Nevins, Jr., *The Mystery Writer's Art* (Bowling Green, OH: Popular Press, 1970), 96; Jacques Barzun and Wendell Hertig Taylor, *A Catalogue of Crime* (New York: Harper & Row, 1971), 418.

note, one amplified by its twist in the tail conclusion. Nevertheless, the novel opens in highly traditional fashion, with the butler at St. Margaret's Lodge discovering financier Sir John Smethurst murdered in his study (a "rough plan" of the scene of the murder is included in the book for the reader's convenience). The murder implement is that classic of Golden Age detective fiction, the blunt instrument. Potential suspects include the dead man's private secretary, Geoffrey Hastings, an attractive widow, Rosamund Barretta, and Samuel McCorquodale, a rival financier and competitor with Hastings for the hand of Smethurt's daughter, Emily. All highly traditional, but things soon take a more unusual turn.

{SPOILERS} About two-thirds of the way through the novel, Hastings is arrested and brought to trial. For five chapters, the ebb and flow of Hastings' fortunes at the trial is detailed. When things look darkest for Hastings, Madame Barretta takes the stand to testify that the private secretary is her lover and that he was in her company on the evening of the murder (this information is corroborated by Barretta's maid). Hastings is acquitted and leaves the country with Madame Barretta, first making sure that the investigating inspector receives a letter from him revealing that he indeed is the murderer of Sir John Smethurst, after all! As the prosecution had shown, Hastings had been speculating heavily and was deeply in debt. To prevent the awarding of a Rio concession by the Brazilian government to Smethurst—an act that would have proved ruinous to Hastings' financial interests—Hastings found it necessary to murder his employer. After bludgeoning Smethurst with a life preserver, Hastings stood at the door of the study and pretended to carry on a conversation with his dead employer, knowing that the butler would pass by farther down the hall and witness the "conversation." Additionally, Hastings had rigged a device in the study to make it appear that Smethurst was alive for some time after he actually had been murdered. When brought to trial, Hastings was able to produce his "alibi" with Madame Barretta (of course Smethurst already had been murdered by this time) and secure acquittal, preventing him from ever being tried again for his crime. {END SPOILERS}

*The Verdict of You All* has faults, not surprising in a first novel. The setting is highly conventional and most of the the characters rather stock. The involved mechanics would strike many modern readers as implausibly contrived. Overall, there is an uncertainty of tone in a novel that at times seems meant to be a mordant reflection on the legal system, and at others seems almost farcical, with the author indulging in labored satire at the expense of a pretentious butler as well as in the overly whimsical naming of characters and places (a police constable is named Raffles, a fussy and pompous doctor Blathermore, a bank manager Crabbitt, a Cockney gardener Wollop, a manservant Raggle, a judge Ballence, a pair of attorneys Deeping Waters and Isaac Sharpe—the latter representing the Scots Jew Samuel McCorquodale—and a drunkard Flush, while a country vicar's widow hails from "Dumbleton-cum-Bumble"). Moreover, the novel displays a regrettable instance of anti-Semitism in Wade's flippant announcement that Geoffrey Hastings "loved Scotland as much as he hated Palestine" (this is an attempt partially to explain Hastings' ambivalence toward Samuel McCorquodale); and the writing is sometimes stilted when amorous matters and female allurements are touched upon, as when we are told of Rosamund Barretta that "her features and her figure were alike of a classical loveliness, while her complexion, if lacking the youthful freshness of Emily's, yet needed little help from art to complete a radiant picture."[12]

An example of the artificiality characteristic of the Golden Age country house narrative that still clings to *The Verdict of You All* can be seen in the Freeman Wills Crofts-like concern Wade allows his characters over the important matter of regular consumption of meals in the aftermath of a murder:

> "Thanks, Rosa. . . . But look here, seriously, you must have some breakfast. It's jolly bad to go without your proper meals.

---

[12] Henry Wade, *The Verdict of You All* (1926; New York: Payson & Clarke, 1927), 54-55, 80.

"I quite agree, dear, it is. Of course you've had yours?"

Emily smiled wanly.

"No, I haven't. I couldn't. But you could and you must. I'll ring and tell Jackson. Omelette?"

"Darling, I'll have some of it if you will—not otherwise. Even if it's only a cup of coffee and a piece of toast, it'll keep you going till you feel up to something more."

"All right, I'll try," said Emily.[13]

In contrast to Freeman Wills Crofts and a number of other Golden Age writers, Wade soon learned to dispense with such trivialities and offer readers a more sophisticated, controlled narrative.

{SPOILERS} Despite its flaws, *The Verdict of You All* remains a striking work within the genre for its cynicism. In the novel Wade allows—with something approaching benevolent indulgence—a cold-blooded, premeditated murderer to blithely escape unscathed by the grinding mills of justice. Hastings' confession to Inspector Dobson—made after he has been safely acquitted and has departed England for greener, foreign shores with his paramour—is a masterpiece of ruthless amorality: "I don't think I'm particularly immoral, but I am unmoral. . . . I started plunging [on the stock market] again, and unfortunately [Rosamund Barretta] followed my rotten example, and we were soon both in the soup. . . . Things got so desperate that we decided that the only thing to do was for me to marry Emily Smethurst." When Hastings finds the Rio concession has been offered to Sir John Smethurst, an event that will mean ruin and public humiliation for him, he realizes there is no longer time for his calculated pursuit of Smethurst's daughter. Rather, Sir John himself has to die: "I decided at once that he must

---

[13] Wade, *Verdict*, 58-59. For an amusing commentary on the importance in many Golden Age detective novels of maintaining one's regular meal regimen during a murder investigation, see H. R. F. Keating, *The Bedside Companion Book to Crime* (New York and London: Mysterious Press, 1989), 101-105.

never get that concession. . . . I made an excuse to get him to the writing table and then hit him on the back of the head—I knew just where and how hard to hit him—with the life-preserver." Hastings dismisses his treatment of Emily—the woman he cynically pursued before murdering her father—with a figurative shrug: "She won't break her heart over me—she was a cold-blooded fish, really."[14]

As the above discussion reveals, Wade's bold subversion of genre convention is striking as well in its handling of the "love interest." Normally a reliably bland and boring affair in the hands of such authors as Freeman Wills Crofts, the love interest in *The Verdict of You All* confounds readers' expectations. Falseness and treachery on the part of one of the lovers lies at the heart of the mystery. Instead of lovers reuniting after the young man accused of the murder has been exonerated, in Wade's novel the young man is exonerated, only to reveal that he is indeed guilty after all as he absconds with another woman, the one he truly loved (a middle-aged widow, no less). Emily Smethurst, who in a Crofts' novel would have been amply rewarded at novel's end for her admirable pluckiness, is left utterly in the lurch, dismissed with the cavalierly contemptuous words, "she was a cold-blooded fish, really." {END SPOILERS}

In Wade's second novel, *The Missing Partners* (1928), the author again offers a mixture of the comfortably familiar and the boldly original. *Partners* includes bright young amateur detectives and timetables in classic twenties fashion, yet it also is original in its solution and its depiction of a thuggish policeman. The missing partners of the novel's title are the cousins Henry and Charles Morden, of the Liverpool shipping firm Morden and Morden (Charles actually is the nephew of the wife of Henry Morden's late uncle, who adopted young Charles as his son). Both partners have disappeared when the novel opens, and the police quickly come to suspect that Charles has murdered his cousin Henry and fled the country. Eventually Henry's dead body washes ashore, dreadfully

---

[14] Wade, *Verdict*, 293-294, 296, 305.

injured—"the nose was crushed, one eye had been knocked in, and the jaw was hanging limp"—and Charles, having been discovered and recovered, is detained.[15] A trio of amateur detectives—composed of the bright and modern Helen Mildmay, daughter of Herbert Mildmay, Morden and Morden's office manager and accountant; Tom Fairbanks, Helen's faithful and exploited dogsbody; and William Turnbull, Charles Morden's attorney—sets about exonerating the surviving Morden cousin.

What follows is unquestionably Henry Wade's most Croftsian novel (indeed, the novel gave Wade an undeserved reputation as a follower of Crofts), with occasional thorny passages like the following:

> "Liverpool, 7.5 p.m.—that's the first [train] you could catch. . . . Gets you to Birmingham 9.45. But there's not a train on to Oxford till midnight and even then you have to wait at Oxford from 1.35 p.m. to 7.10 and that doesn't get you to Southampton till 10.31, which is almost sure to be too late . . . this is better. Liverpool 10 p.m., Euston 5 a.m. Waterloo 5.40 a.m. . . . Southampton terminus 8.48. Or you might go to Southampton West and take a taxi—that's the express and gets there at 7.52—yes, that would be much quicker. Now it just depends on what time the Mauretania and the others set sail."[16]

More happily, Wade includes stylistic touches that enliven *The Missing Partners*, and the center of the puzzle does not turn on timetables. While still tending towards stock, the characters are far more robustly presented than those in a Crofts novel (*A Catalogue of Crime* goes so far as to complain of the novel's "disagreeable characters," a criticism that nevertheless supports the

---

[15] Henry Wade, *The Missing Partners*, (London: Constable, 1928), 112.
[16] Wade, *Partners*, 58.

contention that they make an impression on the reader). Helen Mildmay, for example, is far from the conventional bland and dull Crofts "good girl." Rather, she is an aggressive, tough and manipulative professional woman, scorning convention and sentimentality and treating with casual contempt weaker men, such as her doting father, Herbert Mildmay, and her lovelorn follower, Tom Fairbanks. The latter man Helen has entirely in her thrall, so that he even becomes intensely jealous over her admiration for the latest matinee movie idol. "Beastly Dago," he growls of the film star to Helen from his place in the seats, "I can't stick hearing you crack up these oily South American bounders that aren't fit to look at you."[17] When Helen decides that Charles Morden must be exonerated, Tom proves only too willing to do her bidding (though he fears Helen may have more than a mild altruistic interest in Charles), even if it means jeopardizing his clerkship in the Inspectorate of Taxes. For all his pains, however, Tom is just one among many "friends" to Helen.

Helen Mildmay is similarly able—and cheerfully willing—to manipulate her extremely indulgent father, who throughout his life has made great sacrifices for her:

> It was a source of perpetual wonder to [Herbert Mildmay] that two such insignificant people as he and [his wife] could have brought into the world a creature so lovely, so intelligent, so exquisite as this enchanting daughter of his. All the money that he could save from his generous salary . . . was spent upon her upbringing. Her nurse, her governess, her school, her technical college, even her clothes, would not have disgraced the daughter of one of his employers, and it was almost with regret that he consented to her entering the employment of the firm in which he himself had served.[18]

---

[17] Barzun and Taylor, *Catalogue of Crime*, 421; Wade, *Partners*, 3.
[18] Wade, *Partners*, 17-18.

The author allows that Helen loves her father, but decidedly only after the casual fashion of the times: "She was sufficiently grateful to him for all he had done for her; she looked after him as well as her modern education enabled her to, and she was dutiful and obedient whenever it suited her to be. For the rest, she ordered her life according to her own judgment and experience, had her own latchkey, and was very well able to take care of herself." Helen's flippant outspokenness about sexual subjects is a continual source of mortification to Herbert Mildmay, as when she and her father are speculating on the whereabouts of Henry Morden:

> "Slept at the club last night, she says. Sly old fox, I bet he didn't!"
> . . . .
> "I told you he didn't! He's been out on the tiles, the old rip. Ugh, he's not my choice for a *petit ami*—still, it takes all sorts to make the world go round."
> "Helen, really, I must ask you . . ."
> "All right, father, keep your hair on. 'My strength is as the strength of ten, because I don't do all I talk about.' Shakespeare!"

Or when Helen suggests going to the docks to investigate Henry Morden's disappearance:

> "Perhaps I'd better go there, dear. It isn't quite the place for a young girl—they're a rough lot, these dock hands and sailors."
> Helen laughed.
> "'Once aboard the lugger and the girl is mine.' All right, my cautious parent, off you trot and I'll hold the fort. But don't go swapping smutty stories with naughty sailor boys."
> Mr. Mildmay blushed.
> "Helen, dear, I wish you wouldn't talk like that."

"I know, it's so unladylike.... But then you know what we poor typists are."[19]

The character of Superintendent Dodd is even more unconcerned with offending "delicate" feelings. *A Catalogue of Crime* actually targets Dodd for specific criticism on the grounds of disagreeableness. In truth, he comes far closer than most police detectives of the Golden Age to the brutish, potentially dishonest cop Julian Symons advocated depicting in British detective fiction; and whether or not such a depiction is a merit or demerit very much depends on the aesthetic sensibilities of the reader (to this reader, he offers a welcome contrast with the idealized Golden Age norm). On his first appearance in the novel, Superintendent Dodd is described as "a tall, rather stout man, with heavy cheeks, a drooping black moustache, and small eyes." Conceptions of abstract justice mean nothing to Dodd, who is concerned only with securing a conviction and whose personal well of compassion runs quite shallow. A crude bully by nature (as those small eyes are meant to suggest), Dodd has a quick temper and enjoys intimidating citizens when he can. When he thinks Charles Morden's landlady, Mrs. Plunkett, has swept up burnt papers from her tenant's room, his wrath is terrible, at least by Golden Age standards:

> But it was to the grate that the detective first turned his attention; in it was a neatly-made coal "fire," with white paper surround, all ready for lighting. Dodd stared at it, his face slowly turning to a brick red, his small eyes almost disappearing in the swelling flesh. An oath of the first water burst from him; then he turned on his heel and dashed out on to the landing.

---

[19] Ibid., 18, 20-21, 29. Helen's "strength of ten" quotation, which she facetiously attributes to Shakespeare, ironically actually comes from Alfred, Lord Tennyson's poem "Sir Galahad," in which Tennyson pays tribute to the chaste Arthurian knight on grounds Helen herself likely would not have valued as highly as the great Victorian poet. "My strength is as the strength of ten," righteously states Tennyson's Sir Galahad, "Because my heart is pure."

"Hey, you, Plummer, or whatever your silly name is!" he shouted. "What have you done to this grate? I thought you told me he'd burnt papers in it. If you've cleared them away I'll skin you alive."

The horrified landlady leant against the wall and gasped.

"I-I-haven't touched them, sir," she stammered.

"But the grate's clean—newly laid!"

"In the sitting-room, sir?"

"What sitting-room, blast you?"

"Mr. Morden's, sir—next to his bedroom—that's where the fire was."

"Why the hell didn't you say so then?"[20]

When he finds that the charred remains in the sitting-room fireplace are broken "into something like powder," Dodd's first instinct is to direct his frustration against the landlady: "'If that old fool's been nosing about in here, I'll . . .' he began, then checked himself, as if realizing that he had once already allowed his feelings to carry him too far and that there was no sense in antagonizing a useful witness." At another point in the novel, the author reminds readers that "Dodd could always be friendly if there was anything to be gained by it."[21] Even when the Superintendent is polite to a witness, then, it is not from any finer feelings on his part, but rather coarse calculation.

Indeed, it quickly becomes clear that Dodd has no "finer feelings" whatsoever. When he encounters Herbert Mildmay looking "white and shaky" after his ordeal of identifying Henry Morden's horrifically battered and decomposed body, Dodd's words of "comfort" are not much help: "You mustn't let yourself get upset by a little business like that. That's all in a day's work, you know; what should we become if we were turned up by every sea-green stiff we

---

[20] Ibid., 40, 54.
[21] Ibid., 55, 73.

had to handle?"[22] Dodd finds great amusement from his observation, chuckling deeply, though Mildmay fails to see humor in it.

Herbert Mildmay—who, as his name ("mild as the month of May") suggests, is of a nervous and sensitive disposition—becomes the favored target for Dodd's mental torture as the novel progresses. The Superintendent finds "the prospect of a little fun" in intimating that the meek and painfully respectable Mildmay might be the murderer, even though he does not even consider the office manager a serious suspect. Dodd's chief suspect remains Charles Morden, and late in the novel the Superintendent balks at investigating a line of inquiry that might absolve Morden, telling his Chief Constable: "'I don't know that it's exactly our job. It supports Mr. Turnbull's theory rather than ours.'"[23] The Chief Constable is forced to respond shortly to Dodd that "it's our job to find out the truth, even if it doesn't suit our theories. Let me know what you find."

Ultimately a solution is found and a confession obtained, in a fairly-clued denouement that probably few readers will anticipate. On the whole *The Missing Partners* is an impressive performance, though there are a few blemishes here and there. One comparatively minor deception hangs on a character's having a twin, surely rather a cheating device that certainly should have been dispensed with by 1928 in a serious detective novel. Moreover, a Pinkerton detective is named Hiram P. Quackett, continuing an unfortunate tradition in British detective novels of the period of including ponderous humor over improbably cumbersome American names.[24]

{*SPOILERS*} Most tiresome of all is Charles Morden's chivalric determination to sacrifice himself for Henry Morden's patently

---

[22] Ibid, 119.

[23] Ibid., 121, 237.

[24] The unfortunate British mystery tradition of ponderous American names, complete with insistent initials, continues as late as Ruth Rendell's 2002 crime novel *The Babes in the Wood*, where at a possible crime site Rendell's Chief Inspector Wexford discovers a book, *Purity as a Life Goal*, written by an American evangelical Christian named Parker T. Ziegler. One likes to imagine this gentleman is descended maternally from Hiram P. Quackett.

undeserving widow, the scheming Lilith, who makes Helen Mildmay look soft-boiled. Henry and Lilith Morden had planned to have Henry, who was in financial difficulty, fake his murder, framing Charles (of course, Henry ended up *actually* murdered); yet Charles, on learning this unpleasant truth about his adored in-law, tells his attorney he will not have her brought into court, even though what she knows and refuses to disclose would exonerate him. Moreover, he wants to give her James' share of the business, even though she is not legally entitled to it:

> "I'm not going to save my skin by tarring Lilith."
> . . . .
> Turnbull looked at him with dawning, though reluctant, admiration.
> "And you want to make over to her her husband's share in the business?"
> "I do. And if she won't take it as a gift I'll marry her, if she'll have me."
> "My God!" said Turnbull, aloud this time. "You are a white man."

Another description perhaps might occur to the modern reader. Lilith herself, when told the news by an admonishing Helen Mildmay, reacts with scornful mirth: "You're suffering from an overdose of the movies. 'Perfect English gentleman, soul of honour, dies in silence rather than allow a breath of scandal to smirch the name of his lady-love!' You little fool, do you believe that sort of rubbish?"[25] Even 'twenties readers might have had difficulty swallowing Charles Morden's honor or the praise of him as a "white man," as opposed to derision as a damned foolish mutt, but again this is only a minor character implausibility in what is on the whole a bracingly cynical tale. {*END SPOILERS*}

Treachery and honor feature in Henry Wade's third novel, *The Duke of York's Steps* (1929), which has been cited as his best

---

[25] Wade, *Partners*, 242, 248.

detective story. While *Steps* like its predecessors suffers from some period flaws, it nevertheless signals a significant advance by the author in terms of thematic sophistication, being the first of Wade's novels to serve as an explicit critique of modernity; and it also introduces Wade's most important recurring character, Detective-Inspector John Poole. The novel's murder victim, Sir Garth Fratten, is, like Sir John Smethurst of *The Verdict of You All*, a London financier, but he is employed by Wade in a much more interesting manner. Fratten, chairman of the "family" bank bearing his name, symbolizes sturdy, safe, impeccably honest traditionalism in finance and occupies "an assured position in the esteem, not only of [his] exclusive club, but of the 'City' generally." Moreover, he has as well kept up with the times, so that he understands "the rapidly changing conditions of post-war finance." Both "his opinion and his approval" are "valued very highly, not only by individuals, but even at times by the Treasury."[26]

Fratten collapses and dies on the Duke of York's Steps, beneath "the tall column from which the soldier-prince [Prince Frederick, second son of King George III and noted military reformer during the Napoleonic Wars] gazed sadly out over the London that had forgotten him." His doctor, Sir Horace Spavage, declares that Fratten has died from a burst aneurysm. At his London memorial service the fallen financier is given a grand send-off into the Hereafter: "The church was packed with City men of all types and standings. . . . Every member of the staff of Fratten's Bank, which was closed for the day—a unique circumstance—was there, from the chief cashier to the latest-joined stamp-licker. The City felt that one of its big men had gone—one of the fast-disappearing pre-war type—and it was, beneath its inscrutable surface, genuinely moved."[27]

One of the admirable qualities of Fratten is his openheartedness to the novel's Jewish character, Leopold Hessel, who is, like Fratten,

---

[26] Henry Wade, *The Duke of York's Steps* (New York: Payson & Clarke, 1929), 8.
[27] Wade, *Steps*, 46, 51.

a London financier. Hessel, one of Fratten's directors, is described, in what is meant to be taken by the readers as positive terms, as a man with "dark eyes and sensitive hands, but none of the more exaggerated features of his race." As a German (and a Jew), his standing in society had been jeopardized over a decade earlier, during the Great War, a period "when the position of men of even remote German descent had been extremely difficult." Fortunately for Hessel, Fratten insisted that his friend retain his position in the directorate of his bank. This action by so prominent a citizen as Fratten was "regarded as a certificate of Hessel's patriotism" and saved the German-born Jew "from the worst of the ignominies that were the lot of many less fortunate than him."[28] Appropriately, Hessel is by his friend's side on the Steps when Fratten collapses. But it turns out that Fratten in fact was murdered, and fingers of suspicion start pointing at multiple places, including not only in the business world but Fratten's own household.

Leopold Hessel arguably is the most interesting character in *The Duke of York's Steps*, and I would argue that Henry Wade is, in contrast with the typical view of the Golden Age English detective novel, a strong critic of anti-Semitism in his work, as evidenced not only by *The Duke of York's Steps*, but by two contemporaneous Henry Wade short stories, "The Three Keys" and "A Matter of Luck."

In *Steps*, Wade lays considerable stress on the bigoted treatment to which Leopold Hessel has been, and continues to be, subjected in England. When the author refers to "ignominies" suffered by the British citizens of German—and more particularly German Jewish—extraction as a result of World War One domestic xenophobic hysteria, he is clearly using condemnatory language.

Wade also makes manifest that discrimination against Hessel and other Jews followed in the wake of the war, with Jews continuing to be blackballed in Fratten's exclusive City Constitutional Club. Hessel is reluctant to himself undergo the ordeal of application,

---

[28] Ibid., 9.

despite Fratten's support, though Fratten assures his friend that he would be accepted: "Is it Wendheim and Lemuels? They weren't blackballed because they were . . . because of their religion. It was simply that this club has always asked for other qualifications besides wealth and business success. . . . of course they got pilled—not the sort we want here. You are—you'd get in without the least doubt" (Wade's attribution of hesitation on the part of Fratten in even referring to the possibility of Jews being blackballed because they are Jews, having him instead make a delicate reference to "their religion," is a nice touch). Later in the novel, Fratten dines at Hessel's "rather large-hearted club, the "Wanderers" (the name is neatly suggestive of the Wandering Jew), and the author uses the occasion to emphasize the personal benefits that can flow from a policy of tolerance. After Fratten praises the "first-rate China tea," Hessel smiles and points out to his friend that "that's one of the advantages of being not too exclusive. . . . We've got members from all parts of the world and in all sorts of business; it's rather a point of pride with us that each member who can should help the club to get the best of everything."[29]

Anti-Semitic discrimination in English clubs is an element in one of Henry Wade's short stories from the same period, "The

---

[29] Ibid., 10, 44. On the treatment of Germans in Britain during World War One, see Panikos Panayi, "The Destruction of the German Communities in Britain during the First World War," in Panikos Panayi, ed., *Germans in Britain Since 1500* (London and Rio Grande, OH: The Hambledon Press, 1996), 129. {*SPOILERS*} It must be admitted that Hessel had to be there on the Steps with Fratten, his being in fact the mastermind of the banker's killing. Hessel has been leading a double life, with one life as a respectable banker, and the other as a dishonest financial shark, a director of the shady Victory Finance Company [VCF]. Fatally for Fratten, the respected banker had been asked by one of VCF's dupe directors, an old school friend and key shareholder, to join the board of VCF. Once a member of the board, Hessel realized, Fratten would be bound to discover VCF's underhanded operations; so Fratten had to die. The revelation of Leopold Hessel's treacherous masterminding of Garth Fratten's death has given rise to charges of anti-Semitism against Henry Wade, charges that I find, as explained in the main text, misguided. In *The Duke of York's Steps*, declare James and Joan Gindin in Wade's entry in the *Dictionary of Literary Biography* [*DLB*] "Cosmopolitan Jews, in

Three Keys." {*SPOILERS*} In this story it is the gentile, Herbert Phillips, of the diamond firm Levi, Berg & Phillips, who proves to be the criminal. Herbert is a clerk, brought into the firm by his older brother, George, a partner who came in during the Great War, when another of the partners, Aaron Berg, was interned and outside capital was badly needed. Besides making Levi and Berg innocent victims of a rascally gentile's criminal acts and allowing Levi to remind Inspector Poole (with "quiet dignity") that the pair do not need a holiday at Easter, as they are not Christians, Wade takes time to note empathetically that Levi's and Berg's sports club, the ironically-named "All British Sports Club," "provided entertainment and exercise for many who would not be readily welcomed elsewhere."[30] {*END SPOILERS*}

Another story, "A Matter of Luck" (1930), offers a particularly striking instance of Henry Wade's original thinking, in that it paints a sympathetic picture of possibly the single most reviled archetype in Golden Age British mystery fiction, the Jewish moneylender. Regrettably, the moneylender, Isidore Cohen, is afflicted with the stereotypical "Jewish" lisp of the period, but, nevertheless, the author portrays the man as an honest and

---

particular, are suspect, seen as one of the forces unleashed to debase the social and economic structure.... [T]he machinations of an assortment of financiers, headed by a Jewish banker who had seemed to flourish under Fratten's broad-minded confidence and who was actually holding Fratten's arm as they walked down the steps in their silk hats, are revealed as the agents destroying the English world." See James Gindin and Joan Gindin, "Henry Wade (Henry Lancelot Aubrey-Fletcher)," in Bernard Benstock and Thomas F. Staley, eds., *Dictionary of Literary Biography*, vol. 77: *British Mystery Writers, 1920-1939* (Farmington Hills, MI: Cengage Gale, 1988), 303. As I stress in the text, however, Wade actually provides Hessel with considerable sympathetic back story, something the Gindins overlook. One of the novel's characters, a (non-Jewish) Great War veteran and co-conspirator with Hessel in both financial skullduggery and the murder of Fratten, attempts to explain Hessel's behavior: "I was on my beam ends, like many other soldiers. [Hessel] was on them too—psychologically, and for a different reason. He had had a devilish time in the war—'German Jew' and all the rest of it. His one idea was to get his own back." Wade, *Steps*, 346.{*END SPOILERS*}

[30] Henry Wade, *Policeman's Lot* (London: Constable, 1933), 132-136.

upright individual, and an undeserving victim of a callous and calculating premeditated murderer, Dr. Richard Enterfield. Contrasting himself with another firm of Jewish moneylenders, one that goes under the oh-so-British but unfortunately spurious name of Gordon, Kitchener & Co. Financial Agents, Cohen announces simply, "I call myself what I am: Isidore Cohen, Moneylender. I think my clients trust me. But others like to be deceived." At a later point in the story, after the ruthless and unscrupulous Enterfield has fatally stabbed the moneylender, Wade notes in passing yet also with point that Enterfield owed the ownership of his "expensive practice" to Cohen's bounty. There is not the trace of a sentiment within "A Matter of Luck" to the effect that the moneylender to some extent deserved his demise or that his murderer is partially deserving of the reader's sympathy, making the story a remarkable instance in the genre's tales involving moneylenders. The anonymous reviewer in the *Times Literary Supplement* accurately noted of the "Jew moneylender" in the tale: "He does his money-lending with such whimsical detachment and takes a risk to his life with so much dignity and self-possession, that when he is to be taken for his ride to visit the mysterious stranger [which of course is a ruse intended to lead him to his death] one would like to warn him—and of few Jew moneylenders in fiction can that be said."[31]

In *The Duke of York's Steps* Wade indicates considerable dissatisfaction on his part with the state of English society in the wake

---

[31] Wade, *Lot*, 160, 162; *Times Literary Supplement*, 3 August 1933, 524. Compare the author's attitude in "A Matter of Luck" with, for example, that of Freeman Wills Crofts in his story "The Case of the Avaricious Moneylender." "In most cases," pronounces Crofts' detective, Chief Inspector French, "it's a satisfaction to me to run to earth the man who has committed a murder. But this is not always so. When I brought in Charles Mallory for croaking Ben Isaacs, I was really sorry. If ever a man deserved his fate, Isaacs had done so, and though I could scarcely let my superiors know it, all my sympathies were with Mallory." Crofts makes the murderer, Charles Mallory, an entirely sympathetic victim of the moneylender he later murders. Mallory, it seems, fell into

of the Great War. The author classes Leopold Hessel and other British Jews of Germanic derivation among the Great War's victims. (Yet another such victim of unjust British internment policy during the Great War is the art patron Sir Otto Geisberg in Wade's 1933 crime novel *Mist on the Saltings*, for the author notes that a demoralized Geisberg died during the war in a British prison.)

Although he clearly portrays Sir Garth Fratten in an admirable light as a guardian of what is good and right in English society, other traditionalists in the novel come in for ridicule. Fratten's doctor, Sir Horace Spavage, is a pompous ass who misdiagnoses his patient and refuses to admit the possibility of error under questioning by Inspector Poole: "This is beyond sufferance! . . . You come here and cross-question me about the way I carry out my duties! Me, a Physician to His Majesty the King!" Shortly afterward, the Physician to His Majesty the King is exposed in all his majestic ineptitude at the Coroner's Inquest. Another bulwark of tradition held up to the author's scorn is Major-General Sir Hunter Lorne, K.C.B., D.S.O., a dummy shareholder in the Victory Finance Company. Wade allows that Major-General Lorne "had done well in command of a division in France," but then immediately undercuts this concession with the sardonic observation, "or, what was considered the same thing, the division he commanded had done well." Later, when Lorne is harshly rebuked for inviting Fratten into the VCF, Wade notes scornfully that "Sir Hunter was palpably taken aback." Not since a Corps Commander in the Great War had reprimanded him for squandering lives in what he, Lorne, had

---

Isaacs' sharp hands not through any improvidence of his own ("All his life he had been a worker, and though he knew that such labour as his could not bring wealth, he had hoped at least for a modest competence with which to end his days"), but through his having backed a bill for a defaulting friend and signed his name to a contract with Isaacs that he had not understood. Freeman Wills Crofts, *Murderers Make Mistakes* (1947; rpnt., London and New York: House of Stratus, 2000), 100, 106. Wade's murderer, by contrast, is presented as someone who knew exactly what he was doing when he borrowed his sum and willfully determined to cheat the moneylender.

considered a "successful raid" had the Major-General "been so thrown off his balance."[32]

The central problem that Henry Wade seems to see in a post-war world thrown off its balance by a calamitous martial conflagration is a fundamental loss of belief in the values of honor and human decency. This vision is crystallized in miniature form in Wade's most celebrated short story, "Duello" (1930). In this tale, two men are found dead, apparently victims of a duel. "Like the good old times, isn't it," sardonically speculates Superintendent Cox to Inspector Poole, whom he has brought into the case. "All for the love of a lady." Of course this *crime passionel* turns out to be nothing of the sort. {*SPOILERS*} The two men were, respectively, a woman's husband and her lover, but there was no duel, both men having been murdered by the love triangle's female component, philandering wife and suburban siren Quirril Horne, a sensation-seeking, self-dramatizing nightclub and cinema addict. When Poole goes to question Mrs. Horne, he is immediately repelled by her behavior: "Tears, sobs, heaving shoulders—all the reactions familiar to the devotee of the cinema. The woman was evidently quite incapable of feeling. . . . Utterly disgusted, Poole decided to cut the 'scene'; he would probably have to return to it, but he wanted fresh air—morally as well as physically." Later, after Mrs. Horne is revealed as the culprit and has dispatched herself with another revolver shot, Poole diagnoses her malady to Superintendent Cox: "War-time adolescence and post-war demoralisation. . . . I've seen them in London—night clubs full of them—though they don't generally go to such lengths. Lots of good qualities in her, too—brains and pluck—up to the eyes in pluck." {*END SPOILERS*} Realizing that Cox had suspected something underhand the whole time, Poole asks the superintendent what provoked his suspicion. Driving home the author's point about the loss of honor in the modern age, Cox replies simply, "People don't fight duels nowadays."[33]

---

[32] Wade, *Steps*, 30, 35, 79.
[33] Wade, *Lot*, 3, 13, 23, 24.

More than mere glimmers of Wade's pessimism about the modern era could be glimpsed in the earlier works *The Verdict of You All* and *The Missing Partners*, but *The Duke of York's Steps* is the first of his novels in which the author seems to be consciously striving to develop this pessimism as a unifying theme; and it is a quite interesting and unusual genre effort on that score. Judged solely on its merits as puzzle, *Steps* has much to commend it as well, though again, as with his prior pair of novels, there are some flaws. As with *The Missing Partners*, too much time is given over to rather flippant amateur investigators (in *Steps* Fratten's daughter, Inez, steps into Helen Mildmay's pumps as the amateur ringleader). Wade attempts to lend dramatic heft to Inez Fratten's role by having her secretly harbor a passion for Ryland Fratten, thought to be her half-brother though in reality her stepbrother. Inez has long known the true relationship between them, but it is still rather creepy, especially when she makes a passionate declaration of love for him only some twelve hours after he has learned he is not actually her blood brother. One wishes more time had been spent with the striking Leopold Hessel, rather than with Garth Fratten's family. Nevertheless, *The Duke of York's Steps* is an exceptional work.

A final point that lends significance to *The Duke of York's Steps* is its introduction of Wade's most important police investigator, Inspector John Poole. In creating Poole, Wade actually preceded Ngaio Marsh, creator of Roderick Alleyn, by five years in ushering into detective fiction the idealized genteel policeman still with us today in modern times in the late P. D. James' sensitive poet-policeman, Adam Dalgliesh. "Ngaio Marsh's creation of Roderick Alleyn marks a new kind of hero in detective fiction," insists one authority, too selectively:

> Heretofore the professional police force had been conventionally portrayed by writers as ignorant, lower-class men not clever enough to solve a crime without the assistance of the bright, witty gentleman amateur. . . . It is Marsh who brings detective fiction into greater harmony with the vicissitudes of

twentieth-century life by creating a clever, well born, professional policeman. . . . By creating Alleyn's character as an Oxford educated policeman, Marsh . . . promotes the ideal of professionalism so reluctantly accepted in British society in modern times. More than any other Grande Dame author she transcends the formulaic detective fiction genre.[34]

To be sure, Marsh's Roderick Alleyn is one of the genre's most important English detectives, but before he himself did any path-clearing, the path had been cleared for him by John Poole. Wade admittedly was no "Grande Dame" but he clearly has a greater claim to the title of originator of the "clever, well born, professional policeman" in Britain than does Marsh.

Like his better-remembered followers, Poole is strong yet sensitive; dogged and diligent like Freeman Wills Crofts' Inspector French, while also more intellectually and socially refined (in his leisure time he reads Mary Webb and Henry James, shoots and plays golf); and conspicuously lacking the bold eccentricities that had traditionally lent color to so many "Great Detectives" in the days since Sherlock Holmes. The very physical description given Poole by Wade emphasizes these qualities:

> Standing about five feet ten inches, he had the straight hips, small waist and wide shoulders of the ideal athlete, though his clothes were cut to conceal, rather than accentuate, these features. His face, except for the eyes, was not remarkable; the chin was well-moulded rather than strong, the mouth quietly firm, and the forehead of medium height. But the

---

[34] Kathryne S. McDorman, "Roderick Alleyn and the New Professionals," in B. J. Rahn, ed., *Ngaio Marsh: The Woman and Her Work* (Metuchen, N. J. and London: Scarecrow Press, 1995), 138-139. McDorman's overly ambitious claim for Marsh is illustrative of the error that can result from a too-exclusive focus by historians of the British detective fiction genre on a handful of "Crime Queens."

> eyes were . . . an indication of his character—grey, steady eyes that looked quietly at the object before them, with a curiously unblinking gaze that allowed nothing to escape them.[35]

John Poole is the son of a comfortably-placed country doctor who was able to send John to "one of the smaller public schools" and later Oxford. In college athletics Poole got a Half-Blue as a hurdler and he also played cricket, though "without conspicuous success."[36] Like his creator, Poole evinced an interest in the theater and joined the O.U.D.S., taking a small part in a Shakespeare play (in Poole's case *The Winter's Tale*). The young man's initial career ambition was to join the Bar, but he gradually became interested in police work itself. At the time of *The Duke York's Steps*, Poole, still under the age of thirty, has worked his way through the ranks of the Metropolitan Police and Scotland Yard to the position of Detective-Inspector.

John Poole would appear in four more Henry Wade novels in the 1930s, as well as two in the 1950s. However, Wade's next detective tale, *The Dying Alderman* (1930), introduced yet another recurring Scotland Yard detective (though one subsidiary in importance to Poole), Inspector Herbert Lott. Lott is an older, less appealing version of Poole: insensitive, sardonic and sarcastic, and of more left-wing political inclinations. Wade describes him in *The Dying Alderman* as follows:

> He was rather tall, slim, fair-haired, and thirty-sevenish; his complexion was pink and white, his eyes blue and inclined to goggle—an inclination accentuated by the convex pince-nez attached by a golden chain apparently to the right ear. He was dressed in neat black, with a winged collar, black and white tie and pointed shoes. He looked, in fact, like

---

[35] Wade, *Verdict*, 68.
[36] Ibid., 63, 64.

a Government clerk, of refined education and Fabian tendencies."[37]

Lott appears as the lead investigator in only one more novel, 1932's *The Hanging Captain*, and then is confined by Wade to merely a passing appearance in a Poole novel, where we learn that Poole greatly dislikes Lott. While Lott indeed is not particularly likeable, his refined needling of the somewhat bumptious local constabulary in *The Dying Alderman* is a source of amusement for the reader.

*The Dying Alderman* takes place in "Quenborough," the county town of Quenshire, (obviously a stand-in for Buckinghamshire). With this setting Wade brought a vast amount of authority and experience as an important county landowner and councilor and produced his first unquestionable masterpiece in the genre, a work that is simultaneously a clever satire of provincial society and politics and a deftly-clued murder puzzle. With perception critic Charles Shibuk chose *The Dying Alderman* as Wade's best early novel, noting that it "is written and plotted with great clarity and precision, and remains surprisingly fresh today." *A Catalogue of Crime* [*COC*] concurred, praising the novel's "narrative economy, . . . sufficient characterization, unbroken suspense, subdued wit, local color, and . . . first-rate plot with a fine twist at the end." Like Shibuk, *COC* found as well that the book remained fresh, declaring of it that it "holds up extremely well."[38] A few years later, Jacques Barzun selected *The Dying Alderman* in his series *One Hundred Classics of Crime Fiction*.

By the time Henry Wade published his fourth detective novel, his fame as a detective novelist had spread considerably and he was deemed, by both British and American authorities, one of the major figures in the genre. On the jacket of *The Dying Alderman*, the author's American publishers assured potential readers that "Wade's books have received the highest praise, not only from

---

[37] Henry Wade, *The Dying Alderman* (New York: Payson & Clarke, 1930), 85-86.
[38] Shibuk, "Henry Wade," 91; Barzun and Taylor, *Catalogue of Crime*, 420.

converted arm-chair detectives but from those who seldom venture into the field of detective and mystery fiction." In Britain, *The Verdict of You All* had been called "an admirable book" and *The Missing Partners* "an excellent yarn," while *The Duke of York's Steps* was greeted with absolute superlatives. "It would be difficult to overpraise it," gushed Gerald Gould in the *Observer*. "It is well written, and so well constructed that the excitement grows steadily as the mystery deepens. A book from which it is, literally, hard to tear oneself away."[39] When the Detection Club formed in 1930, the same year *The Dying Alderman* appeared, Wade, like the other authors in this study, G. D. H. and Margaret Cole, became a charter member.

*The Dying Alderman* more than lived up to its praised predecessors and confirmed Wade's high standing among British detective novelists. The novel opens with a stormy meeting of the Quenborough Council. There are the usual imprecations from Tom Garrett, the council's one Socialist councilor, heartily despised by the rest. This time he insists that one of the councilors or aldermen must be leaking information about the Council's working class housing plans to land speculators. The mayor, local country squire Sir John Assington, indignantly denounces Garrett's accusation, declaring that it "must be repudiated by every decent-minded man and woman on the council." Far from assenting to Assington's affirmation of public piety, however, Alderman Basil Trant declares that he agrees with Garrett. In the process Trant grossly insults the Mayor, telling him contemptuously:

> You may be satisfied, as you say, Mr. Mayor; I can well believe you are. But I am very sure that no other man, woman or mouse in this chamber is. No wonder public money was wasted; no wonder public affairs were muddles, when we left them in the hands

---

[39] See the dust jacket of the Payson & Clarke edition of *The Dying Alderman* and the critical notices excerpted in the 1930 popular edition of *The Missing Partners*, published by Constable.

of gentlemen of leisure, with no knowledge and experience of business and no desire except to get through things with as little fuss and trouble as possible. Thank God, things are different now. You are Mayor of this Borough, Sir John—you are the figurehead—and if I may say so, a very handsome figurehead; but please leave the management of the borough's affairs in the hands of businessmen who have got their eyes open and their ears unstuck.[40]

Spurning the Mayor's assurances, Trant insists that as an auctioneer he knows something about speculative land purchase and the council most certainly is facing a case of it: "I know that that land has been forced up to a fictitious value, and I agree with Mr. Garrett that the rise is due to leakage of information and probably to worse." Trant adds significantly that he has "a strong suspicion as to the source of this leakage" and that he "shall not rest" until he has exposed the malefactor, "however securely entrenched he may consider himself to be."[41] At this point, any experienced mystery reader knows that Trant has effectively signed his own death warrant; and, sure enough, during the tea interval Trant is discovered still at the alderman's dais, dead from a knife wound in his neck. Employing a device later associated with the ingenious American detective novelist Ellery Queen, Wade has Trant managing to have left a dying message with a pencil: two scrawled letters on a piece of paper.

As his tirade during the council meeting already revealed, Trant was a highly objectionable person who gave cause to dislike him to numerous people, including Sir John Assington; the Deputy Mayor Voce Mardyke, a Quenborough solicitor; Hallis, porter of Quenborough Town Hall, and Trant's own wife, Mary. The investigation is conducted by a trio of well-conveyed policeman, whose by-play throughout the book is quite enjoyable. The Chief Constable,

---

[40] Wade, *Alderman*, 14-15.
[41] Ibid., 15-16.

Captain Charles Race, owes his recent appointment to the support of Sir John Assington, Race having served during the Great War in the same regiment—the Quenshire Light Infantry—as Assington's only son, who was killed in the conflict. Facing a case affecting some very important county figures, Race decides to call in Scotland Yard, much to the outrage of his dogged but rather bullheaded superintendent, Vorley. The Scotland Yard man, Inspector Lott, is aware of Vorley's resentment of him and does not hesitate to take his amusement at the superintendent's expense. Not only at odds personally, Lott and Vorley find themselves locking horns in the case they are investigating; for the two men have differing theories of the case and are resultantly pursuing different suspects.

{SPOILERS} In the end, however, it is Race who discovers the murderer, though the truth becomes clear only after two suicides have taken place. The mayor, Sir John Assington, proves to be Trant's murderer. Revealed in the last line of the novel is that the dying message left by Trant—the letters "M" and "A"—referred not to Trant's wife "Mary" nor to "Mardyke" but to "Mayor." Since Assington was never ruled out as a suspect, his eventual unmasking does not come with the sort of jolt to the reader's assumptions that often occurs with an Agatha Christie novel; yet, after she has finished *The Dying Alderman*, a reader can go back over it and appreciate the adroitness of the clueing that subtly but fairly points to the Mayor. Additionally, the revelation of Assington's guilt lends interest to the tale not "merely" as a puzzle but as a more serious novel. {END SPOILERS}

Often in the Golden Age, mystery writers plotted their tales without thought of conveying any broader theme or statement about life. This is not the case with *The Dying Alderman*, where Assington's diminishment symbolizes the decline and fall of the aristocracy in Britain, a process amply documented by David Cannadine in *The Decline and Fall of the British Aristocracy*. The decade of the 1880s (the decade of Henry Wade's birth), seeing as it did the "sudden and dramatic collapse of the agricultural base of the European economy," the rise of a "new and fabulously rich international plutocracy" and the extension of the franchise with the Third Reform Act of 1884-5, was, according to Cannadine, the pivotal period in the gradual displacement of Britain's landed gentry as the country's ruling elite. Not only did the traditional land-based aristocracy lose control at the national level, it lost much of it as well at the local level. Admittedly, Cannadine has found that from the 1890s to the Second World War there was an upswing in the number of aristocratic mayors, but Cannadine links this development to the deliberate adoption by local aristocrats of non-partisan, above-the-fray political stances, as well as the desire on the part of the professionals and businessmen who now dominated municipal politics to make use of the rich pageantry of symbolism that accompanied an aristocratic (albeit politically neutered) mayor:

> [Professionals and businessmen] . . . were much concerned to proclaim the greatness and the unity of their communities by appealing to history, to pageantry, and to glamour. . . . [The mayor] embodied the unity and the greatness of the community; he must be able to carry off the social and ceremonial side of his duties with dignity and panache; and he must have the resources to entertain lavishly, and to subscribe generously to charities, clubs and associations. . . . The ideal mayor should be a man of ancient lineage, high social standing, and impeccable connections. Seen in this light, the election of a titled mayor was the embodiment, not the negation, of municipal pride, as aristocratic privilege was used for the furthering of civic dignity.

Cannadine bluntly concludes that "most aristocratic mayors were largely ornamental."[42]

The fate of Sir John Assington in *The Dying Alderman* reads like an illustration of Cannadine's thesis. Described by Chief

---

[42] David Cannadine, *The Decline and Fall of the British Aristocracy* (1990; rpnt., New York: Vintage, 1999), 26, 564.

Constable Race to Inspector Lott as "Sir John Assington, 12th Baronet, late M.F.H. [Master of Foxhounds], head of the oldest and richest county family in Quenshire, descendant of generals, ministers, Privy Councillors, Chairman of this, that and the other," Assington is one member of the landed gentry who has managed to hold on to much of his family's wealth and position, acknowledgment of which had been made with his mayoral appointment in 1929. Yet there are cracks in the Assington edifice of power. As Trant was rude enough to point out to his face in public, Assington does function rather as a figurehead on the council (though, to be fair, one alderman reflects that Assington, while "not a clever man," has "no ax to grind" and thus is trusted "absolutely"). Assington is respected for his heart (except by the contemptuous Trant), but no one speaks respectfully of his brains, as the very name "Assington" surely is intended to suggest. Worse for Assington, he is the last of his line, his brother having died in the Boer War and his son on the Western Front in 1918. Wade expends effort to make the reader feel the poignancy of this extinction of a family dedicated to service of country:

> Walking to the door, [Sir John] turned down an electric switch. Instantly the dark walls became alive with Assingtons throughout the ages, revealed by well-shaded lights. Assingtons in armour; Assingtons in doublet and hose; Assingtons in beards; Assingtons with side-whiskers; soldier Assingtons; political Assingtons; sporting Assingtons. In the latter category, a portrait of Sir John in a pink coat, presented to their retiring Master by the subscribers of the Quenshire Hunt, held a prominent position. Sir John paid no attention to it; a portrait of a boy in service dress was his objective.
> 
> "My poor boy, Edward," he said.
> 
> Race looked with interest at the picture of his brother-officer, (Temporary) Captain Edward Assington, 5th Batt. Quenshire Light Infantry, killed in action near Solesmes, 12th October, 1918. 20 years

of age. The portrait, painted on his last leave in August 1918, was a remarkable one and struck a chord of vivid memory in Charles Race's mind. The features were those of a boy; the eyes were the eyes of a man of forty.

"It's very like him, sir."

Sir John was silent and Race, stealing a glance at him, saw that his lip was quivering.

With a sudden straightening of the shoulders the last of the line of Assingtons swung on his heel and strode towards the door.[43]

Clearly Wade's inclusion in *The Dying Alderman* of a passage such as this one is at odds with the contention that Golden Age mystery novelists sought in their "escapist" works to lull their readership into forgetting all the unpleasant things in life (the murder itself being presented as a "game"). Besides war, another unhappy reality of life addressed forthrightly in *The Dying Alderman* is corruption on the part of politicians and the police. In the novel it is matter-of-factly stated that not one person on the council—the dutiful and conscientious Sir John excepted—can be assumed to be above a little abuse of the public trust here and there (in this respect *The Dying Alderman* anticipates the exploration of civic corruption in H. C. Bailey's *The Sullen Sky Mystery*, 1935). Perhaps even more striking is this cynical exchange between Lott and Race, in which Lott acknowledges, to his superior's unease, that police may have little interest in actually discovering the "truth":

---

[43] Wade, *Alderman*, 18, 79, 163. On the heavy mortal impact of World War One on Britain's gentrified elite, see Cannadine, *Decline and Fall*, 83: "The British aristocracy was irrevocably weakened by the impact of the First World War. Not since the Wars of the Roses had so many patricians died so suddenly and so violently. . . . In terms of relative numbers of lives lost there is no doubt that the titled and territorial classes made the greatest sacrifices." Cannadine notes that "by the end of 1914, the [World War I] death toll included six peers, sixteen baronets, ninety-five sons of peers, and eighty-two sons of baronets." Ibid., 74.

"Know anything about this Mrs. Stoole, sir?"

"Nothing beyond what Vorley told me. She sounds a blood-thirsty hag."

"May be something behind that. I mean she may have some reason for hating your Sergeant-major [the porter Hallam, suspected by Vorley of Trant's murder]."

"I'll tell Vorley to look into it."

"He'll not find anything to discredit her, sir. She's his best witness."

"You're a cynic, Lott."

"I know policemen, sir. I'm one myself."

Race thought it better to leave this rather unsavoury theme.

This "unsavory theme" is not dwelt upon by the author at length in *The Dying Alderman*, but at least he addresses it forthrightly, which is a far cry from Julian Symons' declaration that Golden Age writers "would have thought it undesirable to write about [police misdeeds], because the police were the representatives of established society, and so ought not to be shown behaving badly."[44] Contrary to Symons' assertion, meditations on bad behavior on the part of the police are a recurring aspect in Henry Wade novels in the 1930s.

The most important theme in *The Dying Alderman*, however, indisputably is the diminution of the aristocracy in British social and political life. {SPOILERS} When Chief Constable Race—over the course of the novel increasingly suspecting, to his horror, Sir John of the murder—sends a note to Assington telling him of Lott's impending arrest of Voce Mardyke for the crime, the baronet commits suicide, leaving a confession for Race. Assington explains that during the tea interval he had returned to the council chamber,

---

[44] Wade, *Alderman*, 159; Julian Symons, *Bloody Murder: From the Detective Story to the Crime Novel* (1972; 3rd. rev. ed., New York and Tokyo: Mysterious Press, 1992), 108.

where Trant was alone at the dais, to try to reconcile with the alderman:

> It cost me a bit of an effort, Race, to make that advance to a man like Trant. He looked at me—looked me up and down as if I was a bit of dirt—and said: "I don't want any soft soap, you rotten parasite."
>
> The blood rushed to my head, as if he had slapped me on the face. I hardly know what happened. I can just remember seeing the knife lying there and then I struck him.

Assington's greatest shame concerns what he believes his intemperate action has done to the family name: "I've done a terrible thing, Race. I've dishonoured my family—and no man could do a worse thing than that. To think of my boy—Edward—what he did; and now, I, his father, have let him down. It is worse punishment, that thought, than anything the law could do to me." Polite to the end, however, Assington spares a moment in his letter for his protégé, apologizing to Race for having given him "such a wretched start in your new job" and closing by wishing him, with poignantly absurd good form, "Good luck in your career."[45]

A work like *The Dying Alderman* challenges the oft-repeated assertion, derived from W. H. Auden's overly-influential "The Guilty Vicarage" essay, that Golden Age detective novels inevitably gave readers happy resolutions, with a pleasingly familiar status quo satisfactorily restored. One closes the pages of Henry Wade's fourth novel with a feeling of regret for the pathetic fate of the proud but essentially decent Mayor of Quenborough and a melancholy-tinged reflection that a doomed epoch has, far from being restored or stabilized, irrevocably passed, taking with the bad much as well that was good. It does no justice to Henry Wade as an author to unthinkingly include him with unchallenging writers of the period, writers who never gave thought, as Wade clearly did, to exploring deeper human dilemmas in their works. {*END SPOILERS*}

---

[45] Wade, *Alderman*, 283, 284.

Wade's "decline and fall" theme would be further explored by the author in his next novel, *No Friendly Drop*, which reintroduced his readers to the intelligent and sympathetic John Poole and takes place in "Brackenshire," an even more obvious Buckinghamshire stand-in than the "Quenshire" of *The Dying Alderman* (suggesting the interchangeability of the two locales, Major Faide, Chief Constable of Brackenshire in *No Friendly Drop* and a later novel, *The High Sheriff*, appears in the earlier story "Jealous Gun" as the Chief Constable of Quenshire). With his fifth novel Wade staged the hoariest clichéd setting of the Golden Age, still mocked (affectionately and otherwise) today: the country house. Yet Tassart, the ancestral home of the Grayles in *No Friendly Drop*, is a country house with a difference, one occupied not by sawdust puppets, but flesh-and-blood people who draw the reader's empathy. The present Lord Grayle, Henry, is, like Sir John Assington in Wade's previous novel, a respected man, yet one who does not quite command the respect once simply given as due to his illustrious ancestors. On his first appearance, Lord Grayle is described as a man of sixty who looks his age, with grizzled hair and moustache and "lines of suffering about his mouth." He has a charming though wan face, reflective of his life:

> After leaving Cambridge he had sat in the House for a few years in the Liberal interest, but was unfortunate enough to succeed his father when only thirty. Returning to Tassart, he gave himself up to watching an extremely competent agent manage his estate, and taking a mildly useful part in the county affairs. In the War he played a similar part at Rouen, ill-health rather than timidity keeping him out of the line.... Everybody liked Henry Grayle, many people loved him; he had not an enemy in the world—but he was a sad man because he knew he had not made use of his natural ability and opportunities.[46]

---

[46] Henry Wade, *No Friendly Drop* (London: Constable, 1931), 13-14.

Lord Grayle takes a sedative, Di-dial, to help him sleep when suffering from his painful attacks of neuralgia. One morning he does not wake up, and it is assumed that he died from either an accidental or self-administered overdose of his sleeping medication. However, a post-mortem on his body detects the presence of the drug scopolamine, in an amount normally insufficient to kill a man but fatal when combined with the Di-dial Lord Grayle had taken. Though Lord Grayle was a well-liked, inoffensive man, someone had to have killed him; and it becomes Inspector Poole's task to find out just who that person was, Scotland Yard having been called in by the gentry-shy local constabulary.

Tassart is a home to its share of family unhappiness and antagonism, emotions realistically portrayed by the author. Lord Grayle's wife, Helen, is an exhaustingly forthright and hearty country sportswoman who continues to maintain a lavish lifestyle even as family revenues diminish. The Grayle's son and only child, Charles, and their daughter-in-law, Catherine, are not particularly appealing specimens. They have especially prickly relations with Lady Grayle, who finds them hopelessly priggish and dull and cannot resist twitting them on their visits to Tassart, even over such mundane matters as cocktails:

> "Your own fault if the cocktail's spoilt," said Lady Grayle. "I couldn't wait for you."
>
> "We don't drink cocktails," said her daughter-in-law, a hint of superiority in her voice.
>
> "Don't We? What about our Consort?" asked Lady Grayle. "Come on Charles, it'll do you good, put a little go into you."
>
> She filled a glass and handed it to her son. Charles sipped it and made a wry face.
>
> "It's terribly strong," he said, "tastes of a hairdresser's shop—vanilla or something, I suppose."
>
> "Vanilla! That's Syrop d'Orgeat—a 'Perfect Peach,' Henry's latest."

"I still don't like it," said Charles, putting down the glass still half-full and coughing nervously.

"No guts, that's your trouble," said his mother.[47]

Based on personality, at least, Lady Grayle seems a more obvious murderer's choice than her husband, but it is Lord Grayle who dies. Potential suspects in Lord Grayle's death include his wife, his son and his daughter-in-law, as well as the unctuous butler, Moode, and the family doctor, Norman Calladine. None really seems a likely candidate, however. Lady Grayle, for example, though she is known to spend rather more lavishly than even her indulgent husband liked ("She keeps up exactly the same standard of life as when they had twice the income and a quarter of the taxation," the local vicar regretfully informs Poole), seems genuinely bereaved by his death and, in any event, did not financially benefit from it, most of the estate going to Charles Grayle.[48] And Catherine Grayle is known to be ambitious for her husband and has a Bachelor of Science degree from Cambridge, but would she really have risked hastening her father-in-law's death through murder? Poole instinctively dislikes the butler, Moode, but what is there actually against him?

{*SPOILERS*} Vigorous investigation by Poole convinces the detective inspector that Moode was involved in a criminal scheme of removing heirloom furniture from Tassart (under the guise of repairing/restoring it) and selling it to wealthy American buyers, later replacing the originals with skilled fakes. As Poole closes in on Moode, the butler suddenly dies, poisoned like Lord Grayle (however, this time the poison is extremely painful hydrocyanic acid). It is assumed that Moode killed Lord Grayle, then, fearing exposure, committed suicide; but Poole discovers that the real truth is more shocking.

Lady Grayle, not Moode, had been involved in the furniture faking scheme, which was part of a desperate attempt on her part

---

[47] Wade, *Drop*, 11-12.
[48] Ibid., 85.

to get out from under the crushing weight of debt she had accumulated without her husband's knowledge. The prying Moode had discovered what she was up to and was blackmailing her. Having some scopolamine left over from when, during the War, she had run Tassart as a "Lying-in Hospital for unmarried mothers" (a fact deftly dropped by Wade early in the novel), Lady Grayle decided to put a dosage of it in the butler's early morning tea, to see what effect it would have on him (she hoped to work her way up to a fatal dose). Tragically for Lady Grayle, that same morning the spout on Lord Grayle's teapot was broken and Lord Grayle was instead given Moode's teapot, the one Lady Grayle had dosed already with scopolamine. The scopolamine in combination with the dose of Di-dial Lord Grayle happened to take the previous evening killed him. Later, Lady Grayle did poison her original intended target, Moode, this time using sure and painful hydrocyanic acid, which she procured from a vet, meaningly telling him she needed something with which "to kill a dog."[49] After Lady Grayle confesses all these grave misdeeds, she manages to surreptitiously abstract some scopolamine from her cache before handing it over to the police, giving her the opportunity to commit suicide. The author closes with Lady Grayle's hand slowly reaching out toward the phial, recalling the novel's title, a quotation from Shakespeare's *Romeo and Juliet*: "What's here? A cup, closed in my true love's hand?/Poison, I see, hath been his timeless end:/O Churl; drunk all, and left no friendly drop/To help me after?" {*END SPOILERS*}

*No Friendly Drop* is an exceptionally sophisticated detective novel, both in its puzzle structure and its treatment of character and theme. {*SPOILERS*} The novel continues the aristocratic "decline and fall" theme from *The Dying Alderman*, with the increased taxation, attributed to the war, working in combination with Lady Grayle's own character flaws to produce her and her husband's destruction. Wade does not attempt to hide Lady Grayle's personal failings; indeed, in many ways, she is deliberately made an off-putting figure ("Your latest protege?" she cattily asks her despised

---

[49] Ibid., 62, 339.

daughter-in-law of her fashionable medical specialist, "What's become of that Jew-boy you were so keen on last year?"). Yet Lady Grayle is not essentially evil and Wade conveys through Poole's reflections her miserable ultimate fate with considerable intelligence and empathy: "[Poole] had begun to feel sympathy—almost affection—for [Tassart]," writes Wade. "[T]hough it was impossible not to feel horror at the callous cruelty that had already destroyed two lives, it was also difficult not to feel some sympathetic understanding of the provocation that had led up to it."[50] {*END SPOILERS*}

Throughout the novel, Inspector Poole shows a pronounced sense of refinement concerning police work, in passages where he reflects on the (admittedly necessary) sordid aspects of his job. Anticipating similar reflections in the works of Golden Age authors Dorothy L. Sayers, Margery Allingham and Ngaio Marsh, as well as their modern descendant, P. D. James, these self-recriminatory passages should strike a familiar chord with readers of these women's works:

> Poole felt slightly uncomfortable at this description of his methods. To "wheedle" a man's life out of an old woman was not a pleasant idea.
>
> Mrs. Moode hesitated, and unconsciously Poole put on his pleasant smile—then wished he could tear it off his face, as he saw the woman's own face soften and knew that he was again playing a Judas trick.
>
> "I'm sorry your husband's wasting his time and money over a thing like that," he said. "I suppose that means he keeps you short?" *What gross impertinence*, thought Poole.
>
> He hated the part that he had played himself, and he knew that he had gone very near the boundary of

---

[50] Ibid., 12, 343.

what was allowable in the collection of evidence. . . . He had not trapped her into thoughtless talk; if she had anything to hide, she had had the chance to hide it. But it had not been an agreeable part for him to play.[51]

This sensitive yet dutiful detective's dilemma occurs even in the lighter sections of the novel, when Poole is engaging in banter with the Grayles' pretty and personable social secretary:

> "When you say 'lately,' do you mean since Lord Grayle's death . . . or before?"
> Irene Hollen looked steadily at her companion.
> "Must you always be detecting?" she asked.
> Poole flushed.
> "I know; it's beastly," he said. "But I've got to do it."[52]

{SPOILERS} *No Friendly Drop* also resembles a novel by a British "Crime Queen," past or present, in that the solution to its puzzle pivots on the keen attention paid by the lead detective to the finer points of domestic detail, in this case household habits of brewing tea. Only when Poole discovers from a previously overlooked second footman every last step in the process of tea making and serving on the fatal day does he finally solve the mystery of who killed Lord Grayle:

> Poole looked down at the quaint, old-fashioned tea service, the flat, blue teapot that had been the vehicle of death for the man who had loved it all through his married life. The spout, Poole saw, had got the end knocked off. It must be the devil of a messy job to pour tea out of it. Automatically, Poole

[51] Ibid., 190, 197, 200, 204-204.
[52] Ibid., 157.

picked up the pot and tried to pour tea into the cup; it slobbered down the spout and made a mess in the tray.

William watched him, first with curiosity, then with something stronger; his jaw dropped.

"Good sakes, I'd forgotten that spout," he said.[53]
{*END SPOILERS*}

As the above revelation from William suggests, servants in *No Friendly Drop* have the wit to provide genuinely useful information to investigators and are not portrayed as easily-panicked ninnies or grasping ignoramuses. Indeed, the most unambiguously negatively-portrayed characters in the novel, Charles and Catherine Grayle, come indisputably from the upper crust. Wade represents the younger Grayles as entirely selfish and essentially futile human beings, as can be seen in an early clash of arms the pair has with Poole when they attempt to pressure him into dropping the investigation, in an outrageously anachronistic display of aristocratic hauteur:

> "Lady Grayle and I—my wife and I, that is—have considered the matter carefully and have decided that these investigations need not be continued. We are satisfied that my father's death was due to an accidental overdose. . . . There is not, therefore, any necessity for you to remain in Tassart; your presence in the village . . . is unsettling to the village people and undesirable. . . . I shall send a communication to the Commissioner informing him that you have done your duty with discretion, according to your light."[54]

---

[53] Ibid., 331.
[54] Ibid., 149-150. {*SPOILERS*} Granted, the butler Moode is grasping—he has two women in his life to support—but he is far from an ignoramus. {*END SPOILERS*}

Poole, who as a mere underling the couple did not give the courtesy of offering a chair, is "uncertain whether to be most amused or irritated by this performance." He easily holds his ground against these pale descendants of the country's faded ruling class. Faced with the inspector's unbreakable resolve, the younger Grayles quickly collapse. Charles is dismissed so his wife can be questioned separately about her father-in-law's death, when she finally is reduced to a pitiful attempt to kindle a sense of "esprit de class" on the genteel inspector's part: "It will cause a terrible scandal. . . . People talk so loosely nowadays; there is no restraint, no decency. The common people discuss us freely, as if . . . it is these dreadful newspapers that are responsible. . . . At present everyone thinks it is an accident, why not let it remain at that?"[55] Catherine's gambit, like that of Charles, fails miserably. For Poole as for Wade, life's difficulties cannot be so easily resolved.

Wade's next novel, *The Hanging Captain* (1932), saw the return of the sardonic Inspector Lott, investigating another case of murder among country gentry, this time at the Midlands domicile of Ferris Court, "the Tudor home of twelve generations of Sterrons." Currently residing at Ferris Court are Captain Herbert Sterron, retired from the British military, and his wife, the ironically-named (the reader will see) Griselda. When Sterron is found hanging from a curtain rod in his study, it is first thought that he committed suicide, but a rather officious houseguest, Sir James Hamsted, soon shows that Sterron was actually murdered. The most obvious suspects in the murder of the hanging captain are Sir Carle Venning, baronet and High Sheriff of the county, who seems to have been rather personally close to Griselda Sterron, and Herbert Sterron's brother, Gerald, recently returned after two decades from Shanghai. (Evidently referring to the 1932 hostilities between China and Japan, Gerald Sterron declares to Sir James Hamsted, "I saw what was coming just before the others did and sold out while there was still something to sell—and Americans with dollars to buy it.")[56]

---

[55] Ibid., 152.
[56] Henry Wade, *The Hanging Captain* (New York: Harcourt, Brace, 1933), 6.

Also frequently on the scene at Ferris Court is Father Luke Speyd, a fervent Anglo-Catholic minister and counselor to Grisdelda. With such people of prominence involved in the affair it is not long before Scotland Yard, in the person of Inspector Lott, is called in by the Chief Constable of the county; and once again Lott is competing with a local policeman, this time one Superintendent Dawle, in a race to catch a killer. Dawle is no dim copper, however, so Lott has his work cut out for him. Once again, Wade presents a sound problem with believable characters (both suspects and investigators), though I think overall the novel is a less memorable one than its three most immediate predecessors. Frustratingly, Wade suggests that Lott finds a love interest among the winsome chorines of Birmingham, but we never learn the outcome, as *The Hanging Captain* was the last novel with Lott as its investigator (he later is referenced briefly in a Poole novel).

Although the usually Wade-friendly *Catalogue of Crime* pronounced of Wade's ambitious 1933 novel, *Mist on the Saltings*, that "this ambitious attempt at a novel of character, combined with crime and detection, must be judged a failure" because "the elaboration of the marital tangle, on the one side, and of the disagreement of the police, on the other, has a perpetually retarding effect which kills suspense," other modern critics have been far kinder. Charles Shibuk in *Twentieth Century Crime and Mystery Writers* deemed the novel a "masterpiece" with "penetrating characterization, superb East Anglian marshland atmosphere, and a powerful and deeply moving climax"; while crime writer Martin Edwards more recently called *Saltings* "a study in character . . . ahead of its time." In its own day, *Saltings* divided critics over whether Wade had succeeded in writing, in effect, a "crime novel" (though that term was not used). From her post at the *Sunday Times*, Dorothy L. Sayers rather surprisingly thought not; however, the anonymous reviewer for the *Times Literary Supplement* deemed the novel a complete success:

> Mr. Wade's latest is something more than a brilliant exercise in detection. . . . Dallas Fiennes' corpse is

not found until the thirteenth chapter.... The first part of the book is an attempt, and a very successful one, to restore to the detective novel the background of psychology and atmosphere, which the masters of the craft have tended to sacrifice in favour of pure complexity. In these chapters the reader is introduced to solid and convincing characterizations.... Further, Mr, Wade describes with unusual feeling the lonely stretch of coast, the muddy channels, the stillness, broken only by the cry of the gulls, of the scene where the crime is committed.[57]

*Saltings* essentially concerns a love triangle composed of a struggling middle-aged artist, John Pansel, his wife, Hilary, and the despicable amorous author, Dallas Fiennes, who comes between them. The affair is played out in the remote East Anglian fishing village of Bryde-by-the-Sea, a fictional location Wade conveys with authority:

> Bryde-by-the-Sea, though nominally a harbour, lies nearly a mile back from the ocean which surges invisibly against the line of low sand dunes limiting the northern horizon. In between lies a wide expanse of weed-grown mud, intersected by a maze of channels which at high tide are full to the brim of salt water and at low are mere trenches of black and treacherous ooze. These are the Saltings....[58]

Murder intrudes late, halfway through the novel, when Dallas Fiennes is found dead, his face pressed down in that black and treacherous ooze of the trench-like Saltings. At least three men

---

[57] Barzun and Taylor, *Catalogue of Crime*, 421; Martin Edwards, "Harcourt and Henry Wade," *Do You Write Under Your Own Name*, 10 January 2008, http://doyouwriteunderyourownname.blogspot.com/2008/01/harcourt-and-henry-wade.html; *Times Literary Supplement*, 26 October 1933, 734. Shibuk's praise was prominently "blurbed" on the 1985 HarperCollins paperback edition.

[58] Henry Wade, *Mist on the Saltings* (London: Constable, 1933), 15.

had motive to kill Fiennes: John Pansel, whose wife, Hilary, is widely believed to have had an affair with the seductive writer; local fisherman and man-on-the-make Christian Magdek, who finds himself in urgent need of funds to pull off a marriage coup he has long been plotting; and Frank Helliott, the local struggling squire, whose request to borrow money Fiennes humiliatingly rebuffed. Police finally arrest one man, but the truth is only discovered in the last few pages of the novel.

Contrary to the assertion in *A Catalogue of Crime*, *Saltings* seems to me to maintain a steady level of suspense to the very end of the tale, when the author presents readers with a finely turned piece of sad irony as a finale. Whether one believes that the time Wade devotes to dealing with the various characters' emotional entanglements is excessive depends on one's aesthetic view of the detective novel. To Golden Age traditionalists like Barzun and Taylor, Wade diffuses the interest that properly should be devoted to the mechanics of the crime problem; but more modern readers, raised on writers like P. D. James, Ruth Rendell and Reginald Hill, are more likely, it seems to me, to applaud Wade's pioneering effort to craft a novel of character with crime interest.

While in the earlier novels *The Dying Alderman* and *No Friendly Drop*, Wade created some compelling characters, like Sir John Assington and Lady Helen Grayle, they tended to be people from the familiar country house milieu (an exception is Hallam, the intelligent and pugnacious porter in *The Dying Alderman*). In *Saltings*, Wade moves beyond the country house to look at the denizens of an insignificant fishing village, from the "arty" types like painters and writers to the plainer folk like Christian Magdek; and he allows himself ample time to develop these characters, even if it means drawing our attention away from the police investigation (and, earlier, allowing the buildup to the murder to take up half the novel). Wade also manages to find room for his perennial theme, the baleful effects of World War One. It is no surprise that this author compares the Saltings, with their "black and treacherous ooze," to trenches.[59]

---

[59] Wade, *Saltings*, 15.

We see the corrosive impact of World War One literally in the case of John Pansel, whose digestive system never really recovered from a wartime wound, a "severe abdominal laceration." Besides inflicting permanent physical damage on Pansel, the war also, Wade informs us, destroyed his promising career prospects. Pansel's "reputation as a painter had been firmly established before the war came to smash everything that was beautiful and of good repute in the world." He had won a traveling scholarship from the Lambeth Art School and gone to Paris, where he won the Prix du Louvre. The renowned art collector Sir Otto Geisberg "had sent for him and encouraged and advised him, offered to finance him for a further two years study in Rome." But war came and hurled away the golden ball. Pansel's patron Geisberg perished in a British internment camp in the war, "of unhappiness and horrible food and loneliness and the ugly side of a life that till then had been, for him, nearly all beauty." Semi-recovery from the horror of war and his lacerating wound cost Pansel time, and then came the economic slump and taxes "that were to have come down" but "didn't come down."[60] Paintings, Pansel found to his growing dismay, were among the first things to be sacrificed when the wealthy economized.

When Pansel married Hilary after the war, the newlyweds thought it would be charming to buy a cottage at Bryde-by-the-Sea, where the lights ("greys and mauves, pale yellows and quiet greens") were wonderful for painting and the food plentiful and cheap. And "for the first three months," Wade notes, with a jab at a popular contemporary American romantic novelist, the couple had found "a happiness that had seemed almost impossible except in a book by Gene Stratton Porter."[61] But years of myriad privations—the lack of money, the lack of domestic help for Hilary, the lack of a delicate diet for Pansel—take their toll on the marriage. John becomes morose and embittered, Hilary quietly unhappy. Into this deteriorating marriage comes the charming—to Hilary—

---

[60] Ibid., 4, 5, 9-10.
[61] Ibid., 8, 9.

presence of visiting author Dallas Fiennes, a cheerfully amoral rogue who spends his time, when not writing successful middlebrow novels, planning seductions of any attractive females in his midst.

Much of the novel revolves around these three characters, all well-conveyed by the author: Fiennes, suitably odious, if superficially attractive; Hilary, warm and sympathetic, even when erring; and Pansel, who possesses that frustrating mixture of virtues and flaws that has made Thomas Hardy's Mayor of Casterbridge, Michael Henchard, so perennially fascinating. Wade does justice to other characters in the novel as well. For example, the fisherman Christian Magdek, with his ambitious—if not always ethical—plans to advance himself, is a noteworthy figure in his own right, particularly as he is far from the ignorant forelock-tugging rustic yokel traditionally associated with Golden Age British mystery.

Also of interest are the local gentry, Frank Helliott and his sister Beryl. Like the declining aristocratic family in Shelia Kaye-Smith's English bestseller *The End of the House of Alard* (1923), the Helliotts have found themselves in increasingly straightened financial circumstances with every passing year. They have managed for the time to hold on to the ancestral home, Brulcote Manor, but Frank has for all practical purposes devolved in status from leisured gentleman to a mere working farmer—and not a very successful one at that. Wade does especially well with Beryl, whose ultimate futility as a person gives him a chance to indulge in some satirical (and perhaps a touch chauvinistic) humor. Beryl, he tells us, is twenty-nine, short-sighted and "too depressed with poverty and dullness to take any trouble about her appearance, which in any case was homely. Hilary had called her a nice girl, which meant she was sorry for her and could not under any conceivable circumstances feel jealous of her." Beryl, we learn, has "passed her life in keeping the wolf from the doors—front, back and side—of Brulcote Manor and trying to make her brother remember that he was a gentleman before he became a farmer." Hilary's attempt to get the frustratingly obtuse and determinedly self-denying Beryl to attend a performance of "The Yeoman of the Guard" with her and Fiennes

(Pansel has pridefully refused to go, playing into Fiennes' hands, but Hillary has made her acceptance contingent on getting Beryl to go with her) is amusingly done:

> "Then you'll come?"
> "But I've nothing to wear."
> Beryl was in the woman's Last Ditch.[62]

Overall, however, *Mist on the Saltings* is a grim and gloomy novel, one of the most uncompromisingly such of the Golden Age period. It is worth noting not only that Wade was unable to find an American publisher for this genre masterwork but that after the publication of the more traditional detective novel *Constable, Guard Thyself!* in 1934, he never found another for any of his books again until the 1950s, when influential *New York Times Book Review* critic Anthony Boucher helped spur an American revival of his work. It seems not farfetched to suggest that Wade's novels had become too challenging for American publishers of mystery fiction in the 1930s, being no longer easy for them to pigeonhole. No doubt from an English hand they would have much preferred a "straight" detective tale called *Murder on the Saltings* to the marital-drama-with-murder Wade instead had offered them with *Mist on the Saltings*.

In Britain, meanwhile, Henry Wade's prestige continued to grow, at least among connoisseurs. His 1934 detective novel, *Constable, Guard Thyself!*, was singled out for special praise in the newspapers by no less than Dorothy L. Sayers and Francis Iles (Anthony Berkeley Cox). Sayers, who had felt the year before that Wade's earnest effort at depicting characters of greater emotional depth had reduced parts of *Mist on the Saltings* to "bathos," had no such reservations about *Constable*, which she postulated "might serve as a model of the classical detective story." The novel had, she believed, "a perfect unity of tone and action; neither reaching out to the larger and looser universe of the straight novel [as *Saltings* had done], nor shrivelling to the dry and restricted

---

[62] Ibid., 48, 50.

two-dimensional circle of the mathematical puzzle." Iles similarly found the tale excellent ("just about as good as a detective story can be") and concluded, with language tailor-made for future Wade publishers, that "a new novel by Henry Wade is now an event, as well as a joy."[63]

*Constable, Guard Thyself!* is, like Sayer's *Murder Must Advertise* from the previous year, an important genre milestone in that it is an early example of the "workplace mystery," a mystery where much of the interest is to be found in the authenticity and detail of the workplace setting where the murder takes place. In the case of *Murder Must Advertise,* the setting was that of an advertising agency, a milieu with which Sayers could claim earlier professional experience. With *Constable*, the locale is a county police station, a setting with which Wade had great familiarity because of his own background in county and municipal government. As Sayers noted, "Mr. Wade, unlike many of his colleagues, has taken pains to acquaint himself with the precise workings of the complicated police machinery. . . . This provides the reader with that extra interest and sense of reality which always comes of 'seeing the wheels go round'."[64] Additionally, Inspector Poole is called in to aid the investigation, and his sympathetic and intelligent presence is always a welcome one.

When Chief Constable Scoles of Brodshire (yet another stand-in for Buckinghamshire) is shot in his office, the problem presented appears to be something in the nature of a locked room puzzle. Local police assume the murderer must be Albert Hinde, a man recently released from jail after serving twenty years, who had been convicted on Scoles' testimony (Scoles had committed perjury when testifying against Hinde, the reader also learns). How, Poole finds himself asking, could a rustic ex-lag like Hinde have gotten into the station to shoot Scole and out again to make his escape,

---

[63] *Sunday Times*, 22 July 1934, 7. The Iles review is excerpted in the 1972 Hutchinson reprint of the 1938 Henry Wade short story collection, *Here Comes the Copper*.
[64] *Sunday Times*, 22 July 1934, 7.

without being noticed by any of the policemen? The solution Poole comes to suspect is that, in an occupational variant on G. K. Chesterton's famous detective story "The Invisible Man," Scoles' murderer was not Albert Hinde, but a member, like Scoles himself, of the Brodshire police force. In the course of his investigation Poole stumbles on to a paper suggesting that some sort of financial fraud has been going on in the force, and he believes that a policeman must be implicated in the fraud. If Scoles had suspected who that person was, that man had reason to silence Scoles; and, as a member of the police force, his presence in the station naturally would have raised no alarm.

{SPOILERS} Wade's willingness to raise the specter of police corruption is yet another testament to his artistic commitment to realism, but he ultimately lays the specter to rest by making the corruption plot line a red herring laid by the murderer, who turns out indeed to be one of the Brodshire policeman, but also Albert Hinde's younger brother, who had been sentenced to a jail term as well on Scoles' evidence. Convicted of a lesser charge, Hinde had been released to fight in the Great War, and was thought to have been killed on the western front. To the contrary, far from having died in the war, Hinde survived and created a new identity, later joining the Brodshire police force, nursing plans for revenge against Scoles that he finally acted upon twenty years later. Thus Hinde is in the police but not of the police, as it were. As he himself tells Poole, "I'm an old lag.... I'm on their side; a policeman only for my own convenience." This development, whereby the murderer is not a policeman in the "spiritual" sense, if you will, but rather a longtime mole for the criminal "side," is an interesting idea (interesting enough to have reappeared in the Oscar-winning Martin Scorsese film *The Departed*); yet the inherently melodramatic plot device of a "long revenge" undermines the novel's sense of realism. At the time of *Constable*'s publication Charles Williams noted this flaw, commenting in his review of the novel that "in the end [*Constable, Guard Thyself!*] rather retreats, since one policeman is hardly a policeman at all, or only one in the sense that the devil, as well as Mr. Wade, can quote scripture for

# THE SPECTRUM OF ENGLISH MURDER 69

his purpose."⁶⁵ However, it should be recalled that Wade reveals Chief Constable Scoles twenty years earlier had perjured his testimony against Hinde (Scoles wanted a dramatic conviction of murder against a member of a poaching ring, not merely one for manslaughter), and was supported in that perjured testimony by several members of his police force, who put a higher value on occupational loyalty than truth and justice. At the time and the place he was writing, this was a fairly daring authorial decision on the writer's part. {END SPOILERS}

After completing *Constable, Guard Thyself!* Wade would not return to the pure detective novel form until after the Second World War. His next novel, *Heir Presumptive*, is an "inverted" mystery novel, one of the classics of this mystery subgenre. Inverted mysteries, in which the reader knows who the murderer is or will be from the beginning of the novel, making the narrative focus not "who done it" but how s/he will be caught (if at all), became popular after the 1931 publication of Francis Iles' much lauded *Malice Aforethought*. Wade's inverted tale received a goodly share of enthusiastic praise in Britain, though the novel is today unjustly overlooked, like so much of Wade's work. Writing in the *Sunday Times*, Milward Kennedy, Dorothy L. Sayers' successor as crime fiction reviewer, declared flatly that "no one ... excels Henry Wade as a writer of detective stories" and that the author's "venture into Iles-land" had produced a novel "much more exciting and nightmarish than many which seek to deserve such epithets."⁶⁶

With a wickedly satirical plot that will be familiar to viewers of the 1949 Alec Guinness film *Kind Hearts and Coronets*, *Heir Presumptive* concerns the efforts of the unscrupulous Eustace Hendel to secure the title and estate of his ninety-year-old first cousin (twice removed), Baron Chandos. The pair of male relatives

---

⁶⁵ Henry Wade, *Constable, Guard Thyself!* (1934; rpnt., London: Hutchinson, 1971), 307; Charles Williams, "Passionate Policemen!", *Westminster Gazette*, 3 August 1934, in Jared C. Lobdell, *The Detective Fiction Reviews of Charles Williams, 1930-1935* (Jefferson, NC and London: McFarland, 2003), 114.
⁶⁶ *Sunday Times*, 3 November 1935, 9.

standing closest in line to the Baron, a father and son (respectively third cousin and third cousin once removed to Eustace), happily have just drowned in a bathing accident when the novel opens, leaving only two additional distant cousins in his way. Eustace begins to plot murder, with the "moral" support of his equally amoral mistress. Wade again makes excellent use of his personal knowledge, this time concerning what surely are to most of us arcane matters of aristocratic inheritance. Wade himself did not become "heir presumptive" to the Fletcher baronetcy until his Uncle Henry died in 1910, when the future author was twenty-three years old; and he must have spent some idle moments in his youth studying family genealogical tables. (Appropriately, the first edition of *Heir Presumptive* includes an elaborate fold-out family tree of the Hendels.) I shall refrain from divulging more about the novel's clever plot, beyond adding that the there is one chapter, involving a murder during a stag hunt contrived to look like an accident, that is truly gruesome and a standing refutation to those who tend to dismiss British detective novels of this period as invariably "cozy" affairs.

Having proven himself a master of the inverted tale, Wade turned next to the police procedural subgenre, which places primary importance on the accurate portrayal of police investigations of credible crimes. Sadly, the author has never received his due as a police procedural pioneer. Most recently, Stephen Knight's commentary on the author (in Knight's recent "comprehensive analytic survey of crime fiction," *Crime Fiction, 1800-2000: Detection, Death, Diversity*) is woefully inaccurate and inadequate. Admittedly, Wade, as Professor Knight states, did not "create" the procedural subgenre (though surely it is impossible to assign exclusive creative agency to one person); he nevertheless was one of its key pioneers, based primarily on three works that go unmentioned by Professor Knight: *Bury Him Darkly* (1936); *Lonely Magdalen* (1940); and his second and final short story collection, *Here Comes the Copper* (1938). (Wade's first short story collection, *Policeman's Lot*, also contains several tales that are more in the nature of police procedurals.) *Copper* neatly follows the professional career of Police-Constable

John Bragg, who over time rises to the ranks of the C.I.D. The thirteen stories collected therein are entertaining, if minor, pieces in Wade's canon, reminiscent of former Scotland Yard Assistant Commissioner Sir Basil Thomson's Inspector Richardson novels, published between 1933 and 1937.[67] *Bury Him Darkly* and *Lonely Magdalen* are more ambitious works, each portraying in broad scope the massive mechanism that is a Scotland Yard murder investigation. Because of the stylistic similarities, I shall discuss *Magdalen* with *Darkly* (*Magdalen* at far greater length), even though Wade published two additional novels between *Darkly* and *Magdalen*.

Both novels employ John Poole as the central investigator, although in them we get far more of a depiction of Poole as a mere cog in the great machinery of justice, rather than an all-powerful Great Detective. Of the two works, *Lonely Magdalen* is much the superior. While *Bury Him Darkly* succeeds in giving the reader the realistic feel of an actual police investigation, it makes for rather dull reading. With *Lonely Magdalen* Wade is much more successful both in depicting authentically styled police work as well as in spinning an engrossing tale with compellingly portrayed characters. In his introduction to a 1965 edition of *Lonely Magdalen*, the late Michael Gilbert, an attorney and himself one of the great post-Golden Age mystery authors (several classic police procedurals were penned by him), pays tribute to Wade's mastery of this difficult form. "The process of crime detection by the police is largely mechanised," Gilbert explains:

> The machine employs a number of specialists—photographers, pathologists, laboratory technicians, finger-print experts, and, ultimately, lawyers. . . . [T]he man who works the machine, and without

---

[67] For Stephen Knight's take on Wade, see his *Crime Fiction, 1800-2000: Detection, Death, Diversity* (New York: Palgrave Macmillan, 2004), 153. For more on the John Bragg tales, see John Cooper, "Henry Wade's Police Constable John Bragg," *CADS* 69 (January 2015), 17-20. Cooper has discovered a fourteenth, previously uncollected John Bragg short story, "Cotton-Wool and Cutlets," originally published in 1940. See Cooper, "Bragg," 19-20.

> whose skillful handling it would not operate at all, is the policeman, sometimes in plain clothes, sometimes in uniform. . . . But however they are dressed, and wherever they come from, they work in the same way. They ask a lot of people a great number of questions, and they record and analyse the answers. If this produces no very satisfactory result, they start again, and ask questions of more people; and more. Nobody knew this better than Henry Wade.
>
> . . . .
>
> The difficulty which faces the writer of a police story lies in transforming those steady, plodding, mechanical, routine operations into an exciting book. You will observe, I think, with admiration, the way in which Henry Wade has achieved it.[68]

Gilbert goes on to discuss how Wade structured *Lonely Magdalen* into its highly readable form. With great skill, Gilbert notes, the author devised a narrative which

> wedded a straight story, told in a flashback in the central portion of the book, to two pieces of investigation. The earlier investigation works backwards from the discovery of the unknown woman's body, though the process of identification, to her early life. The later investigation brings the characters of the central portion forward again into the present, since many of them are found to have motives for wanting the woman concerned out of the way.

---

[68] Michael Gilbert, introduction to Henry Wade, *Lonely Magdalen* (1940; rpnt., London: Hodder & Stoughton, 1965), v-vi. {*SPOILERS*} Moreover, in *Bury Him Darkly* Wade again raises the possibility of police corruption as the explanation for the crime, only to dismiss it in favor of a less interesting solution. {*END SPOILERS*}

Gilbert concludes with the forceful declaration that he could "think of no instance in which the double [narrative] journey has been accomplished, and with such firm construction, as in *Lonely Magdalen*."[69]

As in the case with *Mist on the Saltings*, *A Catalogue of Crime* registered disagreement with such high praise, asserting that while *Lonely Magdalen* could boast of "good detection and realistic treatment of police work," its "large dose of routine human interest" was "excessive."[70] What we are again faced with here is an aesthetic debate. To Barzun and Taylor, Wade had erred in *Magdalen*, as he had in *Saltings*, in putting too much emphasis on matters not strictly criminous. Naturally, critics who have wanted mystery authors to break out of the bonds of their genre and produce more than "mere puzzles" have been more sympathetic to experiments like Wade's. My own view is that, while *Lonely Magdalen's* puzzle is not comparable in ingenuity to that of earlier novels like *The Dying Alderman* or *No Friendly Drop*, both the police investigation and the characters are of strong interest, making the novel, like *Mist on the Saltings*, one of Wade's most noteworthy tales.

The first part of the novel, entitled "Working Back," concerns, as Michael Gilbert indicates, the Yard's investigation into the death by strangling of a prostitute in London's Hampstead Heath. This bare summary alone indicates that we are in a grimmer world than that traditionally associated with Britain's Golden Age mystery stories, though of course such sordid affairs were much more a part of the real world than blustering baronets bludgeoned in their country house libraries. But then "realism" is the keynote of this first section of *Magdalen*. The novel opens with the sort of milieu much favored by John Street, but up until now avoided by Wade, that of a working class London pub, "The Red Knight." A radio announcer gives a police notice about the discovery of the dead woman in Hampstead Heath, concluding after the notice is given:

---

[69] Gilbert, introduction to *Magdalen*, vi.
[70] Barzun and Taylor, *Catalogue of Crime*, 421.

"And now here is Professor Harold Dickerson, who will give the second of his weekly series of talks on 'Woman and Her Sphere To-day'." "Not 'ere 'e won't," declares one of The Red Knight's patrons belligerently, "Switch it off, Ted." The same man sourly damns "these effin police" for interrupting the previous program with their message and not waiting until the nine o'clock news.[71] Clearly we are not among genteel and complacent country house society.

Wade does not hold back on details and observations that some readers of the time might have found unpleasant to have to think about when reading "escapist" fiction. Looking down on the murdered woman's body, Chief-Inspector Beldam declares bluntly, "this poor woman's a prostitute or I'm a Dutchman." Likewise, when told that the man who discovered the deceased is a barrister and churchwarden, Beldam offers the cynical observation that "churchwardens may have their weaknesses like the rest of us . . . and I've seen a barrister in the dock before now." During an interview with the estimable barrister-churchwarden, Beldam asks the man if he had ever noticed any soliciting (not of the lawyerly variety) in the neighborhood. The man professes to be shocked at the very idea, declaring piously "this is a respectable locality, I hope and believe." Beldam finds himself wondering whether the fellow "would regard murder as respectable, though soliciting was not." For his part, Inspector Poole discovers from a witness that one of the dead prostitute's customers was "a black man." When another witness, a woman, fails to mention this detail to him, Poole reflects sardonically to himself that this lady "had presumably been so unfortunate as to miss that particular piece of scandal."[72]

A "Red Knight" patron who had been visibly disturbed by the police message heard in the pub was Bert Varden, a dissolute bruiser who supports himself with occasional jobs as a bookie's bodyguard (or "racing tout"). Varden soon becomes the focus of the police investigation. As Poole says, "the odds are that this is

---

[71] Wade, *Magdalen*, 3,4.
[72] Ibid., 12, 14, 36, 50, 57.

just a case of some vicious brute, a more or less casual bit of violence that went too far."[73] But the case against Varden peters out, leaving Poole at loose ends.

Poole decides to investigate farther back into the past of the dead woman (her name, Bella Knox, is clearly fictive), which ultimately leads the reader to the "flashback" middle section of the novel, titled "Twenty-five Years Ago." This section details pivotal earlier events in the woman's life that led to her sorry present of trying to scrape by as an aging, physically scarred prostitute. {*SPOILERS*} With *Lonely Magdalen*'s flashback section we do indeed again enter the confines of that reputed holy of holies of the Golden Age, a baronet's country house (in this case the house is called Chatterleys, the author evidently invoking D. H. Lawrence), and we learn just how far Bella had fallen before her pathetic death. {*END SPOILERS*} Once again the Great War plays its central role in disrupting the stability of society and wrecking people's lives. "Poor lonely Magdalen," reflects Poole to himself ("Bella Knox" once pertly informed a clergyman who asked her name that it was "Magdalen"), "how bitterly she had paid for the wild folly of her youth."[74]

In the final section of the novel, titled "Working Forward," the genteel Poole finds himself faced with the possibility that an appealing, well-born couple from Bella's past may be implicated in her murder, a prospect that appalls him:

> [T]hat people of gentle birth should do such a thing was terrible beyond Poole's experience . . . a soldier who had won the military cross . . . a woman who had worked in France throughout the war . . . what explanation could there be of such ghastly warping of two characters? . . . [T]heir creed, their birthright, was to control passion. *Noblesse oblige.*
>
> Much of that old tradition had, of course, perished since the war and this could only be a case

---

[73] Ibid., 33.
[74] Ibid., 260.

where the evil spell of war had disintegrated all that was good in two human beings.[75]

Eventually Poole finally finds a clue that seems to put a suspect on the scene of the crime, and another clue is uncovered (one that had been lost due to inter-service hostility in the Yard bureaucracy), leading to the busting of an alibi. A suspect is arrested, a trial occurs and a conviction is obtained. Along the way, Wade depicts Chief-Inspector Beldam violating the Judge's Rules by harshly interrogating a person he knows he will charge. Poole "was frankly appalled," writes the author, "This was the nearest thing to 'third degree' that he had experienced since he joined the C.I.D . . . and he hated it. But he could do nothing; he was Beldam's subordinate." At the trial, the defendant's solicitor challenges his client's statement to the police, arguing that it had been improperly obtained by Beldam, but Poole, testifying, supports his superior: "He could not bring himself to let Beldam and the force down; he declared that there had been no bullying; the questioning, though close, had been fair; when he left the box he was sweating and miserably conscious of having been as near perjury as ever he had been in his life."[76] Six years after his involvement in the events detailed in *Constable, Guard Thyself!*, Poole finds himself replicating the actions of those Brodshire policemen who had supported Chief Constable Scoles in his perjured testimony, the only difference being that in the current case the person charged with the crime likely committed the crime. Poole can take some ethical solace in that fact, admittedly; nevertheless, Wade was clearly illustrating for his readers an unseemly fact of police work: policemen violate the Judges Rules and lie on the stand to get convictions. Nor does Wade, like other Golden Age authors such as Freeman Wills Crofts, portray these police illegalities indulgently; he recognizes that a moral and ethical cost is incurred.

---

[75] Ibid., 258.
[76] Ibid., 313, 315.

Of Wade's two remaining pre-war novels (*Lonely Magdalen* was actually published in 1940, but I classify it as a prewar work), *The High Sheriff* (1937) and *Released for Death* (1938), the former is one of his strongest works, the other less so; but both novels have elements worthy of notice. Together, the pair of novels explore the higher and lower ends of the British social strata, but *The High Sheriff*, which involves the lasting costs of the Great War and unearths secrets and shames of the group with which Wade was most familiar, county landed gentry, is the more successful of the two. *Sheriff* opens with a prologue set on the western front during World War One detailing the breakdown of Captain Robert D'Arcy and his attempted surrender of his smashed company after its day-long resistance against overwhelming odds. A sleep-deprived, nerve-shattered D'Arcy agonizes over whether to surrender: "Had he not done enough? Could he not with honour surrender now? Was it not only fair to his men? To hold on was sheer waste of human life; they could do no more good." D'Arcy wants fervently to surrender but cannot bring himself to do so. For the men in the trenches, Wade tells us, surrendering "needed even greater moral courage than waiting for the end called for physical courage." Finally, however, another, this time surely crushing, artillery barrage starts; and D'Arcy, screwing his moral courage to the sticking post, staggers out of his trench with a white rag. His arm rises, then "a violent tug on his coat-tail hurled him back into the trench . . . he saw a white, snarling face before him, a khaki arm raised to strike, then . . . oblivion."[77]

The novel moves forward to 1936, to the pomp and pageantry of the ceremonial assumption of the office of Brackenshire High Sheriff by Lieutenant-Colonel Sir Robert D'Arcy ffollihood Speke D'Arcy, Baronet. D'Arcy feels a swell of pride at this moment, but even now "nothing could drive from [his] mind the picture of himself, on the point of cowardly surrender, being struck down by one of the men whom he was there to lead." After eight months in a

---

[77] Henry Wade, *The High Sheriff* (1937; rpnt., London: Howard Baker, 1972), 22, 23.

German prison and a long recovery, he found himself unable to talk about what he believed to be his shame, and thus no one told him "that he was being absurd, that there was no cowardice in his act, that his defense of the redoubt for twenty-four hours in the midst of overwhelming hordes of Germans had been an act of epic heroism." D'Arcy could only try his courage "at the court of his own tortured conscience, than which there could be no more inexorable judge."[78]

With this scene, Wade establishes the novel's central theme: how a man of genuine honor and courage lets pride and vanity create in him a false belief in his own shameful past cowardice, leading to disaster. Robert D'Arcy rides others as hard as he does himself, determined not to tolerate "weakness," whenever and wherever he finds it. Early in the novel, Sir Wilbraham Bagot, Judge of Assize, asks D'Arcy his opinion on Bagot's upcoming sentencing of "this man Pinwell," a schoolmaster in one of the villages on D'Arcy's estate, who has been found guilty of an unspecified outrage—presumably, from the context, a sexual offense of some nature against a student. "I'm no great believer in psycho-analysis myself," explains the judge, "but there is a psychological side to [cases of this kind] which one ought not altogether to ignore." Noting that he has "more than once, on local advice, bound a man over for medical treatment, with quite satisfactory results," Bagot asks D'Arcy's opinion in this case. Feeling himself "stiffening with annoyance" at Bagot's's words, the baronet cannot believe what he is hearing: "Psycho-analysis! Medical treatment! Good God, what were English judges coming to, to talk such piffling nonsense? What the man needed was imprisonment with hard labour that would sweat some of the dirt out of him." D'Arcy is more than happy to see Pinwell in the dock, the man being "one of those opinionated, socialist fellows that the teaching profession threw up from time to time." When he calms his thoughts, D'Arcy stiffly warns Bagot of "the effect on public opinion" if Pinwell is "let off." The judge, now himself irked, explains there was no suggestion on his

---

[78] Wade, *Sheriff*, 25-26.

part of letting the man off: "If he were bound over on condition of his undergoing a course of medical treatment it would also be conditional upon good behavior; if there was any recurrence he would automatically come up for punishment." D'Arcy waves aside this explanation with the falsely self-deprecating smugness of the proudly parochial: "We are ignorant, old-fashioned people in this part of the world. We expect a man who is convicted of a . . . an infernal offence like this to be punished . . . and severely punished. . . . [The parents] want his blood and if he doesn't go to gaol I won't answer for it that they won't get it." Bagot, "taken aback by the vehemence of the reply" and disliking the "dictatorial note" in D'Arcy's voice, comments shortly, "I see. No nonsense about mercy in Brackenshire."[79]

D'Arcy's sixteen-year-old son Peter, whom the baronet finds unacceptably anxious and weak-tempered, similarly hears "no nonsense about mercy." His favored, elder son, John, had been killed in a flying accident a year earlier, so that, frustratingly for D'Arcy, his line now depends on the weak reed of the nervy younger son, Peter. To the baronet's surprise, he finds that his berating and publicly humiliating Peter does not have the character-building effect he expected it to have, indeed rather causing his son to become moodier and more timid and unsure of himself than ever. D'Arcy much prefers his confident daughter, Ann, but of course as a female she cannot keep the family name and the title alive.

Social stratification in this "old-fashioned part of the world" that is Brackenshire is still pronounced; and both Robert D'Arcy and his wife, Helen, believe in observing the myriad unwritten rules of county class distinctions. One of these is treating the horse dealer Gerald Barton as a distinct social inferior. When Ann D'Arcy begins to become infatuated with the handsome Barton, Wade informs us that Lady Helen never notices, because to Lady Helen "a man like Barton was so completely beyond the pale that she did not think of him as an attractive man at all." After suffering an unmistakable social snub from Lord D'Arcy, an infuriated Barton

---

[79] Ibid., 29, 32-33.

goes to the baronet and tells him that he was one of the twelve men, survivors of a territorial division, who had joined D'Arcy's company on the day of the final German assault against the company's redoubt; and thus he was a witness to D'Arcy's attempted raising of the white flag. "It would make a pretty story for Brackenshire," Barton sneeringly tells the baronet, "the officer who waved a white flag to the Germans and was knocked out by an N. C. O. Nice sort of officer! The High Sheriff of Brackenshire!"[80] Barton's demands for his keeping silent are galling to the proud baronet: that D'Arcy purchase one or two of the horses offered by him and his partner, Jim Lake; that he recommend their business to his friends; that he have him, Barton, over to D'Arcy's manor house on occasion to dine and shoot. Mortified by the possibility of his shame being revealed to county society, D'Arcy acquiesces, very unhappily. But when Barton later raises the ante to include the hand in marriage of the infatuated Ann D'Arcy, the baronet baulks. A few weeks later Barton is fatally shot during a woodcock and rabbit hunt held by Sir Robert.

The police investigation of this incident is conducted by Chief Constable Faide and Superintendent Clewth, police officials Wade depicted previously in the novel *No Friendly Drop* and the story "Jealous Gun." Earlier events in *No Friendly Drop* are referenced in *The High Sheriff* by Faide and Clewth. {SPOILERS} The two men meditate calling in the Yard, but decide that the tragic outcome of Inspector Poole's investigation of the Grayle case argues against the advisability of doing so: "Poole did his work well enough, but once we get the Yard in the case it is to all intents and purposes out of our hands," complains Faide, always conscious of the feelings of county gentry. "Good God," he adds, "We don't want . . . we can't have another case like that. . . ." The deferent Faide cannot even bring himself to refer directly to the horrifying events of the Grayle case, when he had seen Poole "slowly strip the fine mantle of honour from the shoulders of one of his own most

---

[80] Ibid., 61, 66.

treasured and respected friends, bringing the case to a climax more dreadful even than the murder of Lord Grayle himself."[81] Faide cannot abide another such outcome for a county family of quality, and thus is determined to keep the reins of the investigation in his and Clewth's hands if possible. {*END SPOILERS*}

Happily for county complacency, the jury in the coroner's inquest finds that Barton died from "the accidental discharge of a shotgun" and that "there was no evidence to show how that accident occurred." The investigation can now be dropped, with no embarrassment for anyone. Yet Faide, while thankful for the result, cannot suppress a sinking feeling in his heart that D'Arcy for some reason had indeed murdered Barton and that he, Faide, had chosen "a weak and cowardly course."[82]

While Faide's professional conscience pricks him, the fortunes of the D'Arcy family take a happy turn. Ann returns from abroad (she had left before Barton's death to think things over), having concluded she really did not love Barton after all. As far as Sir Robert himself is concerned, he has become a changed man after this intensely stressful period, learning to tolerate weakness in himself and others, including his son, Peter. Unfortunately, this brief family emotional flowering is quickly withered by a blast of cruel chance. {*SPOILERS*} Barton's business partner, Jim Lake, learns from Ann that she and Barton had been planning to marry. He realizes now that Sir Robert had a motive to murder Barton, that Barton must have been blackmailing the baronet. He realizes this because, as he tells the baronet, it was he, not Barton, who had been there at the assault where Sir Robert had raised the white flag. Lake had told Barton about the incident, a revelation Barton decided to make use of after repeated snubbing by D'Arcy. Now a vengeful Lake issues Sir Robert an ultimatum: "You killed my friend and you've got to pay for that. . . . I'll give you till the end of the hunting season to take your own way out. . . . If you don't, I

---

[81] Ibid., 181, 279.
[82] Ibid., 280.

shall have to go to the police." Lake adds that D'Arcy will not be able to "put me out of the way as you did with Gerry. . . . I know what you are and I can take care of myself."[83]

Finally cornered, D'Arcy arranges a fatal riding accident for himself. With his last breaths, he tells Lady Helen of his entanglements with Barton and Lake but insists to her that he did not murder Barton. At Sir Robert's funeral, "poor old Faide" looks "broken up," causing the chairman of the Standing Joint Committee to reflect that "it was really time to give him a hint." After the funeral, Clewth, like his superior suspicious that something is being concealed about the D'Arcys, tries to pry information out of Jim Lake, conspicuously absent from Sir Robert's funeral; but he is curtly told by Lake that the horse dealer has "no information to give."[84] The case is absolutely closed.

In the final chapter, titled "Thirteenth Baronet," we finally learn the truth. Lady Helen confides in her son, Peter (now the thirteenth baronet of the title), her fear that his father might have killed Barton, despite his assurance that he had not. Peter D'Arcy tells his mother he knows his father did not kill Barton because he, Peter, himself killed Barton. "I don't think [the police] really suspect anyone [deliberately] shot him," Peter proudly tells his horrified mother, "*And I'm not going to tell them.*"[85] By slaying Barton (whom Peter had overheard insulting his father) and getting away with it, Peter has in his own eyes finally proved himself to be a man worthy of the D'Arcy name.

*The High Sheriff* is probably the most profoundly bleak work in the entire Wade canon. Robert D'Arcy, an essentially unlikable man throughout most of the novel, finally undergoes a personal reformation, exorcising his demons of the past, yet he is still destroyed. And, worse yet, Wade makes clear that D'Arcy's death solves nothing. Indeed, to the contrary, it ends any chance of D'Arcy saving his son from his own failing: what Lady Helen comes to see as a "dreadful kink in the family that she had not realized,"

---

[83] Ibid., 277-278.
[84] Ibid., 297, 299.
[85] Ibid., 310.

a "pride of race" that leads to "madness" and "wickedness."[86] Moreover, outside the family, the kind and decent Chief Constable Faide is left a broken man. {*END SPOILERS*}

One of the premier British crime novels of the Golden Age period, *The High Sheriff* beautifully illustrates how crime in a novel, in addition to providing a puzzle or suspense element, can also be used to illustrate broader themes about society and character. Once again Wade finds much of value in aristocratic culture, such as its *noblesse oblige* and deeply ingrained sense of honor and duty; but nevertheless he probes and exposes failings like smugness, incuriousness, reactionary traditionalism, and a sometimes overweening class and family pride. Never is the author as bravely remorseless with genre readers as in *The High Sheriff*, one of his great works in the genre.

For some, the experience of reading the tale produced a sort of mental vertigo: *just what kind of book is this?* Thus we get what many would see today as a senseless out-of-hand dismissal of the novel as an uncategorizable grotesque by Herbert Read, the sophisticated poet and art critic. "The story [Wade] tells in *The High Sheriff* is a good story," Read writes, "but I do not think it is a particularly good thriller. . . . [T]here should only be enough character in a thriller to "motivate" crime. In this book characterization runs away with the story and the crime is only incidental. . . . [T]he hard-bitten reviewer, faced with his pigeon-holes, can only place it among the misfits." On the other hand, *A Catalogue of Crime*, critical of Wade's other more novelistic efforts from this period, deemed *The High Sheriff* a "classic story" and Charles Shibuk applauded the tale's "depth of characterization" and "dazzling narrative technique." Similarly, the *Sunday Times* praised the novel for its "penetrating study of a proud, perhaps a vain, man" and declared it "one of those welcome books that bridge the gap between the 'straight' novel and the unvarnished detective-story."[87]

---

[86] Ibid., 305.

[87] Herbert Read, "Blood Wet and Dry," 23 December 1937, in Herbert Read, *Pursuits and Verdicts* (Edinburgh: Tragara Press, 1983), 23-24; Barzun and Taylor, *Catalogue of Crime*, 420-421; Shibuk, "Henry Wade," 93; *Sunday Times*, 7 Nov. 1937, 9.

In short, for those reviewers who could accept serious novelistic treatment of life (and death) in a mystery story, *The High Sheriff* proved a laudable book. For those who expected a "thriller" to adhere to its "natural" limitations, expounded years before in the 1920s by Ronald Knox and S. S. Van Dine, the book was an aesthetically unpleasing freak, suitable only to be "put down" (figuratively and literally). In the modern era of the crime novel, however, one would hope *The High Sheriff* might someday receive the acknowledgment from genre scholars and fans that it deserves.

Like 1937's *The High Sheriff*, Henry Wade's 1938 novel, *Released for Death*, continues the author's practice of using murder as a way of psychologically elucidating character, rather than "merely" providing an intriguing mechanical puzzle for readers to solve. Yet the novel also represents something new in Wade's oeuvre, a sustained attempt to explore through its characters the social milieu of England's working class. The first section of *Released* centers on life at Hadestone—suggestive of *Hades* as well as *headstone*—Prison. One of the incidents described is the beating of a simple-minded, inoffensive prisoner by a guard, Officer Fettle. Wade sardonically notes the inevitable outcome of this event: "Petersen [the beaten prisoner] was still in hospital. He would in due course have to be tried and the evidence against him would be overwhelming. No fewer than four Prison Officers had seen him turn and attack Officer Fettle." The rest of the novel follows events in the life of the London Cockney, Toddy Shaw, after his release from Hadestone, for inadvertently short-circuiting a riot. Here Wade produces something on the order of a social realism novel, with a sympathetic depiction of the plights of the working class in the late 1930s. References to unemployment, the dole and unions abound. When Shaw's wife needs an operation, Wade methodically depicts the kind of crippling imposition this can impose on a lower-class family. When Shaw is looking for work, Wade notes sympathetically that it "is easier for a rich man to enter into the kingdom of heaven than for an ex-convict without a reference to obtain employment from the righteous."[88]

---

[88] Henry Wade, *Released for Death* (1938; rpnt., London: Howard Baker, 1970), 46, 121.

Shaw finds himself being led back into a life of crime by a villainous ex-lag acquaintance from Hadestone named "Jacko" Carson. Eventually Shaw is set up by Jacko to take the fall for the vicious mutilation murder of a night watchman, a man who happens to have been Officer Fettle, formerly of Hadestone. The Reverend John Beckley, Chaplain at Hadestone, champions Shaw's innocence, seeing the Cockney ex-lag's "criminal tendencies" as, in the words of the author, "of sporting or adventurous rather than vicious origin." Chief Inspector Holby is satisfied that Shaw is guilty and Carson innocent (he has an alibi), but Assistant Commissioner Leward Marradine (an old friend of Beckley's father's) decides to put another man, John Bragg (from Wade's short story series *Here Comes the Copper*) on to the case, to investigate Carson and his cronies further. Bragg's job becomes a matter of attempting to romance the truth from one of Carson's flames, Beryl Cobb, who provided him with his alibi for the police. This leads to some rather bathetic drama with Bragg's wife, Jenny, who does not at all like the idea of her husband running round with another woman, even in the line of duty:

> "And what about me?" asked his wife quietly.
> "You, Jennie?"
> "I've got a heart, haven't I?"
> "But, sweetheart, it's not serious! I'm only doing it as a duty."
> "Are you sure, John? I can tell you like her and if she's pretty . . . you've been married to me a long time—eight years; they say it's a dangerous time."
> "Oh, Jen!"[89]

{*SPOILERS*} Thankfully for the reader the Bragg's marital crisis passes and Beryl Cobb, spurred by Bragg's revelation that Jacko is carrying on with another woman, decides to inform the police of the truth: that the vicious murderer whom she has been shielding

---

[89] Wade, *Released*, 242, 339.

actually has no alibi. Wade provides an exciting penultimate scene, where Carson savagely attacks Beryl and Bragg, mortally wounding Beryl; yet she lives to tell what she knows and Toddy Shaw is saved. Tragically, Shaw's wife has died while he was in jail, but the resilient Shaw pulls himself together and resolves to carry on the rest of his life honestly and decently. "Toddy Shaw was himself again," concludes the author admiringly.[90] {*END SPOILERS*}

*Released for Death* still stands today as a commendable attempt on the part of a British Golden Age mystery writer to depict sympathetically a working class environment, but the novel enjoys mixed success. On the merit side is the novel's more realistic portrayal of the police, with its recognition that police might beat prisoners and later cover up their illegal acts. Prisoners like Toddy Shaw view these matters cynically. When his money goes missing after he has been taken into police custody, Shaw comments, "I guess I know where that's gone to." Many (though not all) police are portrayed as disdainful of attempts to reform prisoners. The idealistic and conscientious prison chaplain Reverend Beckley, for example, frequently is dismissed by members of the force as a hopelessly naive sentimentalist, particularly when he launches his quest to exonerate Shaw. The novel also evinces awareness on the part of the author of proper legal procedure, informing readers when the police *cannot* do something legally, however convenient it might be for both the police and the property-owning society they protect. Wade's procedural knowledge is one of the book's greatest strengths, lending its scenes dealing with the police and the law a welcome authority, thereby enhancing their interest to the reader. One of the best sections in the novel, for example, is the detailing of the efforts of Toddy Shaw's attorney to find a witness to back up his alibi for Fettle's murder. A woman who claims to have seen him at the time of the murder is found, and she is able to pick Shaw out in an identity parade; but the police find that one of the lawyer's clerks carelessly gave the witness the day

---

[90] Ibid., 364.

of the week she was supposed to have seen Shaw, thereby undermining her credibility. Chief Inspector Holby happily points out to Shaw's dismayed lawyer that the day has been "forced" on the witness—something the police often have been accused of doing by defense attorneys. The rise and fall of Shaw's hopes in this matter make convincing and compelling reading.[91]

Unfortunately the novel deserves some demerits as well. The chief problem is that it seems to have been difficult for Wade to really get into the mind of urban working-class characters as he did with his country gentry. Throughout, Wade's tone is sympathetic yet rather patronizing, *noblesse oblige* in print form. Usually the author refers to Toddy Shaw as "Toddy," not "Shaw," and he makes comments like, "To Toddy and his like....," rather suggestive of an anthropological lecture on some strange aboriginal tribe. Also, John and Jennie are as bland petit bourgeois caricatures in this novel as they are in the *Here Comes the Copper* short stories (in one *Copper* story, "These Artists!", Bragg flushes with embarrassment merely at the thought of the existence of nude artists' models: "How any nice girl could stand up there with nothing on in front of a man, artist or no artist . . . how the artist himself could . . . better not think about it."). Interestingly, John Cooper

---

[91] Ibid., 231. Wade addressed the matter of the police forcing identifications on witnesses in an earlier novel, *No Friendly Drop*, in a sardonic passage suggesting that the author did not necessarily always hold British law enforcement above criticism:

> "'Now, Mrs. Sparks,' said the Superintendent, unbuttoning one of his capacious pockets, 'I want you to tell me whether you recognise any of these gentlemen.'
> "The Superintendent produced, very correctly, eight cabinet-size photographs of men of different ages and types. Seven of these photographs were well-thumbed, dingy affairs, obviously used for a similar purpose by the Paslow police for years, if not generations; two of the 'gentlemen' actually wore mutton chop whiskers, and a third was collared in the style of Albert the Good. The eighth photograph was, of course, the 'made up' one of James Moode. It did not require a conjuror to choose the photograph that had to be 'recognised.'" Wade, *Drop*, 215-216.

has noted that "Wade came to have a poor opinion of the final six chapters of *Released for Death*" and informed a friend in 1946 that he had rewritten these chapters, altering the ending.[92] Still, the novel is a significant and striking departure from the British Golden Age norm, a book, in fact, that should not exist at all, if one ingenuously takes everything in the Julian Symons-Colin Watson school of mystery criticism at face value.

During the Second World War Henry Wade, in service again, published no novels, but he became an active writer again after the war. 1946 saw the publication of a revised version of *Lonely Magdalen*, while the next year his first new novel in seven years appeared, a detective story entitled *New Graves at Great Norne*. While this novel about serial killings in an East Anglian village is rather backward-looking, with a pre-war setting and a plot resolution that already was familiar when it was published and is rather too familiar to mystery fiction fans today, it has good atmosphere and Wade's condemnation of outwardly pious yet inwardly uncharitable citizens of the village of Great Norne is worth noting. "He was, in fact, narrow in outlook and interest, harsh in judgment of his fellow-men, though diplomatically gentle with those who thought and saw as he did," pointedly notes the author of the Reverend Theobald Torridge, Great Norne's Vicar since before the Great War.[93] Once again, Wade offers judicious criticism of the traditional English society from which he himself had emerged and which he still admired in many ways.

In *New Graves*, the local squire, Norris Beynard, is a recessive presence, respected, but playing little active role in village affairs. Beynard is " a thin, stooping man, nearly sixty years of age, a scholar and philosopher, quiet and retiring, almost a recluse." He has withdrawn from Great Norne's "present life, feeling himself out

---

[92] Wade, *Released*, 109; Henry Wade, *Here Comes the Copper* (1938; rpnt., London: Hutchinson, 1972), 5; Cooper, "Bragg," 19.
[93] Henry Wade, *New Graves at Great Norne* (London: Constable, 1947), 3.

of tune with its pace and stridency."[94] By the time of the publication of Wade's next novel, *Diplomat's Folly*, in 1951, the author had had four more years of the post-war Labour government in which to contemplate the fate of England's landed gentry, and his outlook had become bleak indeed. In *Diplomat's Folly* the older generation is more out of tune with discordant modern life than ever, and the younger generation is damned.

*Folly* opens in 1947 with a formal dinner being served at Shackley Manor. The dinner presents an impressive front, but Wade calls it a facade, setting up the novel's theme of the dichotomy between the gentry's glorious past and a "dirty and disappointing" present of economic austerity and servant scarcity. Wade sees the Second World War as having the same negative impact as the First, making human society nastier and more squalid. The owner of Shackley Manor, Major-General Vane Tabbard, is an aging man (fifty-seven), upright and respected, but increasingly at a loss over how to deal with a world that no longer has a true conception of or place for honor. His very name is suggestive of the futility of the old ideals of chivalry (vane, suggests "vain" and "tabbard" suggests "tabard," the ceremonial coat going back to medieval days still worn, emblazoned with heraldry, by Royal officers of arms in modern times). Tabbard goes through most of the novel in a fog of ignorance about much of what is really occurring, such as the sexual affair between his second, younger wife, Lilian, and his best friend, the ambitious diplomat Aylwin Hundrych, as well as the continuing problems of his son, Major Gray Tabbard, a veteran of the Commandos.

It is the ultimate intersection of the difficulties of two of these characters, Aylwin Hundrych and Gray Tabbard, that drives the plot of the novel. Gray Tabbard seems in Wade's eyes a member of a morally doomed generation. In the already demoralized 1930s, Gray had "made a fool of himself at Harrow, got into a fast set and played the dangerous breaking-out and nightclub-game—with the inevitable consequence. He had been on the drift when Hitler saved

---

[94] Wade, *Graves*, 31.

him, for the time being." Amid the chaos and horror of the Second World War, Gray had been reborn, like a martial phoenix, becoming a remorselessly efficient bird of prey. His war record "had been magnificent: raids on the Dutch and Danish coasts, a drop into France and work with the Resistance men ... an immediate D. S. O." Yet a war conducted without rules of civilized behavior also had further undermined Gray's character. Gray, as his name suggests, does not have any fixed belief in right and wrong, black and white. When his father declares that a "well-disciplined unit" would not have pillaged the wine cellars at Aylwin Hundrych's war-requisitioned and despoiled country manor, The Chase, as in fact had happened, Gray is unimpressed. "Discipline of the old-fashioned type had not been [the Commando's] *forte*," notes Wade, "and Gray regarded it as of minimum importance compared with their magnificent fighting spirit, based upon self reliance and individual responsibility." In peacetime, Gray began again to drift, occasionally finding moorage in some unstable commercial enterprise, like a secondhand car dealership or a Parisian cocktail bar run with his shady French resistance friend, Roland Mantenet. "They started a cocktail bar," a bemused and appalled Vane tells his friend Aylwin. "Fine job for a Tabbard. My God, what would my old father have said?"[95] Gray's childhood sweetheart Ann Chesney is even more nonplussed by Gray's aimlessness in life and tells him that she no longer has any intention of marrying him.

Flaws in Aylwin Hundrych's character also are traceable to the 1930s, when, as a member of the British legation in Paris he had a brief political flirtation with a future despised French collaborator with the Nazis, the infamous Pierre Laval. Threatened with blackmail and scandal that could ruin his impending appointment as Ambassador to France, Aylwin turns to Gray Tabbard, believing

---

[95] Wade, *Folly*, 3, 5, 6. On the treatment of requisitioned British country houses by the government during World War Two David Cannadine concludes, "From the perspective of their owners, the result was an unmitigated disaster ... the country houses of Britain were among the prime victims of the war." Cannadine, *Aristocracy*, 628-629.

that Gray, while he has not found his place in peacetime England, nevertheless has the requisite cunning and ruthlessness to deal with blackmailers. Gray consents to take the job, despite the fact that Anne Chesney, after spurning him, had recently become engaged to marry the much older diplomat. On the night the "drop" of the money is arranged, however, things go horribly wrong. A concussed Gray is helped into Shackley Manor by his old Cockney army crony, Fred Jape, who tells the alarmed household that Gray was attacked by someone, presumably the blackmailer or one of his gang. Aylwin is called by phone and found to be all right, having successfully made the drop. The next day, however, Aylwin is found dead at the bottom of the stairs in his home, his neck broken. Initially the police assume his death was an accident, but they soon discover evidence that points to murder as the cause.

{*SPOILERS*} Chief Constable Cannon is quick to suspect Gray Tabbard, especially as he, Cannon, had been involved during the recent conflict in investigating Gray in connection with the British Commando slaying of an Italian civilian turned Nazi informant. But Gray is ruled out as a suspect in the present-day death, since he was laid up in bed with a concussion at the time the crime must have been committed. Instead, Gray's friend Roland Mantenet becomes the prime suspect, as it appears that he was Aylwin's blackmailer and had a motive to kill Aylwin as well, namely revenge for the diplomat's earlier political involvement with the despised Laval.

On hearing of Roland's arrest, Gray rises from his sickbed and rushes to the police to confess to committing the murder. We learn with the police that Gray had devised a clever alibi. His concussion initially was staged and later he sneaked out from Shackley Manor and killed Aylwin. "He opened the door and let me in," Gray explains with chilling complacency. "As soon as he'd shut the door and turned towards me I let him have an upper-cut to the point of the jaw. He didn't drop, because I'd caught him; then I turned him round so that I was behind him and broke his neck. It's quite simple." After arranging the scene of the "accident," Gray departed for Shackley Manor to tell Jape all he had done (including the murder) and implore him to seal the alibi with a good coshing. "Fred hit me a proper crack with a rubber-covered cosh," Gray continues, "We had been taught the gentle art of hitting in the Commandos and we both thought we knew how hard to do it without killing. But it was the hell of a risk, of course. I just had to face it." When asked by the Chief Constable why he did all this, Gray replies simply: "He took my girl from me . . . That man, who wasn't fit to speak to her." Then a "quick smile" lights up his face and he tells the Chief Constable to "blow for your firing-squad."[96]

*Diplomat's Folly* is an excellent crime novel that bears comparison with Wade's better pre-war works. The puzzle is centered on a bravura slight of hand alibi mechanism of the sort used by Christie and Crofts at their best (in respectively, for example, *Death on the Nile* and *Sir John Magill's Last Journey*), while the characters are compellingly presented, if not necessarily likeable. The average reader likely will not warm to the hard-natured and grim Gray Tabbard, for example, but she will be saddened by the futile waste of his undoubted talent and ability. Once again Wade taps one of his perennial themes, the moral debasement brought by war, for a rich vein of story. And once again another country gentry family falls, the latest casualty of a remorseless modernity. Gray Tabbard, the hope of his house, becomes as much a war casualty as Sir John Assington's son in *The Dying Alderman*. {END SPOILERS}

Wade's next several novels are less successful, though each has some elements worth noting. 1952's *Be Kind to the Killer* and 1953's *Too Soon to Die* are jeremiads against specific Labour government policies concerning man's expiration—respectively, the death penalty and death duties. *Be Kind to the Killer* is set in 1948, in a period when, pending passage of the third reading of a Bill to suspend capital punishment for five years, the Home Secretary had announced that he would invariably recommend commutation of death penalty sentences to life imprisonment (the latter sentence would mean in reality a term of twenty years at most). One of the

---

[96] Wade, *Folly*, 294, 295, 296, 297.

beneficiaries of this policy is Gus Swaile, who murdered Detective-Constable Fred Jordan while the latter was in the line of duty. Swaile, "a guilty, callous murderer if ever there were one," would be certain of enjoying "a comfortable, idle life in prison for a few years" before being "loosed on the world again to enjoy another spell of vicious, dangerous existence."[97] Jordan's childhood friend Henry Campion, like Jordan a detective-constable, determines to investigate the criminal gang he blames for Jordan's death, and becomes himself implicated in a murder. The rest of the novel deals with Campion's ultimate fate.

*Killer* is one of Wade's least successful novels, lacking in plotting ingenuity and tiresomely hectoring, but it can be profitably compared to and contrasted with the earlier *Released for Death*, a novel that *Killer* rather resembles in plot structure. Whereas with *Released*, Wade evinced considerable empathy for convicts, sometimes even going so far to doubt the inherent righteousness of the police, *Killer* shows only hostility towards the criminal classes, reserving sympathy solely for a beleaguered police force. "Not only was there a huge increase in the number of crimes committed," writes Wade of the period immediately following the conclusion of the Second World War, "but the element of violence was constantly present and tending, if anything, to increase."[98] Nothing illustrates better the reactionary impulse that gripped many Golden Age British detective novelists after Labour's ascendance to power in 1945 than this transformation of Wade, who, while admittedly conservative, was before the war more difficult to pigeonhole on political and social matters. In the 1930s Wade, like other thoughtful conservatives, believed in the need for measured reform, but Labour's sweeping actions clearly had unnerved him.

Wade's irritation about the death penalty abrogation, which after all had proven to be only a temporary one, pales next to the outrage he demonstrates in his next novel, *Too Soon to Die*, over

---

[97] Henry Wade, *Be Kind to the Killer* (1952; rpnt., London: Howard Baker, 1970), 3.
[98] Wade, *Killer*, 11.

Labour's revisions to the law concerning "death duties" imposed on the inheritance of wealthy estates. Under the Labour government the period of time required to pass for a "gift" of an estate to be exempted from the tax was retrospectively increased from three to five years. In other words, even persons who had made gifts of estates before the legislation passed now had to survive for five rather than three years after the gift had been granted, or else the state would exact the duty anyway, upon that person's death. The artistic impetus behind the writing of *Too Soon to Die* clearly was the author's desire to expose what he saw as the unjust capriciousness of such a law. "It was the retrospective part that made him so cross," recalls his surviving son, Edward.[99]

In *Too Soon to Die*, a gentry family once again is at the center of a Wade novel, the family this time the Jerrods of county Chassex. When the novel opens in 1949, Brackton Manor, we learn, has been the Jerrod family home for some four hundred years. Even in the stetched postwar years of "increasing twentieth-century austerity," allows Wade, "it was still possible for the present head of the family, with an almost literally skeleton staff, to occupy his family home." Yet "inexorably the tide of disaster was creeping in, flowing over the once fair lands and rich investment lists, seeping up towards Brackton itself, with its last carefully guarded possessions."[100] Seeking to save what is left, the head of the family, Colonel John Jerrod, made over most of his estate to his son, Grant, in 1945. But the Colonel has been diagnosed with a fast-encroaching disease, liver cancer, sure to kill him within six months, meaning that he will die before the statutorily required five year term expires in 1950. His gift to his son will be subjected upon his death to an estate tax so crippling that Brackton Manor itself will have to be sold.

Confronted with this dismal news, John Jerrod's son, Grant, comes up with a bold plan, befitting of a daring, even ruthless, character. Grant Jerrod, like Gray Tabbard in *Diplomat's Folly*,

---

[99] Edward Aubrey-Fletcher to the author, 28 November 2004.
[100] Henry Wade, *Too Soon to Die* (1953; rpnt., London: Howard Baker, 1970), 10, 11.

bewilders an aging father educated in the outmoded school of civilized, gentlemanly behavior. Steeling himself for his upcoming interview with his son, Colonel Jerrod finds himself thinking that "there was something about the boy that was . . . almost intimidating." Again like Gray Tabbard, Grant Jerrod had performed spectacularly in special operations during the war. A sapper, Grant had parachuted behind lines, blowing up "bridges, aqueducts, power stations." More troubling to John Jerrod is his son's "bit of secret service work," as Grant dismissively terms it. The old Colonel suspects the phrase is simply a ready euphemism for that which "was not far removed from assassination."[101]

Grant Jerrod's plan is to cheat the Estate Duty Office of its statutory pillage by seeing that his father dies twice. His father will remove himself to Scotland and die privately and secretly under the care of an old friend, while Grant and his father's scapegrace younger brother, Philip, will travel to a Cornwall seaside village. After the statutorily required survival period has passed in September 1950, Grant and Philip will stage a second death for "John Jerrod," this one in a boating accident. This plan goes forward, with one revision that Grant had had in mind all along, but kept from his father and his uncle. The boating death of "John Jerrod" will be more convincing if a drowned body is discovered, so Grant murders his uncle to secure that drowned body. "To keep Brackton," writes Wade, Grant Jerrod "had not, indeed, stopped at fraud, but had pursued it to the logical, the unavoidable end of crime."[102]

The rest of *Too Soon to Die* details, in classic "inverted" fashion, Grant's attempt to evade efforts to discover his crimes, made first by the Examiners from the Estate Duty Office of the Commissioners of Inland Revenue and later by Scotland Yard, in the person of our old friend Inspector (now Chief-Inspector) Poole, who makes his first appearance in thirteen years, since *Lonely Magdalen* was originally published in 1940. {SPOILERS} In this novel,

---

[101] Henry Wade, *Soon*, 21, 22.
[102] Ibid., 76.

Wade is in full tragic mode, and it should surprise no one to learn that Grant ultimately is the loser in the battle of wits with Poole. Despite praise meted to the novel by Anthony Boucher and Charles Shibuk, it is rather a retread of *Diplomat's Folly*, with *Too Soon to Die's* father and son pairing of John and Grant Jerrod bearing very close similarity to that of Vane and Gray Tabbard in the earlier novel and the plot untwisting itself in much the same manner. {END SPOILERS} For me, the greatest interest in *Too Soon to Die* is found in the return of Poole and in the author's unconcealed anger directed at the Labour government.

In his penultimate appearance, John Poole is described as "a man of middle size, with dark brown hair just greying at the temples." His face still is "pleasant," and "a twinkle not often absent for long from his steady grey eyes." Due to his "modesty and pleasant manners," coupled with his "genuine ability," Poole is "one of the best liked and most respected officers in the force." Despite tentative suggestions of romance made long ago in *The Duke of York's Steps* and *No Friendly Drop*, Poole in *Too Soon to Die* is still "a bachelor, living with a widowed sister in Battersea." He seems a solitary figure, a man who draws great pleasure from his walks home through Battersea Park past the power station. Poole finds "an air of undefeated triumph about this massive, stately structure round which for nights and weeks on end the Germans had dropped their bombs without ever achieving their object of destruction."[103]

Perhaps in this resilient monument to industrial progress, Wade found some sense of hope for austerity Britain. Of the recent past (1949-50), however, he finds much to criticize in *Too Soon to Die*. "They're all straight enough, I expect," allows the Jerrod family attorney of the various members of the Labour government, with every indication of the author's sympathetic agreement. "But [they're] wrong-headed and, in matters of finance, downright stupid." Defending his determination to cheat the Inland Revenue of its "due," Colonel Jerrod reflects of the government, "they've

---

[103] Ibid., 129, 133, 175.

turned us all into twisters. All this rationing. How many of us can say we've never wangled a petrol or a clothing coupon? Or bought anything on the black market?" Grant Jerrod is characteristically blunt: "The Government's fair game, in my view. . . . Under these Socialist Chancellors taxation has simply been a political weapon. They mean to kill us, to destroy private ownership, especially of the land." Indeed, Grant has so lost faith in the modern political and social structure that, when his father assures him that Heaton, butler at Brackton Manor for twenty years, is reliable and "true blue," Grant cynically demurs: "He's just as likely to be a Communist." Throughout the novel, Wade takes opportunities to complain of high taxes, goods shortages, loss of efficiency and loss of freedom. For example, when Grant Jerrod, a professional farmer, sits down in the evening, the author notes that it is "to fill in some of the everlasting forms required by some ministry or another." Even a policeman tasked with surveilling Grant Jerrod on behalf of civil authority complains about how government inefficiency and austerity makes effective law enforcement difficult: "God, I wish we'd got those two-way car-radios fitted. This damned economy!"[104]

The author does not condone fraud, noting, as pointed out above, that crime begets more, often worse, crimes. But while Wade in the end does not condone fraud nor, certainly, murder, like other conservative commentators of his day he decries what he sees as Labour's deliberate assault on the landed gentry, a class that, in his view, did not deserve, whatever faults it might have, to be treated as an enemy of the state it so long had served. Writing of Colonel Jerrod's physical appearance, Wade mentions that his "blue eyes were rather prominent, and these gave a definite impression of stupidity combined with obstinacy—an impression not wholly unwarranted." Nevertheless he commends without sentimentality the Jerrod family's hundreds of years of "honourable and useful mediocrity."[105] The Jerrods of England had done their

---

[104] Ibid., 17 28, 29, 143, 268.
[105] Ibid., 5, 10.

honest best, and they merited something better than the calumnious indictments of class warriors and a state-sponsored economic liquidation.

With his remaining three novels—*Gold Was Our Grave* (1954), *A Dying Fall* (1955) and *The Litmore Snatch* (1957)—Wade, perhaps having gotten his political frustrations out of his system and feeling more at ease after several years of renewed Tory governance, concentrates more on plot and less on politics. The first of this final trio of detective novels, *Gold Was Our Grave*, is Poole's last case, an unfortunately somewhat undistinguished one, rather an attempt to return to the form of *The Duke of York's Steps*, but without the same narrative deftness and plotting cleverness. The last of the trio, *The Litmore Snatch*, is better, a solidly-grounded, realistic police procedural about a kidnapping in a provincial city. The most interesting of the three books, however, is *A Dying Fall*, a novel widely regarded as Wade's best post-war tale and worthy of comparison with his finest prewar works. *Fall* won high praise from both Anthony Boucher and Jacques Barzun, men who did not by any means always agree. The latter critic deemed the novel "a beautifully plotted and superbly told affair" with original clues, incidents and concluding climax.[106] The novel would have served as a fine coda for any of the great Golden Age detective novelists.

Conceding the artificiality of the classical Golden Age puzzle novel formula in an age of procedural and psychological realism, Henry Wade in *Gold Was Our Grave* has Poole reflect: "But somehow the theory of a ruined and vengeful shareholder stuck in the detective's gizzard, it was such a very story-book notion, a motive for murder which his younger colleagues probably would have described as 'corny'."[107] In *A Dying Fall*, however, Wade successfully designed a puzzle novel that managed to be up-to-date and credible as well as genuinely puzzling. The overall tone of the novel recalls the author's cynicism of his first work in the genre, *The Verdict of You All*, but the setting is convincingly contemporary.

---

[106] Barzun and Taylor, *Catalogue of Crime*, 420.
[107] Henry Wade, *Gold Was Our Grave* (New York: Macmillan, 1954), 46.

The novel opens in 1952 at the Royal Cup horse race, one year after the Tory restoration to power. Among the racing set there is "a brighter and more hopeful spirit . . . now that Winston was back in power again." In attendance are "people . . . who had not been racing—not regularly, at any rate—for a long time." Optimism is running so high as to make it seem even conceivable that the government "might take a bold plunge and knock a bob off income tax—if not this year, then surely next." One of the attendees, Charles Rathlyn, feels so confident that he has put almost his entire remaining capital on his horse, Silver Eagle. Sadly for Rathlyn, Silver Eagle finishes second. A down-at-his-heels Charles eventually ends up marrying the wealthy Kate Waygold, owner of a great stable of racehorses. A year after the marriage, Kate, a sleepwalker, takes a tumble over the staircase landing balustrade of their home and dies from the fall. Superintendent Hant is not satisfied with the explanation "accident," and looks around for suspects, among whom he quickly comes to number Rathlyn himself; Kate's idle, visiting brother-in-law from her previous marriage; and no less than two in-house private secretaries, a man for business matters and a woman for social ones. ("Why she should have needed two secretaries was something Hant could not understand," writes Wade wryly, "but, then, presumably rich people had needs, fancied needs, that were beyond his comprehension.")[108] A second questionable death within the household follows, a poisoning, but this death, like the other, may have a plausible explanation besides foul play. Hant suspects Rathlyn is a double murderer, but is unable to prove even that murder was committed. The course of the puzzle takes a twist, and then twists again in a final line justly celebrated by critics, including Boucher, Shibuk and Barzun.

*A Dying Fall* is a masterwork of detective fiction, though one befitting its decade, when stripped-down, sparer mystery novels were the norm. Atmosphere and characterization are thinner than they are in Wade's 1930s novels, but the author's aim here is to entertain and delight the reader with an effervescently clever

---

[108] Henry Wade, *A Dying Fall* (London: Constable, 1955), 1, 136.

puzzle, not to edify her with a grim novel of crime and circumstance. Wade's last genre masterwork and one of the finest post-World War Two efforts by a British detective novelist of the Golden Age, *A Dying Fall* makes an admirable epitaph for a great genre writer. Yet Wade was not quite finished, having one more novel in store for his readers.

While *The Litmore Snatch* (1957) is not comparable in quality to *A Dying Fall*, it nevertheless shows that, despite having entered his seventies, Wade was still writing fairly near the top of his game, in contrast to his contemporaries Freeman Wills Crofts, whose *Anything to Declare?*, also published that year, is a tired work, reflective of its then terminally-ill author, and John Street, who still was relentlessly churning out an average of four books a year, usually by this time dull and uninspired tomes. A police procedural focusing on the activities of the law enforcement apparatus in a provincial city in response to the kidnapping of the young son of a newspaper magnate, *The Litmore Snatch* may not be an insistent page-turner, but it is an interesting and up-to-date example of a fifties British police novel. As usual, Wade was meticulous in his presentation of police procedure, and the tale also offers some intriguing glimpses of social change in Britain in the 1950s.

In Wade's final novel, landed aristocrats, decaying or otherwise, are nowhere to be found. Only the *nouveaux riche* Litmores, the targets of the kidnappers, employ servants, allowing them to maintain a drawing room "only mildly removed from Victorian": "There was no plush, but the curtains were of dark, heavy material, the richly papered walls were overcrowded with pictures of too-varied selection; tables and mantlepieces bore ornaments and photographs that most modern housewives, condemned to do their own dusting, had long since swept away." Standing on class clearly is frowned upon in these democratic days. When a friend of young Ben Litmore, the kidnap victim, who witnessed the abduction, is asked how the abductor spoke, he starts to say not like a gentleman, but checks himself and concludes, "not like my father." As the investigation progresses, police interest focuses on "The Dukeries," a formerly august neighborhood where the fine mansions, shelled by German ships in the Great War, have been replaced by bungalows, now often inhabited by the kept women of city businessmen. It is a pair of females residing in a Dukeries bungalow that draws the particular ire of the local police superintendent, however: "There are . . . a couple of women . . . calling themselves sisters. Sisters my foot! One of 'em dresses like a man, looks like a man till you get close to her. Rides a motor-cycle, with sissie on the pillion behind. Nasty bit of work, I call it, but one can't do anything."[109] Fun fairs and the possibly illicit activities occurring at them also play a role in the tale's events. Though rock music, television and juvenile delinquency fail to make appearances, on the whole *The Litmore Snatch* is a successful "modern" performance by an aging author who had published his first novel over three decades earlier.

Interestingly, the police force portrayed by Wade in *The Litmore Snatch* now includes women in significant capacities. One woman in particular, Detective-Sergeant Mary Wittam, plays a notable role in the tale, though in classical Golden Age fashion she clearly is headed toward the marriage altar at the novel's end, with Chief Inspector Vine of Scotland Yard no less. Possibly Wade could have made a successful late series with these newly-introduced police characters, rather in the manner of John Creasey's popular "Gideon" tales, launched two years earlier, in 1955. However, though he lived another dozen years, Wade laid down his pen with *The Litmore Snatch*, retiring before his creative powers had failed him.

Like other serious authors, Henry Wade gave significant thought to the art of writing detective fiction, something clear, of course, from the novels I have analyzed at some length but also seen as well in his correspondence with Dorothy L. Sayers, a fellow detective novelist and charter member of the Detection Club whom Wade admired enormously. When he wrote Sayers on May 4, 1932, the baronet had just read the Crime Queen's *Have His Carcase* and could not contain his enthusiasm for the book. Sayers' latest novel was, Wade assured his fellow author, "genuine vintage wine,

---

[109] Henry Wade, *The Litmore Snatch* (London: Constable, 1957), 20, 28, 107.

such as one rarely meets nowadays." "In fact," he added severely, "during the last three years I could count the bottles on one hand. Some of the most reputable shippers seem to have struck it entirely from their list and confine themselves to a popular wine from the wood, on which there no doubt is a quick turnover."[110]

In contrast with writers satisfied with producing unexceptionable formula fiction for the less discerning, Sayers had bottled something superb with *Have His Carcase*. The plot itself was "excellent," "real workmanship of the highest quality." Wade had blanched when mention of Bolshevists occurred in the book, believing them "second only to 'Chinamen' on the Black List"; but Sayers had provided "complete justification" for her use of that particular thriller cliché. Thinking Sayers was "going to play a sort of Roger Ackroyd trick on us in the person of Harriet Vane," Wade was taken "completely by surprise" at the actual turn of events.[111]

As much as he enjoyed the puzzle, Wade stressed that what most pleased him was "the actual writing and the characterization." In particular he was impressed with the minor characters in the novel, finding them "one and all real and alive." Even the seaside hotel *gigoli* were "not caricatures but human beings with souls." However, in an admission that might not necessarily have pleased the recipient of his letter, Wade added that he found "Harriet Vane the least real of your characters. At times she is a rather common tom-boy, at others she is ravishing Wimsey, a man of taste and experience. I can't understand why he should be so overwhelmed by her." Considering that Harriet Vane is in many ways an ego-projection of Dorothy L. Sayers, it seems fortunate for Wade's epistolary relationship with the author that he closed by begging her to "please forgive my impertinence in criticizing your Harriet," adding that his having done so was "the surest sign of my admiration for your work."[112]

---

[110] Henry Wade to Dorothy L. Sayers, 4 May 1932, Dorothy L. Sayers Papers, Marion E. Wade Center, Wheaton College.
[111] Ibid.
[112] Ibid.

Wade's 1932 letter to Sayers reveals in him a genre aesthetic at work that is far different from that which one at first blush would attribute to a "Humdrum" writer. While Wade places value on an ingenious puzzle and applauds Sayers for producing such in *Have His Carcase*, he nevertheless stresses that it is writing and characterization he values most of all. Hence it should come as no surprise that the next year Wade would produce his own first "crime novel," *Mist on the Saltings*. It is also worth noting Wade's swipe at formulaic genre fiction ("popular wine from the old wood") that is guaranteed a solid sale, but disappoints the more discriminating reader. As I hope this study of Wade's writing has made sufficiently clear, Wade himself sought to write genre fiction that challenged accepted wisdom concerning the genre's limitations. Having produced definitive puzzle masterpieces with such works as *The Dying Alderman* and *No Friendly Drop*, Henry Wade during the rest of his life wanted to make something more than "mere" puzzles.

Despite the baronet's admission of his own puzzlement over the unique allure that is Harriet Vane, Sayers and Wade kept up a semi-regular correspondence into the 1950s, with Wade addressing Sayers as "My Dear Dorothy." Much to Wade's delight, one year Sayers came to visit him at Chilton for three days. Wade's youngest son recalls sitting at lunch with the distinguished lady mystery author, who strikingly "was wearing gold cufflinks in the form of skull and crossbones." In 1940, when Wade learned that Sayers' *Busman's Honeymoon* was to be filmed, he took time out from the war to write to congratulate her. He hoped that MGM would treat Lord Peter with care, but, knowing as he did the Hollywood propensity for clumsily casting big name American actors whatever the material, he dryly predicted that the choice for the film version of the great British detective would be either Clark Gable or Mickey Rooney.[113]

That same year, Wade urged Sayers to turn her "attention back to private crimes" and deliver unto the world another detective

---

[113] Edward Aubrey-Fletcher, 28 November 2004; Henry Wade to Dorothy L. Sayers, 5 March 1940, DLS Papers. The role of Lord Peter in fact went to Robert Montgomery.

novel. He kept up the refrain in letters in 1947 and 1949, provoking in the latter year a nettled response from the harassed object of his literary affection: "As for writing detective stories—there are a thousand reasons why I feel no desire for it: but the chief one is that, like Conan Doyle, I have been so much put off by being badgered to do it when I was wrapped up in other things that the mere thought gives me nausea." Sayers urged Wade to try "new people" like Michael Gilbert, Cyril Hare and Edmund Crispin.[114]

A chastened Wade quickly answered that he "must apologize for worrying you about crime." He assured Sayers that he would try the authors she had suggested, none of whom he had read, indicating his increased isolation from the mystery scene after the Second World War. By this time, the author, scourged as he was by the furies of petrol rationing, increasing deafness and chronic nosebleeds, had ceased attending Detection Club meetings and so had met none of the newer members. Wade's nosebleeds could be quite horrific. When in the next year another one struck, the baronet informed Sayers: "I more or less fainted and lay on the floor choking in blood." In a shot at Labour, Wade noted that "Mr. Bevan took 2 ½ hours to get me into hospital and cauterized." He added with his characteristic sense of irony that at the time the nosebleed struck he had been rereading *Have His Carcase*, "with its delicious description of the uncoagulated blood-covered corpse on the flat iron rock!" Concluding with the news that he had begun a new detective novel himself (*Diplomat's Folly*), he avowed, "My next murder is to be a completely bloodless affair."[115]

---

[114] Henry Wade to Dorothy L. Sayers, 5 March 1940, Dorothy L. Sayers to Henry Wade, 24 October 1949, DLS Papers. Quoted in Barbara Reynolds, *Dorothy L. Sayers: Her Life and Soul* (1993; rpnt., New York: St. Martin's Griffin, 1997), 339.

[115] Henry Wade to Dorothy L. Sayers, 31 October 1949, 16 March 1950, DLS Papers. "Mr. Bevan" refers to Aneurin "Nye" Bevan, who as Minister of Heath under the postwar Clement Attlee government administered the newly-established National Health Service. Sayers emphatically concurred with Wade in his criticism of National Health.

## Conclusion: Henry Wade and *Noblesse Oblige*

Very few of Henry Wade's detective and crime novels are "bloodless," in the sense of their being dry, mechanical affairs that fail to touch a deeper vein of human thought and emotion. Like his literary idol, Dorothy L. Sayers, Henry Wade produced some brilliant puzzles, but he also gifted readers with carefully-themed and well-written novels with characters that are "real and alive" and "human beings with souls." But is Wade too much a conservative apologist for the landed gentry class he compellingly portrays in his novels? Is it true, as the late Leah A. Strong has suggested, that the author "cannot accept the possibility of [murderous] behavior on the part of people of gentle birth"?[116] {*SPOILERS*} In contradiction to Strong's contention, murderers in six of Wade's twenty crime and detective novels can be said to come from the landed gentry class. Admittedly there are, in each case, extenuating circumstances that serve to make the characters' murderous actions, if not sympathetic, at least more morally comprehensible. In two novels, the initial gentry murder is an unpremeditated affair: Sir John Assington kills the obnoxious Trant in the white heat of anger, while Helen Grayle accidentally kills her husband (she had intended to kill—and later did in fact kill—her blackmailing butler; however blackmailers in Golden Age mystery novels are viewed essentially as fair game). Both characters bitterly regret their actions: Grayle because she ended the life of a much-loved husband; Assington because by committing a murder, an act of ungoverned passion, he betrayed that for which his son had, in part, died on the western front, the code of his social class and the honor of his family name. In *The Hanging Captain* and *The High Sheriff*, the murders are premeditated, but there are some mitigating factors present. In the former novel, the murder victim is a scoundrel frittering away the family estate, while in the latter one, the murderer is a neurasthenic teenager warped by his harsh

---

[116] Leah A. Strong, "Henry Wade's John Poole," in George N. Dove and Earl F. Bargainnier, *Cops and Constables: American and British Fictional Policemen* (Bowling Green, OH: Bowling Green University Press, 1986), 122.

upbringing. Finally, in the two postwar novels where a member of the landed gentry is a murderer, that person's moral sense has been fretted by service in the Second World War.

Yet while Wade sympathizes on some level with the plights of his gentry-murderers, he nevertheless does not shirk from examining the flaws that helped place them in their predicaments. The most common thread here is pride, pride in self and often pride in family as well: John Assington stabs a man is a burst of rage after he is personally ridiculed by that man in public; Helen Grayle's commission of two murders results from her obstinate refusal to adjust her spending habits to conform to her husband's modern-day diminished circumstances; Gerald Sterron in *The Hanging Captain* kills to secure the family estate for himself and more particularly his son; Peter D'Arcy, made neurotic by his failure to live up to his prideful, demanding father's expectations, shoots a man to defend the family honor; Gray Tabbard breaks the neck of a man he considers unworthy of his former fiancée; and Grant Jerrod kills as part of his plan to defraud the government of an estate duty that would force the sale of his ancestral home. In each case, the gentry-murderer fails to live up to the proper code of the gentleman (or gentlelady), as Assington himself recognizes in his rueful suicide letter and Helen D'Arcy bitterly reflects when she realizes what her son has done.

Wade often finds other flaws in his gentry as well, whether it is a lack of intelligence (John Assingon, John Jerrod) or an intellectual inalertness (Helen Grayle, Robert D'Arcy, Vane Tabbard) or a certain complacency and snobbishness. Even the likeable if not overly bright John Assington is portrayed as patronizing to social inferiors and is revealed to have cut Mary Trant dead socially after she made the class error of marrying a tradesman like Trant. Yet for Wade these faults are mitigated to some considerable extent by his gentry's profound commitment to the code of *noblesse oblige*. In the matter of war service alone, the cost to the gentry in Wade's novels—as it was in real life—is high. Sir John Assington's son is killed in the Great War and the family line snuffed out, while Robert D'Arcy is emotionally maimed by the conflict (and, through him, his son Peter as well). And the impact of the Second World War is if anything even worse, with Gray Tabbard and Grant Jerrod learning a wartime ruthlessness and amorality they find difficult to leave behind them in peacetime. But while Wade is aware of the good qualities in his quality, he nevertheless does not in his novels excuse the mortal criminal act. Indeed, when his gentry slip and betray their sacred code of honor, Wade looks on with horror, not merely at the criminal acts themselves, but at the identities of the actors. By failing to adhere to the demanding standards of *noblesse oblige*, the gentry in these works can no longer be seen as meriting an elevated position in the social structure, an outcome Wade sees as tragic. {END SPOILERS}

Several tales from Wade's first short story collection, *Policeman's Lot,* further illustrate the author's view of the class from which he himself came. "Jealous Gun" portrays the advantages that are to be found in counties where a relatively traditional sociopolitical structure remains intact. The story is set in Wade's Quenshire, the locale of *The Dying Alderman*, though Major Faide is the Chief Constable in the story, so we should probably think of the setting as Brackenshire, where both *No Friendly Drop* and *The High Sheriff*, novels in which Faide features prominently, are set. "Jealous Gun" opens with the County Council's Socialist member, Tom Speddings, raising a ruckus yet again, like Tom Garrett, his likeminded and like-named fellow leftist in *The Dying Alderman*, "availing himself of the opportunity to wave his little red flag." Speddings wants to know what the Chief Constable really does to merit his wage: "Seems to me he spends most of his time shooting and hunting. Is that what we pay him for? When's he on duty, Mr. Chairman? Tell me that." The Chairman reminds the Socialist upstart that "a policeman, whatever his rank, is *always* on duty." The rest of "Jealous Gun" is devoted to demonstrating the validity of the Chairman's assertion. {SPOILERS} While Spedding is haranguing the County Council about Major Faide, Major Faide is participating—true to stereotype—in a pheasant shoot in the country. With a keen eye for social detail, Wade notes that the beaters have been recruited mostly "from the unemployed of the neighbouring town . . . in these days it was difficult to find genuine rustics to supplement the nucleus of estate woodmen." Faide finds something "off" about one of his fellow participants in the shoot, Captain Hart-Purves, an outsider renting the country house Beadings for the shooting season. The man speaks too loudly near the beat, dresses in "loud" tweeds and drives a "loud" car (a Rolls Royce). Yet, a puzzled Faide reflects, "he was an attractive-looking fellow, a fine shot; everybody liked him." The Major tries to brush off his feelings of disdain for the Captain. After the shooting starts, however, Faide realizes to his disgust that Hart-Purves is a "jealous gun": someone who greedily (though sneakily) poaches other men's birds.[117] His suspicions having been raised by his discovery of Hart-Purves' poor sportsmanship, the Major conducts an investigation of the Captain on his own time and discovers that this undesirable parvenu is actually a thiever of country houses. {*END SPOILERS*}

"Jealous Gun" celebrates the stability and honor of gentry society in a gently humorous fashion. A far more serious tale is "The Tenth Round," which in the space of twenty-seven pages achieves a sense of genuine tragedy. In Charles Shibuk's view this compelling story achieves "classic status." In "The Tenth Round" we again see an invasion of a rural hinterland by an interloper desirous of getting in some shooting. This time the locale is highland Scotland, the objectionable outsider is Harold Speccard, Chairman of the Speccard Motor Company, and the targets of the shooting are stags rather than pheasants. Speccard is perhaps the most odious person in the Wade canon, someone who wantonly yet thoughtlessly slaughters animals, with no regard for the rules of gentlemanly sport. The local laird, MacBlayre, seethes with mounting anger as he witnesses Speccard's atrocious activities on his estate, which adjoins the laird's own: "Mr. Speccard had had enough; he wanted his tea; he was leaving a wounded beast—two wounded beasts—to wander to their slow and dreadful deaths. It was the ultimate crime!" Appalled, MacBlayre asks Speccard "to reconsider

---

[117] Wade, *Lot*, 226, 227, 228.

the practice of shooting running deer," as "it is a very difficult shot and liable to wound rather than kill"; but an enraged and blustering Speccard only rates the grieved laird for having "the blasted impertinence to come here and tell me how to shoot."[118]

MacBlayre, we learn, is another one of Wade's lingering Great War casualties. His son and the hope of his house had been killed in the conflict and MacBlayre, "failing to get killed himself," returned to his home, Glentorr, "to bury himself in his own house and his own forest . . . his only pleasures seemed to be the care of his forest, the improvement of the strain of wild deer that inhabited it." {SPOILERS} "He was," admits Wade of the laird, "a man of unstable mind"; and, indeed, MacBlayre proves himself so when he murders Speccard. Yet Wade comes closer here to rationalizing murder than in any of his gentry-murderer novels, as we see in the laird's poignant explanation for his actions:

> I begged him not to fire at running beasts, to do everything he could do to avoid wounding. Yesterday I watched him again and saw him . . . kill a hind and then empty his rifle after the others, at a terrible risk of wounding several of them. Then I saw him leave his stalker and walk down the hill towards the road by himself. I felt as if he had been delivered into my hands. . . . I put a bullet through his brain.[119]

It should be easy enough for the reader to see the mass slaughter of "beasts" by Harold Speccard, motor manufacturer, as a metaphor for the machine gun massacres of men in the Great War; and it therefore should be easy enough to comprehend how repeated exposure to these shooting episodes caused something in MacBlayre's own brain to snap. Evading the police, the laird

---

[118] Shibuk, "Henry Wade," 92; Wade, *Lot*, 267, 271.
[119] Wade, *Lot*, 271, 272, 285.

reaches "the very summit of Ben Torr, above the sheer face of the eastern precipice." Police for a moment see his figure standing there, then he leaps "out and down, down. . . ."[120] {*END SPOILERS*}

Major Konsett in "Payment in Full" cuts quite a different figure from MacBlayre of Glentorr, but in the end he redeems himself. As we are introduced to the man in the beginning of the tale, Konsett is very wealthy, exceedingly self-regarding, heavily involved in county affairs and really quite debauched. When Police-Sergeant Adams confronts Konsett with the fact that he is aware the Major has impregnated his daughter, the Major immediately begins to calculate to himself: "As a magistrate and member of the Standing Joint Committee he could not allow this scandal to become public—he would have to pay; and Major Konsett, though a rich man, disliked paying for what he might get for nothing. Perhaps a little tact. . . ." Konsett's "tact," however, fails to mollify Adams, especially when the Major suggests to the police-sergeant, "you're a man of the world—you know these things happen. Men will be men, you know, and in these days girls will be girls." {*SPOILERS*} Adams shoots Konsett in the head; then, making certain to himself that his victim is indeed dead, he arranges the scene to make it appear that Konsett has committed suicide and exits. When Adams later arrives on the scene in his "official" capacity, he discovers to his acute distress that through a freak circumstance the bullet never entered Konsett's brain and that Konsett is not only not dead but has recovered consciousness and is waiting to make a statement to Adams' superior, Superintendent Bander. Leaving Adams on pins and needles, Bander goes to hear what Konsett has to say, then returns to tell the police-sergeant that Konsett has expired from shock, after uttering some final words: "Didn't seem to know who I was. . . . 'Tell Sergeant Adams,' he said, 'that I shot myself.'"[121] Konsett has made his "payment in full" to the Police-Sergeant whom he had wronged: *Noblesse oblige* from the deathbed, as it were. {*END SPOILERS*}

---

[120] Ibid., 287.
[121] Ibid., 206, 225.

# THE SPECTRUM OF ENGLISH MURDER

Wade's greatest preoccupation as a writer clearly lay with the parlous state of the landed gentry in Britain following the Great War (and, later, World War Two), but his range of effective characterization extended beyond members of his own class, to, for example, police of high and low rank in *The Dying Alderman, Constable, Guard Thyself!* and *Lonely Magdalen*; the businessmen in *The Missing Partners* and *The Dying Alderman*; the Jew Leopold Hessel in *The Duke of York's Steps*; and sundry members of the working classes in *The Dying Alderman, No Friendly Drop, Mist on the Saltings, Released for Death* and *Lonely Magdalen*. After his first novel, Wade's treatment of servants is thankfully lacking in the sort of heavy-handed humor at working class expense that is present in many detective novels of the period. Also worth noting is Wade's treatment, in contrast with many genre authors of that day, of middle-aged women (like the fifty-five-year-old Helen Grayle) as interesting—and sometimes even sexually alluring—beings.

Wade has sometimes been criticized for stilted, neo-Victorian writing when dealing with romantic relationships between men and women. Even as late as 1955, in his penultimate novel, *A Dying Fall*, Wade could cumbersomely inform his readers that a couple was "in that seventh heaven that is reserved for lovers from whose path insuperable obstacles have suddenly melted away." Dorothy L. Sayers, who dismissed certain passages in *Mist on the Saltings* as "incongruous pruderies," was particularly scathing of Wade's handling of "sexual passion," declaring that the author "plans a seduction like Napoleon—and executes it like the famous Duke of York."[122] No doubt Sayers in part was having fun here with Wade's repeated use in *Saltings* of military metaphors for sex, which admittedly is heavy-handed. Wade also ultimately baulks at having his heroine, Hilary Pansel, go through with her contemplated

---

[122] Wade, *Fall*, 232-233; *Sunday Times*, 5 November 1933, 9. "The grand old Duke of York/He had ten thousand men/He marched them up to the top of the hill/And he marched them down again/And when they were up, they were up/And when they were down, they were down/And when they were only half-way up/They were neither up nor down."

adultery. However, the novel is franker than most Golden Age works in its dealing with sex. Particularly interesting is the relationship between the on-the-make Christian Magdek and the wealthy publican's daughter he wants to marry. Magdek, whose stunning male beauty is emphasized at several points by the author, refuses to have sex with the girl until they are wed—out of respect for her, he says, though actually he hopes her increasingly urgent physical desire for him will compel her to put more pressure on her father to acquiesce to their marriage. During one petting session, Magdek almost loses control of himself, but like Sayers' celebrated Duke of York, he takes himself in hand and marches his men down again. This episode certainly strikes me as far more graphic in its direct depiction of "sexual passion" than most Golden Age detective novels (including Sayers' own).

With no writer has the appellation "Humdrum" been more unfairly applied than with Henry Wade. A skilled plotter like John Street or Freeman Wills Crofts, Wade was blessed with a more adept hand at clueing, giving him some resemblance as well to Agatha Christie. Moreover, even in his earliest novels he clearly gave thought to characterization and theme, whatever the "rules" for detection writing were deemed to be by such higher authorities as Ronald Knox and S. S. Van Dine. Not many years had elapsed before Wade was significantly experimenting with the form of the mystery story, and he became an important pioneer of both the police procedural and the crime novel. In whatever mystery form he wrote, his authorial mood—ranging from the sardonic cynicism characteristic of his earlier works and some later novels like *Heir Presumptive* and *A Dying Fall* to the tragic sense of decline that comes to predominate in *No Friendly Drop*, *Mist on the Saltings*, *The High Sheriff*, *Lonely Magdalen*, *Diplomat's Folly* and *Too Soon to Die*—is striking and unusual, more akin to the works of P. D. James today than the generally blander works of the true Humdrums or the frothy novels of manners of the Crime Queens. Indeed, though removed from her by a generation, Wade shares with the late Baroness James a mordant sense of resignation that a conservative world loved despite its admitted flaws inevitably is lost, in some degree because of those very flaws. It is not a comforting but an uncompromisingly bleak view of life—certainly not one that many of his readers would have found made anodyne reading. That Henry Lancelot Aubrey-Fletcher, sixth Baronet of Clea, was emphatically among the gentry survivors and that his grandson Henry Egerton Aubrey-Fletcher, eighth Baronet of Clea, today serves, as his Grandfather once did, as Lord Lieutenant of Buckinghamshire is one of those ironies—a happy one this time—that "Henry Wade" no doubt would have appreciated.

# CHAPTER 2 // DEATH ON THE LEFT

## G. D. H. AND MARGARET COLE
## (1889-1959/1893-1980)

### INTRODUCTION

IN 1949, WHILE REFERENCING an article by renowned academic socialist G. D. H. Cole ("Laissez Faire," in the ninth volume of *The Encylopaedia of the Social Sciences*), conservative economist Ludwig von Mises—no fan of mystery fiction himself—dismissively labeled Cole "the Oxford professor and author of detective stories." By that time Cole, as well as his wife, Margaret, in fact had ceased dabbling in detection and the couple's mystery novels would soon fall out of print. Cole, who in 1944 had become the first Chichele Professor of Social and Political Theory at Oxford, devoted his last ten years of life to teaching and adding to his already voluminous writings on political and economic matters. Margaret Cole published a memoir of her life, *Growing up into Revolution*, in 1949, several additional works of Labour history in the '50s and '60s and, finally, in 1971, a biography of her husband, *The Life of G. D. H. Cole*. Today the Coles, in their lifetimes both highly committed, active and articulate socialists, take their place in political histories of the British Left; yet their mystery literature (twenty-eight novels, five novellas and thirty-five short stories), though well-regarded in the between-the-wars period, is treated as a footnote, both in books about the Coles (including Margaret Cole's own) and in surveys of the mystery genre. Usually mention is duly made that the Coles were that oddity of the Golden Age, leftist detective novelists, accompanied by an addendum that their political views were not reflected in their fiction. Julian Symons, for example, notes that the Coles, whom he dubs a "collaborative Humdrum," were both deeply involved in the Labour Movement, but then he asserts that "their books never treated seriously the social realities with which in life they were so much concerned." This chapter challenges both Symons' widely-accepted designation of the Coles as Humdrums as well as the view that the couple's political beliefs were never given voice in their fictional works.[1] In truth the Coles are better understood as academic farceurs like Michael Innes (though without the latter's imaginative range), rather than Humdrums; and although they only occasionally treated political themes seriously in their mystery fiction, much of their world view is in fact reflected in this fiction, often in the form of satire directed at Britain's conservative, capitalist establishment. Additionally, while in their books the couple often lacked the technical assurance and superb plotting craft of the true masters of the genre (including not only the Humdrums), they did score occasional hits in this area; and their writing frequently is lively and witty. In my view their detective fiction, out-of-print for decades, is eminently deserving of modern revival.

---

[1] Ludwig von Mises, "Laissez Faire or Dictatorship," *Plain Talk* 3 (Jan. 1949), 57; Julian Symons, *Bloody Murder* (New York and Tokyo: Mysterious Press, 1992), 117. It was, perhaps, Professor von Mises' association of G. D. H. Cole with detective novels that led him to condemn the entire genre as part of the "the artistic superstructure of the epoch of labor unionism and socialization." Von Mises saw a "latent antibourgeois tendency" in the detective novel, in that it introduces "the cheap character of the self-righteous sleuth who takes delight in humiliating a man [the murderer] whom all considered an impeccable citizen." The detective's motivation for unmasking this man as a murderer, von Mises believed, was his "subconscious hatred of successful bourgeois." Von Mises' take on detective novels is a splendid example of a brilliant mind, driven by a powerful ideological impulse, running spectacularly off the rails (he is probably the only commentator who utterly misses the generally conservative bent of the Golden Age British detective novel). Yet, in the case of the Coles, von Mises is quite correct about their being an "antibourgeois tendency" in their work. For Von Mises on the detective fiction genre, see "Remarks about the Detective Stories," *The Anti-capitalist Mentality* (1956; rpnt., Indianapolis, In: The Liberty Fund, 2006).

Admittedly, by Margaret Cole's own admission, the couple did not take their detective novels very seriously. "In between the wars, for no particular reason that I can see, the writing and discussion of detective fiction became a serious study in the intellectual world," Margaret Cole explained rather diffidently in her biography of her husband. "Douglas and I had both become fairly eager readers of this kind of literature; and when he was in the country [in 1923] recovering from a mild attack of pneumonia he proposed trying his hand at it. I bet him he would not even finish a draft; this was of course a challenge."[2] Never one to flag when writing a book, Cole completed the manuscript and sent it to the publisher Collins, who eventually accepted it (after one murder had been deleted). This tale, *The Brooklyn Murders*, was followed two years later, in 1925, by another detective novel, *The Death of a Millionaire*, which carried the names of both G. D. H. and Margaret Cole on the title page. A public mystery-writing partnership had commenced.

The Coles would go on to officially co-author twenty-seven additional detective novels, though in fact they were written mostly by one or the other Cole (see pages 124-125 for the distribution). Writing detective novels proved "a pleasant enough by-line" for the busy couple, Margaret Cole recalled, especially as the books, unlike their more serious non-fictional works, "required no reference books or research." Margaret Cole admitted that their mysteries never became bestsellers in Britain, let alone the United States (though all their novels were published in both countries), adding candidly that this was because "we were not really good enough and did not take the market sufficiently seriously. Our novels were competent, but no more." Despite spending a scant two pages of her three hundred page biography of her husband on their detective novels, Margaret Cole nevertheless apologized for even devoting that much time to them, insisting that she would not have done so "were it not that the mere fact [that we wrote them] comes perennially as a surprise to many audiences." Twenty-two years earlier, in her own biographical memoir, *Growing up into*

---

[2] Margaret Cole, *The Life of G. D. H. Cole* (London: Macmillan, 1971), 135.

*Revolution*, she made similarly modest claims for the mystery tales, pleading that such works had provided her and her husband with "a very innocent form of escapism and a quite satisfactory way of earning a modest competence."[3]

While Margaret Cole wrote somewhat self-deprecatingly of her and her husband's detective fiction, in actuality their work made a sizeable splash in the 1920s, with discerning critics often placing them in the front rank of British mystery novelists. Additionally, the couple became, along with such luminaries as Agatha Christie, Dorothy L. Sayers and G. K. Chesterton, charter members of the Detection Club in 1930. In the thirties enthusiasm for their work waned, yet they continued to prolifically produce titles, publishing usually two or even three mystery novels a year through 1940. In 1941 and 1942, single novels, one by each spouse, appeared; and these were followed over the next few years by a novella, *Death of a Bride*, and a couple of short stories. The great events of the Second World War served to diminish the interest of the highly socially and politically involved couple in their mystery tales. Margaret Cole admitted that during the middle of the war she became so bored with the detective novel she was currently writing that she "stopped halfway through and never began again," while her husband commented in a 1952 newspaper interview that the advent of the war made death "too beastly to write about."[4] Douglas Cole stopped writing mystery novels at this time too and for the couple, that was that. For the literary historian, however, the Coles left, from a period of over two decades, a sizeable legacy of crime fiction to be scrutinized. Such scrutiny is merited, because the Coles were once well-regarded practitioners in the detective fiction genre and because the couple offer a notable example during the Golden Age of British mystery authors of a decidedly left-wing political bent.[5]

---

[3] Cole, *G. D. H. Cole*, 136; Margaret Cole, *Growing up into Revolution* (London and New York: Longmans, 1949), 179.

[4] Cole, *G. D. H. Cole*, 136. Susan Hicklin, "Behind the Whodunits," *Picture Post*, 9 August 1952, 40. Thanks to John Curran, who sent me this article.

[5] Probably the next most notable leftist British detective novelist of the 1930s is Christopher St. John Sprigg (1907-1937), who over the course of his short writing career

# THE SPECTRUM OF ENGLISH MURDER

## Part One: *The Brooklyn Murders* (1923), Superintendent Wilson, and the Question of Collaboration

THE FIRST PUBLISHED Cole mystery novel, written, as explained above, by G. D. H. Cole alone during convalescence from illness, is *The Brooklyn Murders* (1923). The novel (which, it should be explained, has absolutely nothing to do with Brooklyn, New York, "Brooklyn" rather being the name of the family concerned in the criminous events), reads today like a workmanlike Freeman Wills Crofts pastiche, lacking the individuality that would be immediately and pleasingly evident in the next Cole novel, *The Death of a Millionaire* (1925). Of the writing *The Brooklyn Murders*, Margaret Cole recalled, "It was just about the time when Mr. Freeman Wills Croft's [sic] first stories were coming out, and all the intelligentsia were very much excited about them"; so it is not surprising that this novel should so resemble Crofts' own works at this time, particularly 1921's *The Ponson Case*. Of Cole's highly derivative first novel, *A Catalogue of Crime*—often of course the last redoubt of "Humdrum" writers—is pithily dismissive: "Walter Brooklyn is unjustly suspected, but the girl believes in his innocence. It is vindicated, since he loves her and is a playwright. Despite the bright newcomer Supt. Wilson, the unwinding is tedious and marred by the worst flubdub in the Neanderthal period of detection." I find it difficult to disagree with this assessment. As the *COC* suggests, the novel features a plethora of clichéd, dated elements from mysteries of the period (particularly those of Freeman Wills Crofts), including a tiresome love affair between the novel's principals, carried on in the most stilted neo-Victorian rhetoric

---

became a doctrinaire Stalinist. (Today he is best known for the Communist theory he wrote under his pseudonym Christopher Caudwell.) Before his death in combat in the Spanish Civil War, Sprigg wrote seven detective novels. The first six, appearing in a creative burst between 1933 and 1935, are humorous extravaganzas in the farceur tradition of Ronald Knox, Gladys Mitchell, the Coles and Michael Innes. The last, *The Six Queer Things* (1937), written after Sprigg's conversion to Communism in 1935 and published posthumously, is an exposé of spiritualism that is grim in tone, in contrast with his earlier works.

("They gazed at each other, with something of fear and something of embarrassment in their looks, and each was conscious of a heart beating more and more insistently within"); a pair of bright and eager amateur investigators delightedly upstaging the police whom the reader would cheerfully throttle (the female of the pair, seemingly inevitably named Joan, smugly declares at one point, "I'm really beginning to think, Bob, we're rather clever people"); and detection consisting mostly of lengthy, SAT-style alibi-busting ("First, they made a list of every one who had been present at the dinner on the evening of the tragedy. . . . Next came the servants. . . . Next, they wrote down exactly what they knew of the doings of every one of these people, leaving spaces in which they could fill in further particulars as they discovered more").[6] Less characteristic but no less bad is the author's notion that fingerprints could have been found on a rough stone club (evidently the *COC*'s "worst flubdub in the Neanderthal period of detection"), a mistake a true Humdrum, naturally sound on technicalities like John Rhode and J. J. Connington, would not have made.

Though *The Brooklyn Murders* is on the whole a forgettable detective novel, it does have some significance in the history of the genre, for it introduced to readers the Coles' most important series detective, Superintendent Henry Wilson. Though in *The Brooklyn Murders* Wilson, contrary to the *COC*, does not really shine (he foolishly allows his inspector, Blaikie, to arrest a suspect on what he should have realized was obviously faked evidence and has to release the man after the clever amateurs make discoveries the police should have made), Wilson nevertheless became one of the best known fictional detectives in Britain during the Golden Age of the detective novel. Superintendent Wilson and

---

[6] Cole, *G. D. H. Cole*, 136; Margaret Cole, "Meet Superintendent Wilson," *Meet the Detective* (Harrisburg, PA: Telegraph Press, 1935), 118; Jacques Barzun and Wendell Hertig Taylor, *A Catalogue of Crime* (New York: Harper & Row, 1989), 135; G. D. H. Cole, *The Brooklyn Murders* (1923; rpnt., London: Collins, n.d.), 91, 158, 228. Could Robert Ellery, the male half of the amateur detective couple, perhaps have partially inspired the naming of the detective Ellery Queen six years later?

Inspector (later Superintendent) French often are viewed as British detective fiction's great humdrum police twins, and there indeed is evidence to support this view. Interestingly, Wilson's appearance actually preceded that of the better-known French by a year and Wilson clearly influenced Crofts in the fashioning of his own famous detective.

In his first appearance in *The Brooklyn Murders*, Superintendent Wilson is described as "a tall man, with quick, nervous movements, and a curious way of closing his eyes and holding up his hands before him with the tips of his fingers pressed tightly together when he was discussing his case" (this latter quality—a clear Great Detective mannerism—would not be emphasized by the Coles in later books). The "celebrated" Wilson, we learn, has "but a scant respect for most of his colleagues at Scotland Yard," an exception being his dogsbody, Inspector Blakie, "whose pertinacity in following up clues worked excellently with [Wilson's] own skill at putting two and two together."[7]

Wilson remains an essentially featureless personality at work, but we do at least get a glimpse in *The Brooklyn Murders* of his home life, which revolves around his wife and four children. Mrs. Wilson is the very model of the middle class matron, we find, at least as envisioned by Douglas Cole: "a comfortable, motherly woman, inclined to stoutness, and comfortably wrapped up in her children and her home." When Mrs. Wilson appears we are apt to find her sitting in her chair, "knitting woolies for the children in anticipation of the coming winter" or glancing at the pictures and headlines in her favorite newspaper, the *Daily Graphic*. When Wilson finds himself stuck in a blind alley in a case (as he is in *The Brooklyn Murders*), he is wont to discuss his case with her. To be sure, the placid, motherly Mrs. Wilson does not actually contribute any insights of value to her husband, her comments being confined to ejaculations such as "How dreadful!" and such queries as "Who did it?" Yet, by serving as a sounding board for her husband, she helps him mentally find his way. "Her very passivity was the

---

[7] Coles, *Brooklyn*, 29.

best possible help he could have," notes Cole. "As he talked to her, and as she assented unquestioningly to everything that he said, new ideas somehow arose in his mind."[8] Obviously in no way a genre icon for feminists, Mrs. Wilson perhaps served the author as a source of ironic amusement, as the good woman was so very far removed from Cole's own bold, outspoken and sometimes acerbic spouse. She also clearly inspired Freeman Wills Crofts, who the next year, in *Inspector French's Greatest Case*, fashioned as a matrimonial partner for Inspector French one Emily French, a very close cousin indeed of Mrs. Wilson. Like Superintendent Wilson, Inspector French discusses his cases with his wife, though Emily French is less passive than Mrs. Wilson, occasionally, through the miraculous operation of "women's intuition," getting a "notion" that puts Inspector French back on the right track.

In his 1931 genre survey, *Masters of Mystery: A Study of the Detective Story*, H. Douglas Thomson noted the similarity between the Wilsons and the Frenches, observing: "I always think of French and Wilson living in the same street, and of their respective wives paying calls on each other, comparing their husband's cases . . . , the while they knit socks for their lords and masters."[9] Both Wilson and French, as well as their wives, are, by deliberate design of the authors, bland, inoffensive and entirely forgettable, putting them in stark contrast with the many angst-ridden police detectives and partners/lovers of the modern crime novel. There are, however, some discernible differences between the two men. Physically, Wilson is tall and thin, while French tends towards stoutness and is slightly under average height. More significantly, Wilson shares with his makers a partiality to socialism and is generally more intellectually aware than French. Wilson, for example, is capable of discoursing on a *Times Literary Supplement* article on Gnosticism with a clergyman on a train, a feat hard to see being accomplished by French, who while traveling by train is more likely

---

[8] Cole, *Brooklyn*, 127, 128.

[9] H. Douglas Thomson, *Masters of Mystery: A Study of the Detective Story* (New York: Dover, 1931), 246.

to be found burying his nose in a railway timetable in an attempt to determine how X could have traveled from point A to point C by passing through point B. Despite these differences, however, the two men stand as the most prominent examples of the bland and unflappable Golden Age police investigator, normal to the point of dullness.

Margaret Cole humorously addressed the lack of personality of her and her husband's series detective in a 1935 article, "Meet Superintendent Wilson," wherein Wilson himself appears in the railway carriage in which Mrs. Cole is traveling to ask her why he is such a featureless character. "What *am* I like?" demands Wilson of his creator's wife. "How can I dominate your pages if I'm only a bundle of negatives?" Mrs. Cole explains patiently, "We don't want you to dominate them. We want the main interest of our stories to be in the stories themselves, and in the people and their relations with one another. We want you to be the right sort of person for unraveling the mystery; and the less you get in the way when you aren't wanted for that purpose, the better we shall be pleased." Nevertheless, when pressed by the anxious Wilson for some particulars, she amplifies with a few details: "you came of respectable but impecunious, middle-class parents and got a scholarship to a secondary school. You stayed there till you were eighteen, and then chose the police force because you thought it offered more scope for the imagination than sitting on a stool and entering things in a ledger. Very wise of you, in my opinion."[10] Here, we get a glimpse of the Coles' vision of Henry Wilson: the model socialist white-collar man, eschewing life as a cog in the capitalist money machine, preferring to do his part in the promotion of justice as an enlightened voice in law enforcement.

Superintendent Wilson appears in most of the Cole novels and novellas, though in some he plays a recessive role. Of the twenty-eight Cole novels, Douglas Cole entirely or mostly wrote eighteen, while Margaret Cole entirely or mostly wrote ten. The statements made over the years by Margaret Cole concerning the authorship

---

[10] Cole, "Wilson," 123-126. We also learn in the story "Murder in Church" that Wilson was raised as a Methodist.

of the Coles detective novels affirm that, contrary to common belief, the novels primarily were written not collaboratively, but individually. These statements are supported by the Coles' son, Humphrey, in exchanges made with Margaret Cole's biographer, Betty D. Vernon.

The "responsibility" for the detective novels, Margaret recalls in 1949 in *Growing up into Revolution*, "was about evenly divided." (I take this to mean that Margaret Cole means about half the novels were written by her and half by Douglas; this actually overestimates her own contribution.) In her 1971 *Life of Cole* she writes that the novels were continued "until the middle of [World War Two], when I became so bored with the one I was currently writing that I stopped half-way through and never began again. The last one (his) appeared in 1943, and concerned itself, rather amusingly, with a group of European refuges in Oxford and their troubles" (this latter reference is to the novel *Toper's End*, which was published in 1942, not 1943). Finally, according to Humphrey Cole, "The actual process of creation . . . was one whereby each book was wholly written by either Margaret or by Douglas."[11]

The breakdown of the true authorship is, I believe, as follows:

G. D. H. Cole (18 novels)
1. *The Brooklyn Murders* (1923) (Superintendent Henry Wilson)
2. *The Death of a Millionaire* (1925) (Wilson)*
3. *The Blatchington Tangle* (1926) (Wilson, Everard Blatchington)*
4. *The Man from the River* (1928) (Wilson, Dr. Michael Prendergast)*

---

[11] Coles, *Revolution*, 179; Cole, *G. D. H. Cole*, 136; Betty D. Vernon, *Margaret Cole 1893-1980: A Political Biography* (London: Croom Helm, 1986), 64; Curtis Evans, "By G. D. H AND Margaret Cole? Who Wrote What in the Coles' Crime Fiction Corpus," *CADS Crime and Detective Stories* 63 (July 2012): 19-22.

5. *Corpse in Canonicals* (1930) (Wilson, Hubert and Emily Welsh)
   6. *The Great Southern Mystery* (1931) (Wilson)
   7. *The Affair at Aliquid* (1933) (non-series)*
   8. *End of an Ancient Mariner* (1933) (Wilson, the Welshes)
   9. *Big Business Murder* (1935) (Wilson)
   10. *Dr. Tancred Begins* (1935) (Dr. Benjamin Tancred, Wilson)
   11. *Last Will and Testament* (1936) (Tancred, Wilson)
   12. *The Brothers Sackville* (1936) (Wilson, Inspector Tom Fairford)*
   13. *Disgrace to the College* (1937) (Blatchington)*
   14. *The Missing Aunt* (1937) (Wilson, Prendergast)
   15. *Off With Her Head* (1938) (Wilson, Fairford)
   16. *Double Blackmail* (1939) (Wilson)*
   17. *Murder at the Munition Works* (1940) (Wilson)
   18. *Toper's End* (1942) (Wilson, Prendergast, the Welshes)*

Margaret Cole (10 novels)
   1. *The Murder at Crome House* (1927) (non-series)
   2. *Poison in the Garden Suburb* (1929) (Wilson, Tony and Lydia Redford)
   3. *Burglars in Bucks* (1930) (Wilson, Blatchington)*
   4. *Dead Man's Watch* (1931) (Wilson, Sir Charles Wylie)
   5. *Death of a Star* (1932) (Inspector Walling, Blatchington)*
   6. *Death in the Quarry* (1934) (Wilson, Blatchington)
   7. *Scandal at School* (1935) (Blatchington)*
   8. *Greek Tragedy* (1939) (Wilson, the Redfords)
   9. *Counterpoint Murder* (1940) (Wilson)*
   10. *Knife in the Dark* (1942) (Mrs. Warrender)[12]

---

[12] This tabulation is based primarily on Appendix A: List of Books by G. D. H. Cole, in Margaret Cole's biography of her husband. Margaret Cole writes here that she omitted from the list "the nine novels which were wholly or nearly wholly written by

As can be seen from the lists above, between 1925 and 1935, the couple maintained, as Margaret Cole has written, a roughly even rate of production, with nine books by Douglas Cole and seven by Margaret Cole. After 1935, the balance shifts decisively in the husband's favor, with him authoring eight additional novels and his wife authoring only three (although she also authored during this time a short fiction collection, *Mrs. Warrender's Profession*). Another obvious difference between the two authors is that Douglas Cole clearly much preferred Wilson as his detective, having him appear in some capacity in sixteen out of his eighteen books (he plays a recessive role in the majority of the G. D. H. Cole books

(cont.) myself," all of which would be detective novels. However, she listed only 18 detective novels as having been written exclusively or partly by her husband, meaning that ten novels, not nine, were left off the list. My assumption is that Margaret Cole overlooked one novel that she actually wrote. The ten novels I attribute to Margaret Cole (nine of which she must have written) seem stylistically similar. In addition to her marked preference for Everard Blatchington, who appears in four of these novels (and has a very similar character pinch hitting for him in another, *Dead Man's Watch*), there also are recurring characters in *Poison in a Garden Suburb* and *Greek Tragedy* and the amateur sleuth in *Knife in the Dark* is Mrs. Warrender, the elderly heroine of the tales in *Mrs. Warrender's Profession*, a short fiction collection likely authored by Margaret Cole. Margaret Cole also states in her *Life of G. D. H. Cole* and her *Growing up into Revolution* that the bulk of the writing in any given Coles work of detective fiction was by one or the other of them, so I believe the other group of novels can be credited mostly to Douglas Cole. Of the four short fiction collections, *Mrs. Warrender's Profession*, as indicated above, likely was written entirely by Margaret Cole, while the other three collections, *Superintendent Wilson's Holiday*, *A Lesson in Crime* and *Wilson and Some Others*, contain stories that likely were variously authored by both writers. The novella *Death of a Bride* (1945) likely was authored by Margaret Cole. In the couple's 1952 *Picture Post* interview with Susan Hicklin, Hicklin summed up the tangled situation this way: "Professor Cole first had Dr. Tancred, whom his wife couldn't abide, so she created her Mrs. Warrender. Then her husband invented Everard Blatchington who got everything wrong and was a man after Mrs. Cole's heart. Finally they both settled down with Superintendent Wilson of Scotland Yard, who sometimes relies on the brainwaves of his wife." Although Hicklin's chronology is off, she correctly gives the couple's series sleuth preferences.

from 1935 on, however), in contrast with Margaret Cole, who employs Wilson in only six of ten books. It can also be seen that Margaret Cole preferred the aristocrat Everard Blatchington, whom she used in four of ten novels, in contrast with her husband, who employs him only twice. (She also employed an Everard Blatchington surrogate as a major character in *Dead Man's Watch*.) I have asterisked the works that I believe to be the most successful Cole novels; eight of them are by Douglas Cole and four by Margaret Cole. (I also include *Death of a Bride,* 1945, a novella probably authored by Margaret, among the couple's more successful mystery fiction.) Below I extensively discuss the works of both authors, first those primarily by Douglas Cole and then those primarily by Margaret Cole.

Part Two: The Detective Novels of G. D. H. Cole

*The Death of a Millionaire,* the next Douglas Cole novel after *The Brooklyn Murders*, marks the transition of Douglas Cole from Crofts clone to a distinctive and unique writer within the mystery genre. This novel concerns the murder of millionaire Hugh Radlett ("the richest man in America—and that means, in the world") in his room at Sugden's Hotel in London. Radlett, traveling under the pseudonym Restington, had a suite reserved for him by the great Earl of Ealing. In the opening pages of the novel, Sugden's is preparing to welcome the Earl of Ealing, who is scheduled to meet there with Radlett/Restington. Adopting an intrusive narrative voice in the manner of Dickens or Trollope, Cole with mock reverence describes the exclusive hotel as a bastion of Britain's conservative ruling elite:

> Perhaps you know Sugden's Hotel in St. James Square. Or perhaps you have never heard of it. Most people never have; it all depends on the world you move in. . . . It is not large, but it is the best hotel in London. Any one who is any one will tell you so. It is not meant for the likes of us. . . .

> .... It is not like a palace; it is not like a gargantuan lavatory; it is not a hotel in that sense of the term. It is just a quiet, gentlemanly house, the resort of quiet, gentlemanly people who know the best and are in the habit of getting it every day of their lives....[13]

"Sugden's," Cole loftily informs us, "is not in the habit of being put about. It holds itself above the battle of life." Nevertheless, the employees today are "all just a little flustered," due to the arrival on the premises of the great Earl of Ealing, who is asking to see Mr. Restington. Continues Cole:

> Though you may never have heard of Sugden's, it can hardly be that you have never heard of Lord Ealing. ... He is the richest man in England, and president, for the third successive year, of the Federation of British Enterprises. He has been member of several Cabinets—the urbanest of Home secretaries, the most popularly militant of War Ministers.... He owns several newspapers, and knows how to wield the power of the Press. And he is the chairman of the fairest jewel in the crown of British commercial enterprise—the Anglo-Asiatic Commercial Corporation.... Hearts needs must beat faster at such a paladin's approach.[14]

Naturally Lord Ealing over the course of the novel proves to be anything but a "paladin," repeatedly lying to the police and fraudulently manipulating stock prices to add to his already bursting coffers. For Cole, Lord Ealing and his Anglo-Asiatic Commercial

---

[13] G. D. H. and Margaret Cole, *The Death of a Millionaire* (1925; rpnt., London: Penguin, 1950), 9. Sugden's rather resembles the stately, old Bertam's Hotel of Agatha Christie's *At Bertram's Hotel*, published forty years after *The Death of a Millionaire*. Presumably the authors based their respective fictional hotels on the famous Brown's Hotel.

[14] Coles, *Millionaire*, 9-10.

Corporation [AACC] stand for all that is debased and debauched in British political and economic life. Though "a patrician of unblemished descent" (one must glide over the matter of the great-great-grandfather and the flower-girl), Ealing has cynically allied himself with corrupt, grasping parvenus like the obsequious Mr. Benjamin, son of a Whitechapel tailor originally "from somewhere in Central Europe," and the piggish, vulgar Sir James Vanzetti (surely the name Vanzetti, shared with the celebrated/vituperated Italian-American anarchist on death row at the time of the writing of the novel, is not coincidental); and he uses his name and his place in government at every opportunity to benefit the AACC. When Lord Ealing discovers at Sugden's that Radlett/Restington appears to have been murdered in his room by his secretary Rosenbaum, his body carried off in a trunk, the magnate aristocrat's first thought is to find and destroy any incriminating documents concerning his shady financial dealings (Ealing, who was authorized by the AACC to back Radlett's/Restington's gold mine concession from the Soviet Union, had promised Radlett/Restington to use his influence with the British government to obtain advantages in AACC's dealings with the Soviets; and the pair also had planned to manipulate AACC stock prices to their personal advantage). Sugden's manager as well as the arriving Inspector Blakie prove easy enough to overawe and manipulate (the manager is mainly concerned—and desperately at that—that Lord Ealing get some breakfast), but Superintendent Wilson—"At this time easily the most celebrated detective in England"—proves a tougher proposition altogether for the Earl. Wilson, we learn, "knew a thing or two about that nobleman which Lord Ealing fondly believed to be quite unsuspected in official quarters. The Superintendent had few illusions left."[15] Eventually Wilson discovers the truth about both Radlett's/Restington's murder (a resolution that likely will not surprise experienced genre readers) and Lord Ealing's malfeasance. Unfortunately, Wilson is now like the man who knew too much and must pay for his excessive knowledge of

---

[15] Ibid., 10, 39, 68.

the sordid truth of men in high places in capitalist countries. After the current government falls, Wilson, knowing that Lord Ealing will return to the Cabinet and take the position of Home Secretary so that he can suppress any evidence in the Radlett/Restington matter unfavorable to him, resigns from the force and becomes a private detective.

*The Death of a Millionaire* is yet another crime novel that gives the lie to the contention that a so-called "Humdrum" author cannot have produced a novel of any intrinsic interest other than that of its puzzle. The truth is that the puzzle in *The Death of a Millionaire* is rather rudimentary (and owes something of a debt to E. C. Bentley's earlier genre landmark, *Trent's Last Case*). The main interest of the puzzle is in how it helps unfold the novel's satire of British capitalism. In other words, *The Death of a Millionaire* is better appreciated as a satirical novel with crime in it than as a pure "mystery novel."

Cole has other objects of odium in his novel besides the rotten-to-the-core Lord Ealing and his contemptible cronies in capitalist crime. The fact that the secretary Rosenbaum, a Russian Jew, is suspected of Radlett's/Restington's murder gives Cole his opportunity to critique as well the conservative persecutors of Bolsheviks and Jews during recent "Red Scares" in Britain and the United States. Intriguingly, the real life British wartime Director of Intelligence (and future detective novelist), Sir Basil Thomson, comes in for direct excoriation by name during a discussion between the gullible Blakie and his wise superior:

> "Of course, sir, he had accomplices. One of these Bolshevik dens—the enemy in our midst, sir. We must call in the Special Branch."
>
> "My dear Blaikie, don't talk like an article in the *Daily Express*. I'm not much of a believer in Bolshevik dens. Most of these fellows are a harmless lot of fanatics."
>
> "But Sir Basil always used to say—"

> "Oh, yes, I know all about that." Wilson's little differences with Sir Basil had been notorious, and the quoting of Sir Basil as an authority caused him to react at once. . . . "I remember they used to discover at least a couple of great revolutionary plots a week, before Sir Basil went."
>
> "These Bolsheviks are dangerous fellows, sir."
>
> "My dear Blaikie, if you had seen as much of the Special Branch as I have, you'd be more skeptical about Bolshevik plots."[16]

Wilson's "dear Blakie" is easily led, but the Superintendent soon finds a more obstinate, if ultimately farcical, antagonist in Brigadier-General Sir Evan Bunker, Basil Thomson's (fictional) replacement as head of Intelligence. Of the same defensive and paranoid mentality as his predecessor (as the General's surname suggests), Bunker upon hearing the words "Soviet Union" and "Rosenbaum" immediately commences rounding up as many of the kingdom's Bolsheviks and Jews as his men can lay their hands on, under Wilson's scornful eye. Bunker, Cole informs us, "was not an intelligent man—it was said that defect of his had cost several thousand men their lives during the war—but he was immensely energetic . . . the chasing of Rosenbaum afforded a magnificent opportunity for the display of the General's qualities." Bunker's men hit the streets in search of Bolshies, with less then stellar results:

> Every known haunt of advanced opinion in or near the metropolis was raided and searched from top to bottom. A full-dress raid on the King Street headquarters of the Communist Party resulted only in the seizure of a quantity of "seditious" literature. The Liberty Club in Clerkenwell, haunt of a leading Anarchist group, was raided twice, despite the fact—

---

[16] Ibid., 60-61.

unknown to the Special Branch—that its members looked on Bolsheviks as a shade worse than kings or capitalists. The East End of London was combed fine for suspicious characters, and quite an army of Rosenbaums was interrogated, and several detained for a few hours until they could prove their identity. None of them was the man. Even the Nineteen Seventeen Club was politely visited, while Mr. Ramsay MacDonald was delivering a lecture on the horrors of Bolshevism.[17]

At one point, General Bunker believes he has found his man, but all is for naught:

Bunker's crypto-Jew turned out to be a Scotsman of irreproachable antecedents, his Bolshevik desperado a respectable merchant of sound conservative principles and active in the South Streatham Lodge of the Primrose League. His name was not Rosenbaum, but, as he had said, Ivor Rose, and his partners, Lewis and Smith, were not Levi and Schmid, but the one a Welshman and the other a pure Cockney. Rose had a perfect alibi for the night of the crime, which he had spent attending a Wesleyan Conference in Birmingham. And, best of all, the mysterious trunk which he had brought home after the crime and "secreted" in an outhouse, proved to contain, not a dead or living body, but trade samples—of Poggin's Ideal Pickles for the Home—which the worthy merchant was conveying to the United States when Bunker's zealous emissaries arrested him at Liverpool.... Not for the first time in its career, the Special Branch found itself badly bunkered.[18]

---

[17] Ibid., 101-102.
[18] Ibid., 140.

In the face of such a fiasco Wilson cannot resist tweaking the blustering, impetuous and incompetent Special Branch head over the mess he has made:

> "If we don't want him for the case, you can always deport him as an undesirable alien. That's one advantage with these Russians. There's no one to look after their interests. No fuss about *habeas corpus*, eh, General?"
>
> "It would be a jolly good thing for the country if *habeas corpus* were repealed altogether," said the General savagely.
>
> "Oh, I don't know," replied Wilson. "It would come very expensive if we let you imprison everybody."[19]

Cole does not rest content with ridiculing "Great Men" like Sir Basil Thomson and Brigadier-General Sir Evan Bunker for unreasoning fear of foreigners and leftists; lesser folk are lampooned by Cole as well. "A Russian," darkly declares Sugden's manager of Rosenbaum, "in the tone of one who imputes a crime." "Very foreign-looking gentleman, sir" adds a hotel porter. "Queer-looking, as you might say. Not English, I mean." On the other hand, another character in the novel, one Cole clearly means for us to admire, Hugh Radlett/Restington, is reported to have observed that "Russians were the most intelligent people on earth except the Jews—and [Rosenbaum] had the advantage of being both."[20]

Hugh Radlett/Restington is one of three foci of moral conscience in *The Death of a Millionaire* (besides, of course, Wilson),

---

[19] Ibid., 214.

[20] Ibid., 17, 18, 53. It should be noted that the real-life object of Douglas Cole's ire, Basil Thomson, himself enjoyed a writing career as a detective novelist in the 1930s, publishing eight Crofts-like detective novels from 1933 to 1937 about a Scotland Yard policeman named Richardson, who advances over the series from a police constable to Chief Constable.

the other two being Lord Ealing's nephew and secretary, Arthur Wharton, and Radlett's/Restington's business partner, James Pasquett. A document written by Radlett/Restington reveals that the American millionaire was actually born in England and grew up in a coal mining slum town, where he learned the horror of grinding, amoral capitalism. Here Cole clearly is drawing on his familiarity with Labour issues, from the sympathetic perspective of a committed Labour man. Much of the document reads like it was drawn from a study of poor working conditions in late-nineteenth-century industrial Britain:

> My father, John Radlett, was a collier, but we were very poor. Father had been too active in Union affairs, and the overseer always saw to it that he got the worst working place in the pit. There was no minimum wage then. The Unions weren't so strong as I suppose they've grown since. And father couldn't chuck up his job: no one else in the district would have employed him. He was a marked man. . . .
> 
> . . . . My brother Edward was killed in a colliery accident when I was ten. I remember it well. The cage had fallen to the bottom of the shaft. My mother took me to the pithead, where there was a crowd of men and women waiting for the news. I was frightened, and ran away and hid in a shed. My mother found me and told me my brother was dead. After that, there were only four of us to feed.
> 
> . . . .
> 
> I went to work at thirteen. I had some schooling at first, of course, at a rotten hole of a school pretty nearly as bad as our house. It was draughty and leaky and horribly cold in the winter. . . .
> 
> . . . . And, in a few months' time, came a strike.
> 
> . . . . Father was made chairman of the Strike Committee. When the men went back—starved out—there was no job for him. . . . He was turned fifty by then,

but he made up his mind to leave England and go to the States.[21]

James Radlett finds work with an old friend, Merritt, who made a fortune in American mines, though ultimately Radlett loses his life in a violent strike. To his surprise, young Hugh inherits Merritt's money at the latter man's death. Suddenly he finds himself a rich man. After foolishly marrying a woman who proves a worthless gold-digger, Hugh arranges for his own disappearance and departs to engage in new ventures overseas. In Russia he is caught up in the Revolution and imprisoned, but eventually makes his way out, with a valuable gold mine concession, in partnership with his friend John Pasquett.

Pasquett is the pivot on which much of the novel's puzzle plot turns, the anti-Ealing of the novel, and Cole lavishes much sympathetic attention on him. "He was," Cole tells us, "a big, fair man, clean shaven, and of fine physique. But he was much more than that. He had one of those faces which are always half-smiling, as if he was perpetually amused. There was a humorous twinkle in his eye, too, and he was used to making friends at sight." One of those friends at first sight that Pasquett makes is Arthur Wharton, Lord Ealing's nephew and private secretary. Under Pasquett's influence, Wharton too becomes a true moral agent in the novel. Wharton is the son of Lord Ealing's sister, who married a novelist from whom she was quickly estranged. The novelist went off to live in Capri, providing his son, Arthur, with a small allowance but never seeing him. Like G. D. H. Cole, Arthur Wharton attended Balliol College, Oxford; later he was elected to a Fellowship at All Souls, which he relinquished to go to work for his uncle, feeling "conscience of a desire to do things."[22] Wharton soon realizes, when plunged amidst the events described in *The Death of a Millionaire*, that his uncle is corrupt to the core; and that realization leads him to repudiate Lord Ealing and the business world and return to Oxford, where decency reigns.

---

[21] Ibid., 86-96.
[22] Ibid., 75, 114.

Arthur Wharton's relationship with James Pasquett is interesting for nonpolitical reasons as well, for it appears to be, on Wharton's part, latently homosexual. Indeed, in a novel singularly bereft of significant female characters, Wharton functions as the "female" half of the novel's love interest, caught in the classic conflict of loyalty to a parental figure (in this case an uncle, Lord Ealing) versus love for a winning young man (Pasquett). Before Wharton even knows the identity of Pasquett, he is struck by Pasquett's very presence: "Arthur was glad the man with the laughing eyes was to be his fellow passenger. He observed him closely as he stood talking to the mechanic, noting his great strength and physical vigour." After departing from Pasquett's company, Wharton's only "regret is that he had failed to exchange names and addresses" with Pasquett: "The man remained in his thoughts: Arthur wanted to meet him again." Later, after the two become fast friends, Arthur finds himself thinking about Pasquett constantly: "Arthur missed him when he was gone. Lord Ealing . . . laughed at him for mooning about like a girl who has lost her lover. Arthur first blushed, and then said that really he did feel a bit like that." Later, when Wharton comes to fear that Pasquett may be involved, like Lord Ealing, in shady business transactions and even perhaps as well in murder, he agonizes in the manner of a lover: "His uneasy mind suggested to him all manner of dark suspicions. He put them from him, but they thronged back to haunt him. And yet, the worse his thoughts of Pasquett, somehow the greater his affection grew. . . . Arthur groaned in spirit, perplexed between fear and love." Believing that Wharton will reveal what he knows of his Uncle's crooked business dealings, Lord Ealing attempts to manipulate Wharton's doubts about Pasquett to his own advantage, in highly melodramatic fashion: "Have I not seen your affection for him? . . . Would you send him to prison to mark your love for him? . . . I ask you, Arthur, would you send your friend to imprisonment—perhaps—who knows?—to death?"[23] A mortified

---

[23] Ibid., 97, 101, 145, 170, 219.

Wharton decides he must keep quiet about what he knows, in case his beloved friend is implicated, though he tells his uncle that he holds him in contempt and will leave his employ.

Fortunately for the anguishing Wharton, Pasquett is revealed to be virtuous at the tale's end. However, Wharton ultimately must satisfy himself, after Pasquett marries a young lady, with Pasquett's firstborn son being named "Arthur." In the novel's final colloquy between the two men, Pasquett provides Cole's moral, one highly subversive of putative Golden Age verities:

> The trouble about you, Arthur, is that you've been badly brought up. You think you're a bit of an iconoclast; but away down in your mind you've a profound veneration for property, and law and order, and middle-class morality, and all the other things you criticize in those funny little books of yours. I had all that knocked out of me quite early. You see, I was brought up to a be a business man—in America too. I know that law and order and the rights of property, and all the rest of the stuff your uncle puts in his speeches, are just bunkum. You only know it theoretically; when it comes to acting you're a good old Whig like the rest. . . . I judge for myself: I make my own laws. . . .[24]

An obviously deliberate irony here is that Cole is having Pasquett, when making his stirring call to revolutionary action, effectively lecture Wharton about Cole's own "faults." Like Wharton, Cole is an Oxford academic writing about advanced societal reformation in "funny little books." There is another similarity between Cole and Wharton as well, in the area of sexuality. Cole himself seems to have had certain homosexual impulses. "Physically, he was always under-sexed—low-powered," recalled

[24] Ibid., 286-287.

Margaret Cole of her husband in her biography of him. Until Douglas' marriage with her, she admitted

> his physical affections, his desire to caress, had been generally directed towards his own sex; he had fallen in love with various young men, one or two of whom I afterwards met, and had written poems to them. . . . For women generally, except his wife, he never seemed to have any sexual use at all, and by and large to regard them as rather a low type of being. . . . He believed as strongly as any anti-Socialist that no woman (except Jane Austen) had ever achieved first-class honours in art or literature; and he felt that the main purpose in life of a majority of them was to distract man from his proper work.[25]

With the above in mind, it seems clear that in her first essentially solo detective novel, *The Murder at Crome House*, Margaret Cole modeled the character of the protagonist, James Flint, after her husband:

> James Flint was a tallish, slight young man of a year or two over thirty, who looked older by reason of his hairless temples and the steady gravity of his expression. . . . He was a lecturer and tutor in history and economics. . . . [He] had a positive horror, based mainly on . . . practical inexperience . . . of the modern young female of his own class. . . . [T]he Young Woman of the Period he regarded as a monster who would certainly try either to marry him or become his mistress.[26]

---

[25] Cole, *G. D. H. Cole*, 91-92.
[26] G. D. H and Margaret Cole, *The Murder at Crome House* (New York, Macmillan, 1927), 3, 4, 27.

The late Michael Foot, once a Labour party leader, supplemented Margaret Cole's forthright account of her husband's sexuality, recalling that as a professor Cole had "innocent little homosexual crushes on some of his students," including a future Labour party leader, Hugh Gaitskell. This attitude described by Margaret Cole and Michael Foot—that relationships between men were somehow higher and more "spiritual," if you will, than those between men and women—can be glimpsed in other Douglas Cole tales besides *The Death of a Millionaire*. For example, in *The Man from the River* (1928), the country vacation of Wilson and his friend Dr. Michael Prendergast, is treated rather like a romantic, rural "getaway" idyll for the male duo; while in *End of Ancient Mariner* (1933), the sympathetic lead character, Philip Blakeway, rather remarkably thinks to himself, "although he liked his wife well enough, he would unhesitatingly have burned her at the stake if Sam Fowler's interests had demanded the sacrifice" (Sam Fowler is his best friend and business partner).[27]

Cole's next detective novel, *The Blatchington Tangle*, turns for a subject of satire from the world of finance to that classical locus of Golden Age detective fiction, the country house. *Blatchington* is an amusing novel, but also a more derivative and less original work than the preceding *The Death of a Millionaire*, plainly following in the steps of Agatha Christie's country house romp from the previous year, *The Secret of Chimneys*. At a country house party weekend ten individuals—a shady financier, an obnoxious American millionaire, an eccentric aristocrat and his former chorus girl wife, a couple young gentlemen of leisure, a matronly professional houseguest, a plucky girl, a private secretary and an impeccable butler—are enmeshed in violent death (of the shady financier) and

---

[27] Michael Foot, introduction to Betty D. Vernon, *Margaret Cole*, 21; G. D. H. and Margaret Cole, *End of an Ancient Mariner* (London: Collins, 1933), 10. Wilson appears with his friend Michael in two more "vacation" novels, *The Missing Aunt* (1937) and *Toper's End* (1942), as well as eleven short stories, presumably written mostly or entirely by Douglas Cole; no vacations of Wilson with his wife are recorded.

jewel theft (of the celebrated Blatchington Rubies) over an event-filled and comical weekend at Blatchington Towers. Wilson, now the "best-known [private] detective in England" in the wake of his resignation from the Yard at the end of *The Death of a Millionaire*, is called in by members of the house party in the second half of the novel to solve the case (Inspector Peascod not accepting the perennially popular theory with country house sets that the culprit "must have been somebody from outside . . . some horrible tramp"); later he compliantly participates in a cover-up.[28]

Though having no other evident purpose than to entertain, *The Blatchington Tangle* is one of the best Cole works, with genuinely amusing writing and characters and a sufficiently coherent plot. The financier murder victim naturally being loathed by the other house party members ("He was a brute and a bully. He kept the most filthy company. And his business methods—my word!"), the feelings of the private secretary—"he clearly felt no emotion but curiosity at the murder of his late employer"—are representative of his fellow survivors, leaving Cole free to indulge in one of the most high-spirited *Murder? What fun!* narratives from the period. Several comments from the characters are splendid examples of Golden Age *joie de mort*:

> "Bellamy," said Lord Blatchington, "have these clothes taken up to my room. And, by the way, there's a corpse by the window."

> "Arrested!" cried Lady Blatchington. . . . "What nonsense! Oh, I wish that horrible policeman would do what he's come for and go away! I do hate police in the house. . . . They set all the servants gossiping, and it takes weeks to settle them down again."

---

[28] G. D. H. and Margaret Cole, *The Blatchington Tangle* (New York: Macmillan, 1926), 124; 209.

# THE SPECTRUM OF ENGLISH MURDER

[The American, Mr. Wick Ellis, expounding at length, as is his wont, on the superiority of American over British police]: "The entire house-party—all potential suspects, you mark—left to roam at large, no finger-prints taken, the servants let in to dust the very scene of the crime, probably removing the most valuable clues with their unpolished boots." There was an indignant chorus of protest.

"The servants aren't allowed in the library in their boots! How can you be so ridiculous?" said Lady Blatchington.

"And if you're worried about the condition of the library," said Lord Blatchington, "you'll be pleased to hear that it hasn't been dusted. The inspector locked it up as soon as he arrived . . . there's a fool of a bobby locked up in there with my best whiskey."

"Murders *do* break up a house-party," said Mrs. Rivers plaintively.[29]

Here and there a few bits of more subversive satire appear in the narrative. Both involve Lord Blatchington's nephew Everard Blatchington, who would go on to appear in five more Cole works. Everard is an aristocratic dilettante portrayed with far greater sympathy on the part of the Coles than are those nasty financiers, presumably because of the young gentleman's cultured sensibility and sense of *noblesse oblige* leftism, qualities evident in Everard's discussion of the time his Uncle, Lord Blatchington, served as Governor-General of the British West African colony of Malaria. Lord Blatchington, admits Everard, "spent all his time big-game hunting up country, and left his subordinates to do the governing." He adds with remorseless scrutiny: "That's rather the way with our

---

[29] Coles, *Tangle*, 10, 49, 44, 81, 82, 113.

family. Most of us expect other people to do the work while we amuse ourselves *a notre gre*. Take me, for instance. What do I do? Nothing at all. And it's the same with Uncle Chetwynd, though he's a bishop, and Uncle Lothian, though he's got a seat in the Cabinet. We're a pack of ne'er-do-weels, I'm afraid." Explaining that after Malaria's native population revolted against British rule "a few experiments in teaching the niggers a lesson" had been made, Everard reflects, "I don't much hold with teaching niggers lessons—that is with airplanes." He also implies that Britain had less than altruistic motives in carrying the British flag to poor Malaria, declaring that "trade . . . has a way of getting a bit mixed up with the flag." Later, seeking to derail Wilson in his pursuit of the solution of the mystery, the imaginative Everard invents a fictional murder suspect that he clearly has drawn right from the pages of the sillier thrillers: "he's a big square Jew with black hair and fleshy lips and a heavy black moustache."[30] Everard knows it is all tosh, but he hopes it will send Wilson haring off in the wrong direction.

In 1928 came the fourth Wilson novel by G. D. H. Cole, *The Man from the River*, an excellent country house/village tale. In this novel Dr. Michael Prendergast is on vacation in the quaintly decayed Essex village of Steeple Tollesbury, outside Colchester, awaiting the arrival of his good friend Henry Wilson, who is still with Scotland Yard (apparently the novel predates *The Death of a Millionaire*). Before Wilson's arrival to join Michael at the local inn, the Old Malting House, a corpse is fished out of the River Toll; and foul play is suspected. The dead man, William Meston, was a partner in a Colchester brokerage firm. It turns out that there are quite a few people who may have wanted Meston dead, including his beautiful wife, Sylvia, who recently left him to take refuge with her relations at Loring Grange, a nearby country mansion. Local law enforcement being a bunch of nitwits, they are soon relying on the vacationing Wilson to solve the case, with the help of his Watson, Prendergast (the latter man would appear in

---

[30] Ibid., 63, 64, 217.

two more novels with Wilson, as well as eleven short stories). Although Cole's narrative in *The Man from the River* is somewhat discursive, the plot is rich and complex, the setting pleasing and the solution fairly-clued yet surprising, making the novel one of the better English village mysteries from the 1920s.

Clean plotting does not distinguish *Corpse in Canonicals* (1930), the Douglas Cole novel that followed *The Man from the River*, but it is a fitfully amusing tale of an English village crime wave that allows Cole to indulge himself in mocking one of his favorite satirical targets: British clergymen, both high and low. As one character aptly describes events, "Upon my word, I never knew life in our English countryside was so exciting. First a corpse, and a parson at that, and then another parson someone's slugged over the head; and Murgatroyd says there's been a burglary too. Edgar Wallace isn't in it."[31]

With this novel Cole also introduces two recurring characters, Colonel Hubert Welsh, Chief Constable of Brigshire and his flirtatious wife, Emily, who has rather a pash on Henry Wilson. (The couple later appears in Douglas' *End of an Ancient Mariner* and *Toper's End*.) The amiable but parochial and not overly bright Colonel Welsh makes a fine vessel for Cole's humor:

> "The last book you lent my wife," said the Colonel, "was about a man who fell in love with his horse. Give me Edgar Wallace."
>
> "Don't pretend to be a fool, Hubert," said his wife. "You know you said you liked Proust."
>
> "I said I liked him in moderation," said the Colonel. "The trouble was, there wasn't any moderation."[32]

---

[31] G. D. H. and Margaret Cole, *Corpse in Canonicals* (1930; rpnt, London: Collins, 1933), 96.

[32] Coles, *Canonicals*, 113. The references to Edgar Wallace anticipate the Coles short story "A Lesson in Crime," in which an Edgar Wallace surrogate is murdered by a fanatical detective story enthusiast (see below).

Cole took farce several steps further in *The Affair at Aliquid* (1933), a novel that is not even truly a detective or crime story, though it was published, quite mystifyingly, by the Collins Crime Club. There is an incidental jewel theft and an investigating police detective, the brilliantly named Inspector Bulkhead, but the focus of the novel is on pure humor in the manner of P. G. Wodehouse, albeit of a cruder order. *The Affair at Aliquid* concerns the misadventures of amiable con artists David and Dorothy Rogers at Aliquid Castle, where they have been welcomed by the philanthropist Duke of Aliquid, who labors under the mistaken impression that the spouses are highly devout African missionaries. Much of the humor of the novel comes from this misunderstanding, for David and Dorothy, an excruciatingly modern young couple, are about as far in morals from religious missionaries as could be imagined. Once he realizes the situation, David lets his imagination soar:

> "Crackenthorpe usen't to have any love for missionaries when I knew him," said the Duke.... "He used to tell us at the club it would be an easy job governing Africa if all the missionaries were lined up against a wall and shot."
>
> "As a matter of fact," said David, "he has shot several. But he and I managed to keep friends."
>
> The Duchess gasped.
>
> "You say Sir Lindsay Crackenthorpe has shot several missionaries," she cried.
>
> "Only black ones, of course," said David, "except one. He was parti-colored."

Dorothy, however, has a little more difficulty masquerading as a "good" woman:

> "Ah, yes, in Africa, said the Duchess. "You were out there for some years, were you not, Mrs. Rogers?"
>
> "Years and years," said Dorothy. "That's where I met David, you know. I was the only white woman for miles and miles."

> "You must have felt very lonely sometimes."
>
> "On the whole I managed to have quite a good time. I do, somehow. Only, of course, it wasn't like jolly old London.... There's something a bit creepy about those black people, don't you think? But I do think some of them are really good-looking when you get used to it. I remember a man who used to play the saxophone...."
>
> "I never knew the saxophone was a native African instrument."
>
> "Oh!" said Dorothy. "That wasn't in Africa.... That was somewhere else."[33]

As the above passage suggests, religion, class and race all are irreverently treated in *The Affair at Aliquid*. Also coming in for ribbing is Freudianism, in the person of the forbidding but daft amateur psychologist Miss Perks, who is also a guest at Aliquid. Clearly the socialist Cole did not have much sympathy for Freudian psychoanalysis and the belief that the key to understanding human nature lay in comprehending the sexual subconscious (rather than class identity), for he never misses an opportunity to tweak Miss Perks:

> "What I maintain is that the Bible can only be regarded as inspired in the purely Freudian sense.... It is, of course, obvious that all savage superstitions have a sex origin. If you wish to persuade a savage to substitute your superstitions for his own, your only course is to get right down to the roots of his subconscious mind. What you will find there will surprise you."
>
> "I'm sure it will," said David.
>
> "Now I, Mr. Rogers, have no sex—absolutely none." The lady turned her steely eyes upon him.

---

[33] G. D. H. and Margaraet Cole, *The Affair at Aliquid* (London: Collins, 1933), 36, 163.

David hovered between "Hard luck" and "How fortunate for you" as the more appropriate comment.[34]

Like Miss Perks, Cole in *The Affair at Aliquid* is rather sexually outspoken, at least by Golden Age standards:

"You can see for yourself [Dorothy's] not exactly cut out for a missionary's wife."
This remark seemed to make the Duke uncomfortable.
"Um," he said. "A bit on the lively side, perhaps. She seems to have plenty of vitality."
"That's the worst of it," said David. "In that hot climate, too. You see, I was kept so busy looking after Dorothy I really had no time for looking after heathen. I sometimes think Dorothy needs a missionary all to herself."

"He was the kind that would carry on with anything in skirts—or preferably without."

"But, my dear Lady Snodgrass, you must realise that it's very undesirable to go about suffering from the delusion that people want to rape you. Especially when it's so impossible."

"Look here, be a good chap and lend me [your braces]—for Dorothy's sake."
"You're not playing fair," said Toby. "I'm sure Dorothy wouldn't want my trousers to come off."
"And don't you wish she would," said David.[35]

---

[34] Coles, *Aliquid*, 57.
[35] Ibid., 172, 250, 257, 274.

Throughout the novel, Cole strikes subversive and original notes for the genre of this place and period. Unlike most Golden Age mystery writers, such as Henry Wade, Cole spares no tears over the tax burden borne by the modern aristocracy: "Nor is [Aliquid Castle] in the best of repair," admits Cole unconcernedly, in his Trollopian narrative mode, "for the Duke, like most Dukes in these days, has immolated a number of under-gardeners and written to *The Times* to express horror that instead of finding other work they are now living in idleness on the dole—which, as a matter of fact, they are not."[36]

In her review of *The Affair at Alquid* (in, it must be admitted, *The Times*), a disgusted Dorothy L. Sayers dismissed the novel, lecturing the Coles that in a farce "the smallest error of taste is fatal" and that their errors of taste in their new novel were manifold: "The mirth is coarse and commonplace, the satire clumsy and brutal." Getting into her stride, Sayers essentially concluded that the Coles had not the proper standing to write such a story: "One must both know and love these bishops, butlers, and noblemen if one's caricature of their foibles is to be anything more than an ill-bred grin through a horse-collar."[37] With *The Affair at Aliquid*, Cole had gone too far; the Establishment had Spoken, and She was Displeased.

To be sure, Sayers was on the mark in censoriously concluding that *The Affair at Aliquid* had "no proper business in the Crime Club list." The best G. D. H. Cole crime novels from the thirties that actually involve *crime* are the novel *The Brothers Sackville* (1936) and the novella *Disgrace to the College* (1937). The genuine mysteries that Cole published between 1931 and 1935 are all

---

[36] Ibid., 19.

[37] *Sunday Times*, 17 September 1933, 7. In praising a Coles novel, *Death in the Quarry*, the next year, Dorothy L. Sayers approvingly noted that the tale was "free from those errors of taste which sometimes mar their work, and the social problems involved are handled with better tact and truth." *Sunday Times*, 13 May 1934, 7. Sayers' reviews of various Coles novels suggest that Margaret Cole was not off the mark when she complained of conservative reviewers carping about the presence of "politics" in their crime fiction.

disappointments. *The Great Southern Mystery* (1931) is tediously complicated and cluttered, while *End of an Ancient Mariner* is an unispired inverted mystery of the type Francis Iles (Anthony Berkeley Cox) had recently popularized. Douglas Cole produced no novel in 1934, but 1935 saw the appearance of his *Big Business Murder*, an apparent attempt by the author to return to the successful capitalism critique of his masterwork, *The Death of a Millionaire*. Unfortunately, *Big Business Murder* is a pale imitation of its predecessor, lacking its zest and gusto and burdened with a particularly dense character, a celebrated cricketer, who chivalrously insists on taking the blame for a murder in order to protect another man's wife, with whom he is not even intimately involved. Still, the author manages a few clever lines. We learn, for example, that Arrow Investments Chairman Lord Tadcaster, who is the firm's selfish aristocratic figurehead, makes a living from serving on boards, since he is hard up indeed, it being doubtful whether Tadcaster "has really any property he can call his own except a most impressive family vault."[38] Admittedly the anti-corporate theme of *Big Business Murder* retains some interest today, but overall the tale is a disappointment, lacking the storytelling flair or plotting ingenuity of a similarly-themed novel from the same period, John Street's' masterful *Death on the Board* (1937).

Cole's next three fictional works, from 1935 and 1936, constitute attempts by the author to produce longer, denser, more consciously literary novels, in the manner of other British detective writers at this time, such as Dorothy L. Sayers, Margery Allingham and Henry Wade. Two of the titles, *Dr. Tancred Begins* (1935) and *Last Will and Testament* (1936), actually are two parts of one extremely long—and extremely dull—family saga cum mystery novel. "*Dr. Tancred Begins* and shows every sign of going on as long as the patience of the long-suffering reader will permit," nastily but accurately carped crime fiction reviewer Ralph Partridge. Much more enjoyable is *The Brothers Sackville* (1936),

---

[38] *Sunday Times*, 17 September 1933, 7; G. D. H. Cole and Margaret Cole, *Big Business Murder* (New York: Doubleday, Doran, 1935), 5.

which retains the authors' trademark humor in addition to offering good writing and lively characterization. The latter, particularly, were qualities increasingly desired by the readership of mystery novels; and they were emphasized in the description of the novel on the dust jacket flap of the American edition. "And apart from the mystery," the "blurb" assures readers, "Mr. and Mrs. Cole have given us a satirical glimpse of life as it is lived in a high class quarter of Birmingham, and in a shabby-genteel house in a respectable London suburb. The story is rich in observation of character." Perhaps not surprisingly, *A Catalogue of Crime* deplored what the blurb writer celebrated. "Evidently the Coles went all out here to do a novel," notes the *COC* icily. "The result is most tedious." My view, however, is in accord with other reviewers who had much more positive reactions, such as Ralph Partridge (who found *The Brothers Sackville* "brilliant in many ways, full of amusing characters and neat situations"), Milward Kennedy of the *Sunday Times* (who declared that the novel ranked "with the best" work of the Coles), and the American reviewer in the *Saturday Review* (who found the "A1" tale a "tantalizing family tangle" with "capital" "characterizations and background" and a "conclusion that startles both sleuth and reader").[39]

Reader interest in *The Brothers Sackville* centers on the two households of the Sackville brothers, Fred and Alfred. The upwardly mobile Fred lives with his wife Bertha in a high-class Birmingham neighborhood, while Alfred, a commercial traveler, lives with his wife, Josephine, and two children in a "shabby little villa" in Brondesbury. When Bertha's wealthy brother, the miserly and miserable John Ainsworth, is murdered, Alfred Sackville, who has unaccountably disappeared, becomes a leading suspect, though Ainsworth's servants are suspicious characters as well. The solution surprised many reviewers at the time, and some complained that canons of "fair play" had been violated; yet, whatever one's

---

[39] *New Statesman and Nation*, 1 June 1935, 836; Barzun and Taylor, *Catalogue of Crime*, 135; *New Statesman and Nation*, 9 January 1937, 54; *Sunday Times*, 6 December 1937, 11; *Saturday Review*, 12 June 1937, 16.

view of that matter (I find the solution legitimate), much enjoyment can be derived from the tale's satire of the pretensions of several characters, particularly the Sackville women, Bertha and Josephine. Josephine Sackville, a desperately devout Methodist, also is mocked for her faith in her minister, Reverend Ebenezer Williams, whose utter worthlessness starkly reveals itself during the course of events. It is easy to discern where the author's sympathy lies in such a Marxian-inflected ironical passage as the one that follows (reflecting Josephine's meditations as disaster falls on her head):

> Alfred was a bit of a Socialist; and Mr. Williams said that Socialism was all wrong because you couldn't make things any better except by saving people's souls, so that they wouldn't mind what happened to their bodies because they would be certain God was looking after them.
> What a comforting doctrine that was!

Elsewhere, Josephine naively reflects: "There was lots in the Bible one wasn't meant to understand. But the Bible was inspired; and when you were inspired you didn't need always to make sense." Eventually, even the foolishly pious Josephine realizes that her minister is a man of straw and renounces the flabbergasted canter, who departs with a typically smug exit line: "Good-bye, dear sister; and pray God to forgive you because you knew not what you said."[40]

Admittedly, the constantly whiny Josephine grows tiresome and Cole's pokes at organized religion are a bit heavy-handed, if pleasingly uncharacteristic of the genre at this time. The novel's truest satirical highlight, in my view, is the splendidly dense, selfish, overbearing and snobbish Bertha Sackville, whose greatest aspiration in life is gentry status, though she herself, a monument of bourgeois ignorance and complacency, is manifestly unfitted for

---

[40] G. D. H. and Margaret Cole, *The Brothers Sackville* (New York: Macmillan, 1937),1, 67, 68, 94.

it by any standard of taste or cultivation. Her exchanges with the prim and proper lawyer Mr. Stowell during her descent on her murdered brother's country home, Blessgrave Manor, are amusingly portrayed:

> "The law is a nuisance," said Bertha. "You can't think what it means to me, being kept in suspense. Of course, a hundred and eighty thousand[pounds] would be better than nothing...."
> "A great deal better, "Mr. Stowell murmured.
> "But there is all the difference in the world between being just able to manage and really having plenty of money. Don't you agree?"
> "In my experience, Mrs. Sackville, some of the people who find it hardest to manage are those who have a great deal of money."
> "That's nonsense," said Bertha. "What I mean by having plenty of money is not having to remember how much you've spent."
> "That, is I may so, is a very—er—perilous definition."
> "But if we don't find work for the poor, who else will? That's what I say," said Bertha, with the air of one producing a wholly irrefutable argument.
> "In these days," said Mr. Stowell, "the unemployed are kept out of the taxes."
> "They could all get work if they tried," said Bertha. "Except the unemployables. They ought to be made to work. But don't let's start talking politics. They make my head ache."[41]

Throughout the novel, Bertha is equipped by the author with a fine stock of *non sequiturs*, such as her fervent insistence, "I don't care how slanderous it is. It's true." She also is a mistress of the

---

[41] Coles, *Brothers Sackville*, 118-119.

insincere sentiment, as indicated in an exchange with the handsome local medico, Doctor Broughton, whom she has called upon, not, as she claims, because she wanted to find out more about a beloved brother's last moments, but because she likes Broughton's brown eyes:

> "I wasn't there, you know. He'd been dead for hours when I saw him."
> "Yes, but I wanted to ask you: Do you think he *suffered* much?"
> "I should say he knew nothing at all about it, after his head smashed on that spike."
> "Oh, how nice to think that."[42]

Another interesting element in *The Brothers Sackville* is the presence in the tale of a socialist policeman, the old labourite Sergeant Westwell. Typically treated in the genre between the wars as figures fit only for caricature, socialists in tales by the Coles are sagacious individuals, worthy of respect and admiration. Sergeant Westwell is described as "a fat, sleepy-looking person, with a large drooping black moustache, and a habit of folding his hands across his corporation when he was in repose." Despite his unprepossessing appearance and his lowly sergeant status (he has been repeatedly passed over for promotion because of his involvement in the Police Union after the Great War), Westwell yet manages to run rings around Tom Fairford, the young, attractive, politically conservative detective inspector to whom he has been assigned, not only in the Ainsworth affair but in other matters as well. When the two briefly discuss politics, Westwell is shown clearly getting the better of his superior:

> "I say, if you're that sort of chap, you ought to meet my sister. She says she's a Socialist. Can't say I see any sense in it myself."

---

[42] Ibid., 148.

"Why not?" said Westwell.

"Oh, well. What I say is, why go upsetting things? We're pretty well as we are, aren't we? Of course, there's this unemployment, and all that."

"There is," said Westwell. "I've got a brother who's been out three years. He's a miner. Six kids too."

"Rotten luck!" said Tom. "But he gets the dole, I suppose."

"Yes. He gets that. Unemployment Assistance they call it nowadays. It's . . . something."

"I suppose things are pretty bad, for some people. But there are an awful lot of rotters too."

"I think men being out of work makes men feel a bit rotten," said Westwell mildly.

"I didn't mean that. I meant these 'I won't works'."

Sergeant Westwell sighed gently. Inspector Fairford was a nice enough young fellow; but it didn't do to say what was really in your mind to your superior officer. He relapsed into silence, while Tom mused regretfully on the fate that had given him this old Bolshie as an assistant instead of his friend Jack Shipton.[43]

With *Disgrace to the College*, a novel expanded from the 1936 Dr. Tancred short story "Too Clever by Half" that was published in 1937 as part of Hodder and Stoughton's "New at Ninepence" series of illustrated paperback "thrillers," Cole turned for the first time in a novel—surprisingly, given his intimate knowledge of the institution—to Oxford University as his setting (the specific College, St. Mark's, is fictional). Margaret Cole later recalled that her husband "was well experienced in the ways of obstructionist Fellows in College meetings" and enjoyed getting some of his own back

---

[43] Ibid., 133, 134-135.

in satirical form in this novel.[44] *Disgrace to the College* not only boasts excellent satire, a firm sense of place and some effective character-drawing, but also a well-clued, rationally deduced murder puzzle, making it Douglas Cole's strongest mystery tale.

The novel is divided into two parts, the first of which concerns the unfolding of various events at St. Mark's that lead to murder. The South African undergraduate Sam Barrett, a clever idler, is in danger of being "sent down" by authorities after discovery of his intimate dalliance with Ellie Symonds, daughter of the late Butler of St. Mark's. The seventy-three year old College Bursar, Jerome Slatters, has been "past it" for some time, but he has no intention of retiring and has invoked ancient statutory authority to forestall his removal. Ellie Symonds, despising life at home with her selfish, gin-soaked mother and her weak rotter of a brother, Percy, is desperate to escape her surroundings by marrying Sam. William Hendry, Clerk to the Bursary, has a son at Cambridge, and is finding it difficult to meet mounting financial exactions. Like Ellie, Hendry also despises Percy Symonds, an assistant clerk in the Bursary, who received the position solely on account of his late father, the respected St. Mark's Butler.

The second part of the novel takes readers forward to the next term at St. Marks, where events have not stood still, though Slatters still is refusing to budge. Sam has indeed been sent down and married Ellie, and the couple is running an inn, the Golden Child, which caters to a large college clientele. Furious at attempted encroachments on "his" Bursary, Slatters finally has an unprecedented fit of temper and an accompanying stroke, forcing him finally to step down from his office. After Slatters' exit, financial irregularity in the college is discovered, and the reader learns that both Hendry and Percy Symonds are implicated in it. Hendry advises Symonds to hide out for the time being at his sister's and brother-in-law's inn.

Converging on the Golden Child are other actors in the coming murder drama, including Everard Blatchington, the amiable

---

[44] Cole, *G. D. H. Cole*, 260.

aristocratic dabbler in murder investigations in the previous Cole novels *The Blatchington Tangle*, *Burglars in Bucks*, *Death of a Star*, *Death in the Quarry* and *Scandal at School* (*Disgrace to the College*, certainly his triumph as a detective, is his last appearance). Everard happens to be stopping at the Golden Child in sight of Sam Barrett when the two men hear a loud bang. Inspection reveals that Percy Symonds, who had been given a room at the inn, is dead from a gunshot wound to the head, apparently self-inflicted. Everard soon suspects murder. After a short but ably conducted investigation, he demonstrates to the police that his suspicion is correct. Everard, who, to be honest, had never before revealed himself to the Coles readership as quite so keen a fellow, is justly proud of himself. "I hope, though, that Inspector Fry, when he puts in his report to his superiors, will include a good mark for me," he declares. "What I need from the police of this country . . . is a little encouragement."[45]

After *Disgrace to the College*, Cole produced only five more detective novels: *The Missing Aunt* (1937), a tedious tale unmemorably reuniting in novel form Wilson and his friend Michael Prendergast; *Off With Her Head* (1938), a disappointingly dull work despite its college setting and the reappearance of *The Brothers Sackville*'s Tom Fairford (who falls in love with a charming woman he encounters during the murder investigation, in the fashion of all young, well-bred police detectives at this time); *Double Blackmail* (1939), an amusing tale of a craven Anglican clergyman, his overbearing wealthy philanthropist mother and the soon-to-be-murdered rogue attempting simultaneously to blackmail them both; *Murder at the Munition Works* (1940), of more interest as a study of labor-capital relations than as a detective novel; and *Toper's End* (1942), a successful return to the country house farce of *The Blatchington Tangle*.

For its political content rather than for any inherent worth as a mystery novel *Murder at the Munition Works* is the most

---

[45] G. D. H. and Margaret Cole, *Disgrace to the College* (London: Hodder and Stoughton, 1937), 90, 127.

interesting of Cole's last known works of crime fiction. The tale deals with the bombing murder of Agnes Sullivan, wife of the hated manager of Anchor Works, an important wartime chemical factory located in Bullbridge, a once sedate college town, now having growing pains due to a wartime influx of factory workers. In this, Cole's penultimate detective novel, the author returned to the form of Freeman Wills Crofts, with a puzzle involving a map and a timetable in the classic manner (unfortunately, in uncommonly unsportsmanlike fashion the author drops the elusive, indeed unguessable, motive into the laps of Superintendent Wilson and the reader in the last few pages of a long novel). *Munition Works* also lacks entirely the Coles' trademark humor, focusing tightly on Wilson's investigation, so that it more resembles a police procedural than most other Cole novels. Although the setting and situation is interesting and unusual, there is very little dramatic impetus to the tale, for the characters all are one-dimensional cardboard cut-outs (also following Crofts), with their goodness or badness depending simply on their relative position on the political spectrum, with Left (Labour) equaling good and Right (Tory) equaling bad. Such a schematic may redress problems of ideological balance in other Golden Age works, but it does not make for a compelling detective novel.

With *Munition Works*, Cole turns the conventional detective novel upside down, making socially conscious workers (i.e., Labour men) admirable and Tory-sympathizing, conservative managers contemptible. This standard applies as well to policemen, with the admirable Wilson and his appealing new assistant, Sergeant Gulliver ("a Yorkshire lad who had worked his way up from an elementary to a state secondary school and thence to the university with a county scholarship"), clearly sympathizing at each turn with socialists; and, conversely, the blockheaded Chief Constable Murnin stupidly endorsing the conservative status quo at every opportunity. Murnin is determined to blame the shop steward William Pearson for Agnes Sullivan's death, as the steward had a notoriously bad relationship with Timothy Sullivan, manager of the Works, and Murnin assumes that Mrs. Sullivan was the mistaken victim of a murder plot actually devised against her husband. Murnin's summary to Wilson of the case against Pearson consists not of true "evidence" but is rather simply a catalog of Sullivan's political biases and workplace grievances against Pearson:

> "You seem to be taking Mr. Sullivan's word for a good deal."
>
> "Well, he's the manager. He ought to know his men."
>
> Wilson sighed gently. He was not forming a high opinion of Chief Constable Murnin's mental endowments. He said, "Tell me again what you have against this man Pearson."
>
> "Quite a lot. As I told you, he's the ringleader among these Reds. He got up a strike at the works just recently by refusing to obey orders and getting himself dismissed. And then the directors had to reinstate him because all the skilled men struck work and there were no other skilled men to be had for love or money, and the others refused to go back without him. Pearson's always tub-thumping at street corners about the wickedness of employers and the capitalist system. You know the sort of rot these fellows talk. . . . He's . . . "
>
> "I was asking you what evidence you had to connect him with the murder," Wilson put in.
>
> The Chief Constable did not appear to notice the sarcasm in his voice.[46]

Murnin is certain Pearson is guilty, but he wants Scotland Yard to do the arresting because of the strong Labour presence on the

---

[46] G. D. H. and Margaret Cole, *The Murder at the Munition Works* (New York: Macmillan, 1940), 17. With his *idée fixe* about Socialists Chief Constable Murnin rather resembles Chief Commissioner Rose (Corin Redgrave) in "A War of Nerves," a 2004 episode of the acclaimed British detective series *Foyle's War*, set during World War 2.

Town Council. "Things aren't what they used to be," Murnin sighs, "when the Council was non-political and they were all sound Conservatives." When the Superintendent first visits his friend Tom Bracket, a fellow in one of the Bullbridge Colleges who has patriotically left his job to enter wartime government service, he learns that Bracket serves on the Council and in his capacity as a councilman has consistently opposed the interests of the "old gang" (which includes Sullivan and Murnin). "Of, course, Tom was supposed to be non-party, because he represented the University," Bracket's wife concedes. "But he always worked with the Labour men, after they first got elected a couple of years ago." Bracket quickly gives Wilson the "politically correct" lay of the land in the world of *Murder at the Munition Works*:

> "Chief Constable Murnin's view seems to be that, being a rank Communist, [Pearson's] certain to have murdered somebody."
>
> "Communist be blowed! Willie's no more a Communist than I am. We're both solid, moderate Labour men. Transport House loves us."
>
> "I'm not sure Murnin would know the difference."
>
> "Murnin's a stupid old goop. He's a fat, easy-going, incompetent old codger that ought to be pensioned off."
>
> "I confess he did not impress me greatly," said Wilson. "He *would* quote Mr. Sullivan at me till I'm afraid I almost lost my temper with him. Mr. Sullivan's views are apparently not very advanced."
>
> "Sullivan's a pest," said Tom Bracket. "He's the worst works manager on God's earth. And he's chairman of the Ratepayer's Association and at the bottom of every bit of iniquity in Bullbridge, besides being a dirty little rip in his off-duty moments."[47]

---

[47] Coles, *Munition*, 21, 27, 30.

As the above bill of iniquities indicates, despite his all round unattractive nature the loathsome Sullivan even has a reputation for "sexual aberrations," as Cole himself puts it, by which term the author means that the works manager is a profligate adulterer ("Lord bless you, dozens of them," the Sullivans' cook rather surprisingly responds when Wilson asks her whether Sullivan has had affairs with "young ladies"). This aspect of the novel is unconvincingly done, as is sexual material in all G. D. H. Cole's novels, the surprisingly fresh and farcical *Affair at Aliquid* excepted. Perhaps one reason Cole's novels are undersexed is that Cole himself became increasingly so over the course of the 1930s, according to his wife. After he was diagnosed as a diabetic in 1931, Margaret Cole wrote, her husband's "asexuality was greatly increased . . . he was warned by the specialist that he must expect far less enjoyment of sex, to which according to his own account he replied, 'Thank goodness'." Admitting that Cole's "sex-life diminished gradually to zero for the last twenty years of his life [1939-1959]," Margaret Cole added that concurrently "he developed by degrees a positive dislike of, and disgust with, any aspect of sex almost equal to that of the early Christian fathers. . . . He came to feel that it was all revolting. . . . 'Womaniser,' I was once told by one of his secretaries, 'was his last word in condemnation of any man'."[48]

That in *Murder at the Munition Works* Mr. Sullivan, ruthless capitalist exploiter and profligate womanizer that he is, does not in fact turn out to be the murderer of his wife might be a surprise to some readers, but Cole manages to pin the guilt on another managerial-level capitalist, who proves nearly equally unattractive and conservative. Though not the murderer, Sullivan nevertheless deservedly loses his employment at Anchor, and the saintly Pearson is resoundingly exonerated. John Parrish, "the energetic young managing director" of the company with which Anchor has merged, reveals to workers that a new day is dawning: "I agree with Mr. Pearson the time will come, maybe quite soon, when

---

[48] Ibid., 35, 174; Cole, *G. D. H. Cole*, 93-94.

places like this factory will belong to the community and we shall all draw our wages and salaries as servants of the public. You see, I happen to be a Socialist, too." Loud cheers greet this "unexpected announcement of [Parrish's] political faith." Sullivan, finally reduced to becoming a traveling salesman, is last seen trying to convince Mrs. Wilson to purchase from him "a new patent vacuum cleaner."[49] When he sees Superintendent Wilson, the humbled man proceeds to beg a fiver from his former nemesis.

Over the course of the novel, Wilson evinces progressive tendencies in other ways beyond displaying overt admiration for socialists and disdain for conservatives. At one point he expresses doubt over the morality of the death penalty. Later, he lectures his friend Tom Bracket about police ethics:

> "You felt justified in telling the girl that, did you, knowing it to be untrue?"
>
> Bracket seemed to be surprised. He said, "Yes, why on earth not? I thought you detectives always told as many lies as you found convenient. I was simply taking a leaf out of your book."

Implicitly setting himself apart from his supposed twin, Freeman Wills Crofts' Inspector French, Wilson (though he himself had occasionally in the past used a bent wire or skeleton key in the French manner himself) sternly admonishes Bracket: "If one of my men told an innocent member of the public a lie like that . . . he'd get into no end of hot water."[50]

As mentioned above, Douglas Cole gives Wilson a new assistant, Detective-Sergeant George Gulliver. Like other newly-introduced police officers from the period, such as John Rhode's Jimmy Waghorn and Freeman Wills Crofts' Sergeant Rollo, the younger man is a graduate of Hendon's Police College, but he is not, Cole assures us, "one of the new band of gentleman detectives" ("at any

---

[49] Coles, *Munition*, 1, 270, 325.
[50] Ibid., 258.

rate in his own eyes"). Rather, Gulliver is "a Yorkshire lad who had worked his way up from an elementary to a state secondary school and thence to the university with a county scholarship." Sergeant Gulliver even retains "his Yorkish accent" and "a certain habit of calling a spade a spade which was not displeasing to Wilson though it had led to trouble with some of his other superiors at the Yard."[51] With the advent of Sergeant Gulliver, Cole set up an interesting work colleague of and ultimate successor to Superintendent Wilson for a post-Tory age, but unfortunately Cole was to produce only one more detective novel before setting down his pen, and this last novel did not include Gulliver.

*Murder at the Munition Works* is a distinctive Golden Age detective novel, not because of the excellence of its plot or its writing, but because of its political ideology. Cole clearly had glimpsed the dramatic social change that was to be wrought by the Second World War, and, unlike many of his Golden Age counterparts, he did not dread, but rather enthusiastically embraced, what he saw coming. As John Parrish tells the stubborn, selfish, backwards-looking Timothy Sullivan, "we're all working for the state nowadays. . . . We've all got to pull together and do our best for the country."[52]

Postwar Douglas Cole mysteries might have differed markedly from those of most of his contemporaries, but Cole published his last detective novel, *Toper's End*, during the middle of the war, in 1942. Unlike *Murder at the Munition Works*, *Toper's End* is a humorous work, a country house murder farce, its tone admittedly rather discordant with its wartime setting. Cole may have conceived *Toper's End* as his own fictional finale, for the novel seems the nostalgic work of a man bidding his readers a whimsical adieu.

*Toper's End* records death and near death at Excalibur House, the Brigshire country home of Dr. Sambourne, an eccentric scientist given to mysterious experiments in chemistry and endless disquisitions on the manifold perfidies of the international banking

---
[51] Ibid., 36.
[52] Ibid., 2.

system. When the novel opens Dr. Sambourne's household consists of an acerbic research assistant, David Oman; a put-upon but plucky secretary, Mary Philip; a slovenly servant couple, Mr. and Mrs. Mudge; and a so-called "menagerie" of distinguished European war refugees (mostly named by Cole after great European music composers): a German couple, the classical economist Johann Meyerbeer and his hausfrau wife, Bertha; an Austrian psychiatrist, Eva Gluck; the mysterious Amadeus Franck, also said to be Austrian; an Italian engineer, Arturo Rossini; a Dutch fine arts professor named de Wauters; and a Jewish Biblical scholar, Kurt Aronson.

Descending on Excalibur House at the time of the murder as well are Dr. Sambourne's unwelcome relatives. These are his exasperating sister, Queenie Moggridge, and her two unpleasant children, the enervated Patricia and the intolerable young Gurth; and his brother-in-law and business partner, George Potts, who is trying to persuade him to agree to allow their company to borrow money necessary for wartime expansion. At dinner with all these guests, an apparently inebriated Rowland Moggridge, the husband of Queenie, shows up too, and has to be put to bed. Next day he is found dead, with two different fatal substances in his system. The local police, headed by the Chief Constable, Wilson's old friend Colonel Hubert Welsh (who appeared with Wilson previously in *Corpse in Canonicals* and *End of an Ancient Mariner*), flounders until Wilson coincidentally happens on the scene, accompanied by his friend Michael Prendergast (of *The Man from the River* and *The Missing Aunt*). With Colonel Welsh's flirtatious wife, Emily, appearing as well, *Toper's End* clearly functioned as a fictional old home week for longtime Coles fans (Inspector Tom Fairford of *The Brothers Sackville* and *Off with Her Head* also is mentioned in passing, as is one of Wilson's old nemeses, General Bunker, from *The Death of a Millionaire*). Additionally, the novel has a good plot and some excellent quasi-farcical humor, so it offered the Coles' readers something more than a nostalgia trip.

# THE SPECTRUM OF ENGLISH MURDER

## Part Three: The Detective Novels of Margaret Cole

In its day, Margaret Cole's detective fiction was as well-regarded as her husband's, with such authorities as Howard Haycraft and Charles Williams praising various works by her (since the couple put both their names on the novels and short story collections, however, the individual authorship of any given work was not then known). In my view the best of Margaret Cole's detective novels are *Burglars in Bucks* (1930), *Death of a Star* (1932), *Scandal at School* (1935), and *Counterpoint Murder* (1940). In several Margaret Cole novels, solutions frustratingly either are handed on a plate to the detective (as in Douglas Cole's own *Murder at the Munition Works*) or are reached through some seemingly miraculous form of inspiration on the part of the sleuth. For example, Margaret Cole's last detective novel, *Knife in the Dark*, boasts a strong character study in a malicious, sexually restive university wife reminiscent of characters in a Ruth Rendell novel, yet the puzzle disappointingly falls flat, with the tale's nominal detective, the Miss Marple-like Mrs. Warrender, arriving at the solution near the very end of the novel through no readily explicable process of ratiocination. To cite another example, in *Greek Tragedy* the author skewers snobbery and anti-Semitism in a striking way, yet the explanation of the mystery is perfunctorily dealt with and the character interest that had been kindled is allowed to damply fizzle. Similarly, in *Scandal at School* the murderer's motive is generously dropped in the detective's lap, though in this case both writing and plotting hold up well enough for the tale to be viewed justly as a success. The greatest exception to this general rule for Margaret Cole's fictional work is her penultimate novel, *Counterpoint Murder*, where the focus is on plot rather than character and the plot is brilliantly carried out by the author. Indeed, *Counterpoint Murder* is, along with Douglas Cole's *Disgrace to the College*, the most impressive example of *detection* in a Coles detective novel. Additionally, *Death of a Star* is an exceptionally accomplished Golden Age proto-police procedural crime novel and *Burglars in Bucks* is one of the finest essays in that challenging form, the epistolary mystery novel, and an effervescent country house crime tale.

These exceptions aside, Margaret Cole's detective novels often are of greatest interest today for their tartly witty social and political commentary, which puts them frequently at odds, like the mysteries authored primarily by her husband, with the modern conventional belief in the genre's all-pervasive, High Tory conservatism during the British Golden Age of detective fiction. From her first novel, *The Murder at Crome House* (1927), Margaret Cole's mystery fiction is filled with unorthodox (by Golden Age standards) political sentiments. In *Crome House*, for example, the protagonist's landlady after denouncing her charwoman's supposed negligence in cleaning a fireplace hearth is chided by the author for expressing anti-labor sentiment presumably typical of her petit-bourgeois class:

> "It was Mrs. Lawson's duty to have mentioned it to me, as I should have thought any one would have known; but with their husbands drawing the dole it's all the same, they don't care whose house they burn down!"
>
> The connection between unemployment benefits and incendiarism was never made quite clear, for at that minute an irritated basement bell announced the milkman or butcher.[53]

In addition to defending that middle and upper class *bete noire,* the dole, Margaret Cole in *Crome House* also takes time to denounce stock market speculation ("he put up a long tale about being an absolute bloody fool and thinking he could get rich quick by some sort of Stock Exchange hanky panky . . . he had a sister who'd been left frightfully badly off through some swindle or other"), celebrate Union membership ("I've joined a Union. I'm a member of the General Labourers. . . . And it's my duty as a Unionist

---

[53] Coles, *Crome*, 8.

# THE SPECTRUM OF ENGLISH MURDER 165

to attend branch meetings regularly") and take a potshot at that citadel of capitalism, the United States of America ("afterwards I didn't feel altogether so keen about making the world safe for J. P. Morgan as some of his countrymen seemed to be").[54] None of these sentiments directly impinge on the main plot, but they certainly provide some left-of-center shading atypical of Golden Age detective novels.

Margaret Cole's next mystery tale, *Poison in the Garden Suburb* (1929), makes the author's leftist politics somewhat more central to the plot. The novel reintroduces that amiable idling young gentleman, Tony Redfern, who first appeared in the story "The International Socialist." In *Garden Suburb*, we find he has a peppery dowager of a great aunt, Lydia Redfern, as well as a sister, Rachel Redfern, who constitutes half the novel's love interest. The other half of the love interest is Rachel's neurotic, limp dishrag of a boyfriend, Martin Delahaye, who, like Rachel, is a Socialist who works for the Bureau for Left-Wing Information, an organization Cole likely based on Beatrice and Sidney Webb's Labour Research Department, with which she and her husband had been significantly involved. When a poisoning murder occurs during a lecture at the Medstead Garden Suburb Literary Institute (the speaker's topic is "Modern Aspects of Eugenics"), Martin becomes the chief suspect; and the plucky Rachel, who loves the tiresome young man for some obscure reason, eventually calls in Henry Wilson, at this time still a private detective, to extricate her errant young lover from the difficulties in which his own stupid actions have placed him.

Socialism is never fully integrated into the plot, but Margaret Cole does introduce a number of interesting asides that are reflective of her progressive social and economic views, on such subjects as lesbianism, abortion, library censorship and that perennial favorite of the socialist couple, financial swindles. Merely the fact that the love interest in the novel belongs to a pair of young socialists is a striking anomaly in Golden Age British detective fiction. One may suspect that Martin and Rachel to some extent

---

[54] Ibid., 122, 156, 174-175.

represent Douglas and Margaret, the latter of whom by her own account had to take the romantic initiative with her somewhat undersexed husband. Certainly the author evinces sympathy for the pair, as in this passage, where Great Aunt Lydia, no economic leftist herself but essentially fair-minded, reflects on the couple:

> [Martin] had been engaged to Rachel now for six months, solely against the will of the latter's father, who regarded him quite simply as another of those damned Bolsheviks who were after his (Mr. Redfern's) money. Miss Lydia had backed young Delahaye, both because he was Rachel's choice and because she regarded her nephew as incurably stupid; but she had never really cared for him, thinking him in her secret heart an unreliable, opinionated cub. There was no denying his brains; he had done excellently at Cambridge, and could probably have made himself a brilliant career in some intellectual calling; but while at Cambridge he had become a Socialist, and as soon as he had gone down had immediately associated himself with this Bureau of Left-Wing Information. . . . But, when all was said, she was forced to admit that none of the faults she saw in him particularly pointed to his being a murderer. . . .[55]

Needless to add, perhaps, young socialist love triumphs (with much help from Wilson); though only after the steadfast Rachel has undergone a considerable ordeal.

Leftist social commentary is mostly absent from *Burglars in Bucks*, the cleverly-titled and delightful soufflé of a country house mystery that Margaret Cole served up in 1930, though in the novel Everard Blatchington does take time, in cataloguing the guests at Headingham Manor, to pen an acid description of the novel's

---

[55] G. D. H. and M. Cole, *Poison in the Garden Suburb* (London: Collins, 1929), 104-105. The relationship between Rachel and Martin obviously has parallels with that of Douglas and Margaret.

grasping finance capitalist (a former war profiteer, naturally) and his wife, in a tone dripping with aristocratic disdain for bourgeois *nouveau riche*:

> But, all the same, some of Peter's collection does fill me with horror. There's a really terrible object called Sir Hiram Watkins, which has a pasty face, a fat belly, a mouth like an advertisement of American Business Efficiency, and the eye of a lecherous old fish. It looks exactly like the caricaturists' idea of a war profiteer, and apparently it is. . . . Its wife . . . is an Enormous cubical object called Doris, coloured like a prawn all over—at least, that's the color that emerges where the powder's rubbed off on the back thereof, so I'm presuming it's all of a piece. As to attire, it looks as though the good Baronet had laid out all his war gains in jewellery and was using his wife as a temporary showroom—and certainly a roomy one. She plays bridge, my God; you can't see the cards for the dazzle. They are a perfectly frightful pair, both of them. . . .[56]

*Burglars in Bucks* is perhaps the best of the tales known to have been written primarily by Margaret Cole. Published in 1930, *Burglars in Bucks* actually preceded by a year Dorothy L. Sayers' own (and much better remembered) experimental epistolary crime novel, *The Documents in the Case*. The tale also shares some of Sayers' interest in Victorian-era literature, recalling Anthony Trollope's *The Eustace Diamonds* in having a plot that hinges on a dispute over the ownership of an aristocratic family's famed necklace. Contemporary crime fiction critic Charles Williams adored *Burglars in Bucks*, dubbing the novel a "glory."[57]

---

[56] G. D. H. and M. Cole, *Burglars in Bucks* (London: Collins, 1930), 25-26.
[57] "Crime: The Real Thing and The Romantic" (June 4, 1930), in Jared C. Lobdell, *The Detective Fiction Reviews of Charles Williams, 1930-1935* (Jefferson, NC, and London: McFarland, 2003), 29. Bucks is an abbreviation of the English county Buckinghamshire.

As indicated above, *Burglars in Bucks* brings back for an encore appearance Everard Blatchington of Douglas Cole's *The Blatchington Tangle* and reunites him with Superintendent Wilson. Everard is a guest at a country house party at Headingham Manor when a jewel theft takes place (instead of the Blatchington Rubies of *The Blatchington Tangle*, this time it is the Pallant Emeralds). Much of the novel is told through Everard's letters to his wife, who is at home at Blatchington Towers, pregnant with the couple's first child, already ambitiously named Christopher Columbus Blatchington. Everard, who hoodwinked Wilson during that convoluted tangle at Blatchington Towers, believes that the Superintendent is suspicious at finding him again on the scene of a country house jewel theft. For his part, Wilson complains in his case notes that the heir of Blatchington "seems to take these things lightly."[58] Like Everard Blatchington, the author of *Burglars in Bucks* also takes things lightly, even going so far as to violate a prime artistic canon of the genre by not even condescending to adorn the tale with a nice murder to go along with the burglary (robbery without violence, as it were). Yet she writes wittily and breezily and keeps the complicated plot strands sufficiently clear, making *Burglars in Bucks* one of the finest essays in Golden Age country house mystery, comparable to Douglas Cole's own *Blatchington Tangle* and Agatha Christie's *The Secret of Chimneys*.

Margaret Cole's next novel, *Dead Man's Watch* (1931), sees the reappearance of certain character types already familiar in her work, and they are again used to allow the author a certain amount of left-leaning social commentary. Again we see an ineffectual but charming leisured amateur detective figure, the dipsomaniac Sir Charles Wylie (clearly standing in for Everard Blatchington), as well as a tiresomely neurasthenic young man accused of murder, Ronald Bittaford, and his relentlessly stalwart girlfriend, a winsome Cockney girl alliteratively named Dolly Daniells. Making note of the romantic pair in *A Catalogue of Crime*, Jacques Barzun and Wendell Hertig Taylor discerningly comment that "the Coles' touch of social commentary takes the form of making the blunt Cockney

---

[58] Coles, *Bucks*, 130.

girl intelligent and generous and the middle-class Bittaford boy whom she loves a pathological weakling." Certainly it seems in *Dead Man's Watch* that Margaret Cole is intent on contrasting Ronald, a drooping white collar drone, with Dolly, a mentally and physically healthy working class girl. On first seeing Ronald, Sir Charles reflects: "'City clerk' was written all over him—in the cut of his clothes and hair, in his cheap, bright blazer and in the whiteness of the skin that showed beneath his shirt. He was a lanky, anaemic-looking youth . . . with a thin face, a long pointed nose, slender shoulders, and the drooping lip of a child or a dog that has not been too kindly treated." To Sir Charles young Ronald seems rather a poor fish, but the plucky Dolly impresses him much more favorably; and soon she is helping Sir Charles investigate the murder in which Ronald is implicated. Later in the novel, when the now reinstated Superintendent Wilson encounters Dolly, we find that Wilson too likes her "at first sight," having "always had an admiration for the Cockney spirit."[59]

Besides his being employed as a city clerk, the other black mark in Ronald's life is his miserable religious upbringing in an exceedingly odd petit bourgeois sect known as the "Pentecostal Hoppers." The Hoppers, as letters from Dolly Daniells to Sir Charles soon make clear, are nothing more than a pack of ignoramuses and/or charlatans. Particularly objectionable, Dolly learns, are a grotesque husband and wife named Mr. and Mrs. Cole. He is "a blanky old fraud, never does a stroke of work but makes the chapel keep him," Dolly informs Sir Charles, while she is "a nigger-driver and an old miser."[60] No doubt Margaret Cole found these particular characters especially amusing. I found much of the humor in *Dead Man's Watch* deplorably heavy-handed, however.

Yet another victim of the capitalist system is suspected of murder in Margaret Cole's detective novel from the following year, *Death of a Star* (1932), one of the most impressive essays in socially realistic, police procedural detective fiction from the Golden

---

[59] Barzun and Taylor, *Catalogue of Crime*, 135; G. D. H. and Margaret Cole, *Dead Man's Watch* (New York: Doubleday, Doran, 1931), 9, 235.
[60] Coles, *Watch*, 122.

Age. In the novel, police look dubiously upon Ted Dougal after the taximan reports to young Constable Wedderburn that he has been driving around London in his cab with a large, sinister-seeming fishbag left in the back seat by a passenger; in the fishbag is the decapitated head of an actress, Rita Morning.

We find that Dougal leads a precarious existence as a taximan, barely managing to keep his wife and two children. A Great War veteran, Dougal complains to Edward Sayle, an artist friend of Everard Blatchington who takes a paternalistic interest in his case, that "they don't want us now, specially not rankers. Got too big for our boots, we did—better to be put in our places, and told not to bother a grateful country." Worried that Dougal might be railroaded by the police despite the presence of a number of other, more socially connected, suspects, Sayle seeks advice from his friend Everard Blatchington, who after his exploits in *The Blatchington Tangle* and *Burglars in Bucks* has developed something of a reputation in society for expertise in criminal matters. Everard's reflections indicate no great faith on his part in the justice system of capitalist Britain:

> "But there's no denying that the police are apt to be a bit rougher with the lower classes than they are with us, and if your friend's a neurotic subject . . . he may be in for a bit of an uncomfortable time."
>
> "It's a pretty rotten state of things," said Sayle slowly, "if a man can be afraid that he's going to get into trouble for something he had nothing to do with."
>
> "It is. But many things in our social system are pretty rotten, including the press, and some of my uncle's companies, and a whole lot more," Everard said.[61]

---

[61] G. D. H. and Margaret Cole, *Death of a Star* (New York: Doubleday, Doran, 1932), 22, 34, 77.

Sayle investigates and finds out more sad detail about the Dougals, later giving Everard a true bill of indictment of the state of things in Britain after the Great War:

> "They've really had a pretty thin time. He was a ranker officer, as you know, and wasn't demobbed until nearly a year after the Armistice, when pretty nearly all the available jobs had been snaffled. He got a job for a time selling cars, married—she was a typist in the office—in '21, lost his job in '22, when the slump came and their first baby was on the way, got another, lost that, and so on, going a bit further down the scale. Then he had pneumonia and was threatened with T. B. and they used up all their savings. He was pretty nearly all in; then he enlisted as a volunteer driver during the general strike, and the firm he worked for kept him on when that was over. There he stayed till about two years ago, when he got the sack over a row and started as an owner driver, buying his cab by installments. Lately, however, he's been unlucky with his work, getting fewer and fewer fares, and so they've run into debt and are in arrears with the cab money, and altogether it isn't too bright."

This long catalogue of then recent British social ills, with its mentions of the slump and the general strike, is uncharacteristic of Golden Age detective fiction, which tended to glide over such unpleasant realities. Dougal's efforts to keep his head above the economic waters inexorably flooding over the capitalist edifice are failing him, and he is drowning, like a rat in a rain barrel. (Unfortunately for Dougal, Cole indicates, he does not see that the solution to these myriad social ills in Britain lies through collective action on the part of labor.) Not altogether surprising is it in such a novel that Dougal's wife has a "cheerful waking dream of [her children] Jack and Daisy without food, their house sold up, Ted dying of tuberculosis, and herself with nothing left but the gas oven."[62]

Cole's portrayal of police procedure in *Death of a Star* is more painstaking than the norm for the period, with the author employing a large cast of superintendents, inspectors, sergeants, constables and other law enforcement functionaries. Henry Wilson is mentioned only in passing, and, with the exception of the kind-hearted Constable Wedderburn, the policemen who do appear in the novel are an unprepossessing lot unlikely to win the reader's sympathy. Cole also deftly etches London high society and the criminal classes alike. While her depiction of several Jewish characters suffers from errors of taste (see my discussion of this matter below), overall the book is an exceptional work for the period, ahead of its time in its depiction of realistic social detail yet also offering readers a good problem in detection. Margaret Cole's immediately subsequent detective novel, *Death in the Quarry* (1934), is competently plotted and features both Everard Blatchington and Henry Wilson (who actually solves the case), but it is altogether less inspired than its predecessor.

Despite any carping one might have about Cole's portrayal of Jews in *Death of a Star*, after Adolf Hitler's ascendance to power in 1933-34, the author's mounting concern with the rise of Nazi Germany and anti-Semitism found expression in three of her four later detective novels, *Scandal at School* (1935), *Greek Tragedy* (1939) and *Knife in the Dark* (1941). Of these three novels by far the best is the first, *Scandal at School*, an amusingly and incisively written public school mystery with an interesting plot. *Scandal* concerns the suspicious death by sleeping draught overdose of an obnoxious fourteen-year-old student, Henrietta Zimmerman, at an absurdly progressive public school, Santley House. Ending up entangled in the case is Margaret Cole's preferred series character, the idle aristocrat Everard Blatchington, whose wife, Margaret, thinks Santley House might potentially be a good future

---

[62] Coles, *Star*, 94, 144.

educational choice for their three-year-old son, Christopher Columbus Blatchington (an "embryo" in *Burglars in Bucks*). Reading a boosting newspaper article on Santley House, Everard is, for his part, openly derisive:

> "Then he gets to the grounds of the school, and goes into ecstasies because he's met, if you please, by a female member of the staff—wearing trousers!"
> "Why shouldn't she be?"
> "Why not, indeed? But why wearing trousers should be accepted as a certificate of educational efficiency, I confess I can't quite see. Then he goes on, and he finds that as it's a jolly summer day, the children in their wisdom have decided not to work indoors, but to 'carry on outside activities.' I should have thought you could have cut lessons to make mud pies without founding a whole new school and calling it an 'educational experiment.' And then he says that all the dear little children make their own dear little rules. Oh, yes. And do all the dear little children obey their own rules? And are they the same rules? Or do they make one lot Monday and a new lot on Tuesday? All the dear little children I've ever known would change their rules once an hour to suit their own convenience!"

Later Everard learns to his dismay that the portly and pink headmaster, Milton Cromwell is a passionate nudist; and the naturally horrified gentleman sleuth spends much of the rest of the novel trying to avoid encountering the man.[63]

---

[63] G. D. H. and Margaret Cole, *Scandal at School* (London: Collins, 1935), 7-8. "[The headmaster's] name is Milton Cromwell," Margaret Blatchington tells Everard, "which sounds pretty ridiculous, but I suppose it's his parent's fault." Coles, *Scandal*, 8. We learn later that the headmaster's real name rather ingloriously is Milton Cromwell *Spink*.

*Scandal at School* might well be called *Satire at School*, for it is a highly satirical tale, with numerous shafts aimed at educators, intellectuals, *artistes*, psychiatrists and philanthropists. Notable is Margaret Cole's unsentimental attitude toward children. She clearly believes that the creatures will degenerate into savage little hellions if left entirely to their own devices and that it thus is necessary for adults to impose some sensible regulation into their young lives. Nor does Cole make the adolescent murder victim remotely sympathetic. Henrietta's own father, the psychiatrist Walter Zimmerman, condemns his daughter as an incipient monster and, indeed, ranks high on Everard's list of suspects for the odious girl's murder (if murder it is).

It is interesting to contrast *Scandal* with later detective novels in institutional settings by P. D. James, such as *Shroud for a Nightingale* (1971) and *Death of an Expert Witness* (1977), written during Margaret Cole's last decade of life. Whereas James invariably darkens her tone when exploring the human miseries and pathologies that lead to murder among professional English men and women in elite institutions, Margaret Cole maintains a lighter, satirical note in her tale, even though she is dealing with the death of a fourteen-year-old girl. Since Cole deals not only with the possibility that Henrietta was murdered by her father but also with the controversial issues of abortion and lesbianism (as late as the 1950s English magistrates on three different occasions ordered copies of *Scandal at School* destroyed on obscenity grounds), it is rather striking indeed that Cole manages to maintain this lighter note. Certainly the material was present to allow Cole to take the tale in a much darker direction, but she chose not to traverse this route.[64]

One character not treated satirically is the Austrian-born émigré sculptor, Felice Quentin, who happens also to be the wife of one of the school's teachers. The daughter of a Jewish Social

---

[64] On the judically-ordered destruction of copies of *Scandal at School* in England in the 1950s see A. D. Harvey, "Not Fit For Our Eyes," *Independent*, 31 July 1994.

Democrat, she found it prudent to flee her home country, pro-German fascism being increasingly rampant. Felice at one point discusses the case with Everard while doing a hideous sculpture of an unattractive Jewish businessman, a Mr. Tannerburn. Everard is surprised that Felice exults in the exquisite ugliness of her subject, a fellow Jew, and has created a bust of the man that resembles "one of the more revolting types of a West African fetish god." Learning of Everard's distaste for the object, Felice asks, "why should I mind? Oh, I see; because it is a caricature of a Jew. You think that a Jew might not caricature a Jew—now, while people are persecuting Jews." Felice explains her contrary view of the matter in this philosophical discursion:

> "He is a very ugly Jew. Must I say he is beautiful because he is being persecuted? Indeed, persecution does not make ugly people beautiful. Generally it makes them uglier, and not even funny. . . . But I think . . . that you mean Jews ought to say all Jews are good and beautiful, because Herr Hitler says that only Aryans are. . . . That is to make yourself the same as the Nazis, only of the other kind, and so we will all wallow together, like pigs, and all drill very badly in ugly clothes and say 'Heil Hitler! Heil Weissman! Heil, Mr. Baldwin!'. . . . I do not wish people to drill or to wallow. I know very many Jews who are ugly and unpleasant. . . . I do not think they should be persecuted because they are unpleasant, but I do not see that I should say that they are good and beautiful. I do not think, even if I could stop Mr. Tannerburn being persecuted by saying he was beautiful, I would do it. All I could say is, "See how you will destroy his charming ugliness."

Through the words of Felice, Margaret Cole condemns what she deems ethnic/national tribalism, whether in the form of Nazism ("Heil Hitler!"), Zionism ("Heil Weissman!") or British Conservatism

("Heil Baldwin!"), presumably seeing this as an obstacle to the formation of class consciousness and mobilization of socialist collective action. (Notably absent is the declaration "Heil Stalin!")[65]

Golden Age critics found in *Scandal at School* an especially appropriate milieu for the intellectual Coles and praised the tale as their finest work of detective fiction in years. "The setting suits the Coles better, I think, than that of any other of their books," opined Milward Kennedy in the *Sunday Times*. "The fact is that they are at their best when they handle characters and situations which are out of the ordinary." For his part, Ralph Partridge in the leftist *New Statesman and Nation* was even more impressed than Kennedy, declaring that the "modern crank school" of the Coles' new novel "provides their talents with the best of settings." Partridge thought it too difficult to deduce the murderer, yet he reflected that after all the Coles belonged "to the romantic school of detective writers, in which character is more important than the structure of the crime"; and with this former aspect of the tale, characterization, the Coles had succeeded admirably. "It is some years since I have enjoyed a book by Mr. and Mrs. Cole as much as I did *Scandal at School*," concluded Partridge.[66]

After an unprecedented gap of three years with no detective novel of her own appearing (during this time Douglas Cole produced five detective novels), Margaret Cole published *Greek Tragedy*, a byproduct of a trip to Greece taken by the Coles in 1937. This tale, which concerns murder on a Greco-Roman tour cruise aboard the *S. S. Gizeh*, raises some interesting issues but is much inferior to *Scandal at School*, being heavy-handed in its depiction of character (as in *Murder at the Munition Works*, people are graded as either angels or devils according to where they fall on the political spectrum) and having a mystery plot that ultimately proves utterly inconsequential. In *Greek Tragedy*, passengers on the *Gizeh* seem to break down into Communist and Socialist college students, proto-Fascist pseudo-

---

[65] Cole, *Scandal*, 196-197. Presumably "Weissman" refers to Chaim Azriel Weizmann, an influential Zionist leader in Britain who became the first President of Israel after World War Two. "Mr. Baldwin" is the conservative British politician Stanley Baldwin, who in 1935 resumed office as Prime Minister.

[66] *Sunday Times*, 1 December 1935, 9; *New Statesman and Nation*, 14 December 1935, 942.

# THE SPECTRUM OF ENGLISH MURDER

and semi-intellectuals, landed gentry and—odd people out—a half-Jewish Nottingham manufacturer and his daughter. Cole portrays the Communists, Socialists and part-Jews sympathetically and the proto-Fascists unsympathetically, while she casts an indulgent eye, as she had before in her novels, at her landed gentry. "Individually and collectively, the landed gentry were nice enough, not in any way obtrusive and kind to the lower orders," the author informs us.[67]

Because the Nottingham manufacturer, Emanuel Downes, is half-Jewish and has a discernible midlands accent, he becomes an object of scorn for the snobbish anti-Semites on board the *Gizeh*, much to the mortification of the novel's initial protagonist, Downes' daughter, Margery. Leaders of the arrogant, anti-Semitic clique are Henry Aveling, the *Gizeh*'s cruise-leader for the Greco-Roman Tours; a fellow cruise lecturer, the "slim and fastidious" art critic Guy Strickland; and Guy's wife, the "slim and athletic" Eva. "I do think, if people of that sort must come on cruises, they might at least keep their mouths shut," complains Eva Strickland of poor Emmanuel Downes. "Did you *hear* his accent?" Later on the cruise, Aveling decides to exclude Downes from a tour party. Even Guy Strickland protests, provoking the following exchange:

> "I can't bear the man, myself; he's an awful little nuisance. But—
> "Look here," said Aveling, "do you want to travel two days in a car and sleep in Napulia with a Jew?"
> "A Jew!"
> "Well, of course he's a Jew. Where are your eyes? A sneaking, grovelling, money-grubbing little Jew, aping at being cultured! I have to put up with his presence on the boat, but I'm damned if I put myself in a position where I have to smell him for thirty-six hours on end! He and his daughter—who I notice has very properly taken up with that greasy rat from the surgery [the Armenian ship's doctor]."[68]

---

[67] G. D. H. and Margaret Cole, *Greek Tragedy*, (New York: Macmillan, 1939), 21.
[68] Coles, *Greek*, 20, 38, 100.

The sheltered Margery, who overhears this conversation, finds herself poignantly reflecting, evidently for the first time, on racism in British society:

> She had never experienced, never imagined anything like this before. She had heard that there were people in England who hated Jews; but she had never met them. She had never thought of herself as having Jewish blood, or of the grandmother who had died when she was a child as having any connection with people of whom one read in Germany. . . . Were all those superior smug people like that underneath—hateful, insolent, obscene?[69]

The Communists and Socialists in the group are, in contrast with the Stricklands and Aveling, virtuous, admirable people. Indeed, the only "fault"—if it can be called such—of Roy Arkell, the student Communist in the group, is that he is so very much better than everyone else as to be overwhelmingly intimidating:

> "Do *you* like Mr. Arkell?" Margery said.
> "I think he's an absolutely first-rate chap," said David warmly. "Gosh! I wish I had half his brains, and he doesn't waste them either. He's done more fine political work of all kinds than any one of his age, I should think. . . . But. . . . I'd be a bit shy of being a close friend of his, because I don't think I'd be able to live up to it, and I'd be scared to death of his running into something that'd be all right for him, but too dashed noble for me to keep it up, see? . . . I'm an ordinary sort of bloke, but Roy's liable to be a hero any time—sort of chap that goes and gets killed in Spain."

---

[69] Ibid, 101.

And, indeed, Cole quickly confirms that the star-struck David spoke "more truly than he knew," because, before that very summer passed, the noble Roy was to join the fighting in Spain, where he would be felled by "a bullet on the Ebro."[70]

To some extent, however, Margaret Cole in *Greek Tragedy* tries to have it both ways, condemning the snobbery directed toward Emmanuel Downes by the Stricklands and Aveling yet going out of her way to make it clear to her readers that the snobs actually are not that well-educated after all and that Downes indeed does not come out of the top drawer—or even the middle one—and can at times be a bit exasperating, really:

> [Downes] . . . had made a considerable amount of money, which had enabled him to gratify a deep-seated and hitherto suppressed desire for culture. This was laudable, and nobody could have objected to it; in fact, one of the avowed purposes of Greco-Roman Tours was to help such as Mr. Downes. But, unfortunately, he had already helped himself . . . he had been studying antiquities on his own account; he had amassed a great deal of miscellaneous information, and what was worse, he had collected a number of theories and evolved more out of his own consciousness. And he was very anxious to talk about them. . . .[71]

For her part, Eva Strickland is scorned by the author for having a voice that is "the product of Wycombe Abbey [a prestigious, conservative English boarding school for girls] and a year abroad," while Aveling is revealed as an undereducated specimen from the lower classes who harbors unseemly jealously of his Oxford and Cambridge betters:

---

[70] Ibid., 67, 76-77. Oddly, Margaret Cole's paragon Roy Arkell shares a surname with William and Martha Arkell, the scoundrel servant couple appearing three years previously in Douglas Cole's *The Brothers Sackville* (see below).
[71] Ibid., 22-23.

> A poor boy whose country school education had not been combined with sufficient application on his own part to get him into anything but a provincial college, Aveling regarded himself as unfairly defrauded by fate of the high academic honours which he believed could easily have been his, and credited all who came from Oxford and Cambridge with a deliberate intention to bar him from contaminating their walls.[72]

All the truly best people, Cole might as well be saying to her Golden Age readership, are in fact leftists.

Paragon characters obviously admired by a mystery author do not, as some contemporary reviewers complained of the Coles' novels, make the best suspects; so it should not be surprising that the murder mystery in *Greek Tragedy*, when it comes, is a disappointing one, with the crime offhandedly fobbed off by the author on a nearly non-existent, inconsequential character. Worse yet, Cole allows her protagonist Margery—by far the most engaging character in the tale—to drift from the center of the story, so that what non-criminous reader interest that remained in the tale recedes into the distance as well. As a crime novel, *Greek Tragedy* can only be seen as a failure, though a rather interesting one, because of sociopolitical content unusual in the genre at this time.

In what is presumably Margaret Cole's next detective novel, *Counterpoint Murder* (1940), Cole eschewed the more colorful character sketches and social commentary of *Scandal at School* and *Greek Tragedy* and concentrated firmly on plotting. Since the plot of *Counterpoint Murder* is something of a corker, this was all to the good for the Coles' readership. Critics again praised the new Coles tale as the best Coles novel in years (likely since *Scandal at School* itself or *The Brothers Sackville*). "The plot of 'Counterplot Murder' has all the appearance of novelty," noted the reviewer for the *Times Literary Supplement*. "The Coles have found a puzzle

---

[72] Ibid., 38, 122. Margaret Cole herself was educated at Rodean School and Girton College, Cambridge, and taught briefly at St. Paul's Girls' School.

worthy of the powers they claim for Superintendent Wilson." The central plot device of *Counterpoint Murder* is a clever one, the original use of which dates back, as far as I know, to Margaret Cole's use of it in this novel. The declaration of the Collins Crime Club that "this is one of the most ingenious plots the Coles have yet produced" is no exaggeration.[73]

Saying much about the clever plot might spoil it for future readers, but I will note that, as the title suggests, the narrative largely concerns two murders and the elusive connection between them. Only after a third murder is committed does Wilson directly involve himself in the investigations of his underlings (the not-encouragingly-named Inspectors Doolittle and Mugge), which he thereupon resolves after some excellent detection. Atmosphere and characterization are thinnish, though Cole succeeds in capturing that unreal period of the "phony war" before the invasion of France (with air raid wardens and blackouts and refugee children from London all being seen as rather silly nuisances), as well as in more successfully portraying police procedure. Stray bits of Coles humor too can be found in *Counterpoint Murder*, as, for example, in the recurring playful naming of characters (such as Doolittle and Mugge), in collegial references to other writers of detective fiction (Chesterton, Crofts, Christie and Sayers) and in this little exchange between Inspector Doolittle and the porter of the gentleman's club where one of the novel's murders takes place:

> "I've some questions to ask you, my man." He sat down at the table and pulled out his note-book. "Name?"
> "Pelley—E. Y."
> "Christian name."
> "Ignatius Dominic Aloysius Francis Joseph Mary."
> "Eh?" said the inspector, caught quite unprepared.

---

[73] *Times Literary Supplement*, 7 December 1940, 619. For the Collins Crime Club statement, see the front matter of *Counterpoint Murder*.

"I'm sorry, sir. Ignatious Dominic Aloysius Francis Joseph Mary."

"Yes, yes, all right . . . of course. Catholic?"[74]

Though he was to appear in one more novel, Douglas Cole's *Toper's End*, and the short story "Birthday Gifts," Wilson found his most fitting swan song in Margaret Cole's *Counterpoint Murder*, seventeen years after her husband had created him.

Margaret Cole's last detective novel, *Knife in the Dark* (1941) is similar to *Greek Tragedy* in that it yokes an intermittently interesting exploration of then-current social and political issues to a perfunctorily-solved mystery. The novel's central inspiration clearly must have been the *Arandora Star* tragedy of 1940. In July of that year, the vessel *Arandora Star* left Liverpool with nearly 1300 Germans and Italians on board (mostly political refugees and pre-war resident aliens of Britain), bound for internment camps in Canada. Seventy-five miles off the western coast of Ireland, the ship was torpedoed by a German submarine. It quickly sank and half the passengers and crew expired. Public uproar over the incident helped lead to a reform of Britain's harsh internee deportation policy, so that in the future enemy aliens were interned only in domestic camps.[75]

In *Knife in the Dark*, Margaret Cole dramatizes the plight of enemy aliens in wartime Britain under Winston Churchill's punitive "Collar the lot!" policy through the character of Marta Zyboski, a refugee Jew whose son was interned in a camp on the strength of accusations made in an anonymous letter. When Kitty Lake, the wife of Stamford University's Reader in Inorganic Chemistry, Gordon Lake, is murdered and it is discovered that she was the author

---

[74] G. D. H. and M. Cole, *Counterpoint Murder* (London: Collins, 1940), 41.

[75] See J. M. Ritchie, "German Refugees from Nazism," in Panikos Panayi, ed., *Germans in Britain Since 1500* (London and Rio Grande, TX: Hambledon Press, 1996), 166-167. The subject of British World War Two interment policy was notably addressed in "The German Woman" (2002), the premier episode of the popular British detective series *Foyle's War*.

# THE SPECTRUM OF ENGLISH MURDER 183

of this and other anti-refugee letters, Marta becomes the prime suspect in Kitty's murder. Ultimately, Marta is arrested, allowing her to deliver a denunciation of the British treatment of refugees that clearly reflects the view of the author: "You need not say any more.... I am a stateless creature with no rights; and the British, who are fighting Nazism, must practise a little now and then, in case they shall change their minds one day and decide to imitate Hitler and not fight him."[76]

Fortunately for Madame Zyboski, old Mrs. Warrender, the novel's putative "detective," (see more on her below in my discussion of the Coles' short detective fiction), somehow divines the truth in the novel's last few pages: {*SPOILERS*} The violently slain Kitty Lake was knifed in the dark by her own husband. Gordon Lake had discovered that Kitty was the author of the spiteful and false anonymous letters and, as a passionate advocate of refugee rights, the Stamford scholar found it necessary to resort to murder to stop his wife—"an abnormally discontented and uninhibited person"—from doing further harm to refugees from Fascist oppression. When Lake learns from Mrs. Warrender that his friend Marta has been arrested, he commits suicide, leaving a confession behind to exonerate the wronged woman. "If only he hadn't gone off his rocker about those foreigners," reflects the novel's Colonel Blimpish official investigator, Colonel Greig.[77]

In their work *The Lady Investigates: Women Detectives and Spies in Fiction*, Patricia Craig and Mary Cadogan mock Gordon Lake's murder motive in *Knife in the Dark* as one "out of proportion to the provocation" and amusingly recall one of the ruthless rhymes:

> Late last night I slew my wife,
>     Laid her on the parquet flooring.
> I was loath to take her life,
>     But I had to stop her snoring.

---

[76] G. D. H. and M. Cole, *Knife in the Dark* (London: Collins, 1941), 180.
[77] Coles, *Knife*, 43, 192.

Yet one needs to consider the novel in the context of the *Arandora Star* sinking—a great needless human tragedy of modern times—and to reflect that Margaret Cole no doubt was personally aware of people capable of putting a great social cause above personal considerations.[78] {*END SPOILERS*}

PART FOUR: POLITICAL AND SOCIAL IDEOLOGY
IN THE DETECTIVE NOVELS OF THE COLES

BOTH THE COLES brought different political and social perspectives to Golden Age British detective fiction, something underappreciated in studies of the genre. It is doubtful that genre readers in the twenty-year period in which the husband and wife published mystery fiction could have entirely missed the left-of-center sentiments in their works. Certainly contemporary reviewers did not miss them, some complaining, for example, that socialist characters in

---

[78] Patricia Craig and Mary Cadogan, *The Lady Investigates: Women Detectives and Spies in Fiction* (New York: St. Martin's Press, 1981), 104. Indeed, rather ironically, given Margaret Cole's forthright condemnation of British World War Two internment policy, when the Coles' friend Rose Cohen, a British citizen living in the USSR, was arrested in 1937 on trumped-up spy charges during Stalin's purges, the couple refrained from signing a letter of protest to the *New Statesman and Nation* (only a pitiful nine signatures were obtained, including that of Margaret Cole's socialist brother, Raymond Postgate), evidently being reluctant to put their personal friendship with Cohen ahead of their commitment to the great Soviet experiment. "Nor am I one of those who, when everything in the new and struggling Socialist community does not go just as they would like, turn their backs on the struggle and proclaim the Revolution is being betrayed," testily lectured Douglas Cole in an article in November 1937, the same month in which a bullet to the head ended Rose Cohen's life after a one-day show trial. "Alas, men cannot make a new civilization without growing pains, or liquidate an ancient tyranny without suffering." Kevin Morgan and Gidon Cohen, "Rose Cohen," *Dictionary of Labour Biography*, vol. 11 (London: Palgrave, 2003), 37-38. {*SPOILERS*} Clearly, the Coles could have understood the motive of someone like Gordon Lake, who did not allow petty personal considerations about "growing pains" to stand in the way of a Great Cause. {*END SPOILERS*} For more on Rose Cohen, see Francis Beckett, *Stalin's British Victims* (Stroud, Gloucestershire, UK: Sutton, 2004).

the Coles' novels could automatically be eliminated as potential villains, undermining the appeal of the books as puzzles. Even crime fiction devotees on the left side of the political spectrum, like E. R. Punshon and Ralph Partridge, registered this complaint. "Dr. Johnson, it is recorded, took care to see that the Whig dogs did not get the best of it," wrote Punshon in his *Manchester Guardian* review of *Murder at the Munition Works*. "The Coles seem a little of the same cast of mind, and indeed in their new story . . . the Tories are so very, very bad, and the Socialists are so wholly compact of sweetness and light . . . that really one feels Dr. Johnson's example has been even improved on." Similarly, Ralph Partridge, mystery reviewer for the leftist *New Statesman and Nation*, continuously complained in his reviews of Coles novels that the left-wing characters were always good and could be immediately eliminated as suspects. Of *The Missing Aunt* Partridge grumbled, "from the earliest pages [the Coles] indicate by their righteous animosity where the guilt lies. Virtue, in the character of a noble hiking hero from Magdalen College, Oxford, is deservedly rewarded with the heroine . . . everyone gets his deserts, except the poor reader who wants to be a little misled." Of *Greek Tragedy* the exasperated reviewer sighed, "Nazis may be liquidated, but the Coles will always put up alibis for the Communists." With *Murder at the Munition Works*, the most overtly political Coles novel of all, Partridge was withering:

> With the Coles a detestable reactionary factory manager has his wife blown to blazes by an explosion in his office at the works. A noble Socialist shop-steward, whom he has just sacked, is suspected of the crime—oh! How unjustly! The list of *dramatis personae* in *Murder at the Munition Works* runs to two pages from which to choose the villain, but as most of the characters are members of the Left Book Club, the field is evidently narrower than might appear at first sight; in fact, proceeding by political elimination,

the candidates for the halter are reduced to a mere two. The scenes of strikes and labour-meetings are well and intimately described, but the Coles' bias to the Left will lead the reader straight to the solution.[79]

Margaret Cole herself was certainly under the impression that the detective novels she and Douglas Cole had written had unorthodox political content. "How often have I read in a review that it is a pity that the Coles 'drag politics' into their detective novels," recalled Margaret Cole pointedly in 1949. "Politics of the Left, is what these reviewers mean."[80] In addition to their quite evident sympathy for socialist characters, the Coles, both atheists, tended

---

[79] *Manchester Guardian*, 13 August 1940; *New Statesman and Nation*, 29 January 1938, 178; 23 December 1939, 934; 10 August 1940, 143. {SPOILERS} It likely will not come as a surprise to anyone familiar with the Coles to learn that the murderer in *The Missing Aunt*, one Barry Latchemere, "wants to be a stockbroker, and is trying to persuade his Aunt Elinor to buy him a partnership in a go-ahead firm of outside brokers." Douglas Cole lays on his distaste for the objectionable Barry with a trowel in the rather precious and intrusive Trollopian narration he sometimes adopted in his novels (see *The Death of a Millionaire* and *Big Business Murder*):

> A rather puffy-looking young man? Likely to run to fat in middle age? Certainly weak, to judge by his chin, and probably obstinate at the same time? Well, well, perhaps the reader is right in not being attracted. But is it really fair to judge a young man by what he looks like when he is asleep with his mouth wide open? In mercy, let us suspend judgment.
>
> But lo! The sleeper wakes; and we steal away just in time . . . he feels for the novel (yes, yes, of course it is by P. G. Wodehouse) that he has let fall to his side. He resumes his reading of *The Clicking of Cuthbert*. We hear a fat chuckle. Truly, my lord deigns to be amused.

G. D. H. and M. Cole, *The Missing Aunt* (New York: Macmillan, 1938), 38-39. {END SPOILERS} Conversely, the hiking former Oxford undergraduate has virtue's crown firmly planted on his noble brow by the doting Douglas Cole. The young man, we quickly learn, is a "free-lance journalist" whose short stories are getting "talked about in certain highbrow circles." Better yet, we find he "started his education at a council school and worked his way up by scholarships" and was sired by a man "still hewing coal somewhere in the bowels of Yorkshire." Coles, *Aunt*, 11.

[80] Cole, *Revolution*, 19.

to portray religious figures, whether high church or low, as either fools or rascals (and frequently both). Indeed, when one reads in the story "Murder in Church" of an orating minister crushed by a collapsed metal pulpit hood, one can well imagine the Coles deeming the manner of this particular man's snuffing out amusingly fitting. Military men as well typically appear as reactionary buffoons, reflecting the distaste of the Coles for British imperialism, as well as the persecution of conscientious objectors during World War One (including Margaret Cole's brother Raymond Postgate, himself an author-to-be of crime novels) and of Communists in the post-war "Red Scare" period in Britain and the United States.

This being conceded, however, it is nevertheless true that the Coles were more characteristic of the Golden Age in other ways, both ideological and aesthetic. As in the cases of other Golden Age writers, their fiction reflected in some ways the social class from which they came, as evidenced by occasional instances in it of authorial snobbery, reflexive anti-Semitism and distaste for such things as cosmetics, Freudian psychology, progressive education and commercial development. Moreover, the Coles tended toward aesthetic conservatism in their stated view of detective fiction, deeming it first and foremost an exercise in puzzle making.

By the time they began writing detective fiction, both Douglas and Margaret Cole were part of the intellectual elite of their country, their very names lending prestige to the genre in which they moonlighted. In photos, Douglas Cole has a certain air of patrician hauteur, looking the very model of the Oxford don, while Margaret Cole often seems to have a intimidating countenance scornful of, as she once put it, "the mess human beings have made in the world." Yet appearances do not always tell all, for, while Margaret Cole was the daughter of an extremely formidable Cambridge Lecturer in Latin, Douglas Cole came from solidly petit bourgeois stock, his father starting professional life as a pawnbroker and estate agent and his mother coming from a farming family. "Douglas Cole was definitely an oddity . . . in his family," wrote his wife in her biography of him, "intellectually above all, but not only intellectually." The family resided in "a sizeable house with a large garden in Mount Park Road, Ealing—a highly respectable street in a highly respectable suburb." No books entered the house, according to Margaret, unless they were Douglas Cole tomes "dutifully presented by the son" and "for the most part unopened" or dusty volumes left over from an estate sale.[81] Douglas Cole's father had as a young man somewhat unorthodoxly been both a Liberal and a Methodist, but after his marriage he had converted to Toryism and the Church of England and settled down to a highly conventional life. Though Douglas Cole certainly rejected his father's political and religious conservatism, in some ways his detective novels would reflect his staid, bourgeois upbringing.

Margaret Cole's father, John Percival Postgate, was no less conservative than Douglas Cole's father, yet he was considerably less conventional. Margaret Cole's fascinating reminiscence of her own life, *Growing up into Revolution*, makes clear, without directly saying so, that she detested the man. Much of the reader's enjoyment of the earlier chapters of *Growing up into Revolution* (arguably Margaret Cole's finest work) consists in anticipating what outrageous thing Professor Postgate will do next. In one Dickensian passage, like something out *of Oliver Twist*, Margaret Cole describes how her father taught her to learn Latin:

> My father . . . was a crusader like his father before him, but a crusader in the linguistic field. He was the great protagonist of the modern pronunciation of Latin by "the direct method," *i.e.*, making the children *talk* Latin as though it were any modern language. . . . Not being a boy, I never had experience of the direct method in class; but I had plenty of it at home. I began Latin on my fifth birthday, by being sent into my mother's room to announce the event in the words "Hodie quinque annos nata sum"; thereafter I had to

---

[81] Cole, *G. D. H. Cole*, 24, 27.

learn to talk on common subjects in Latin, and on Sundays, when such of the children as could sit upright and feed tidily dined downstairs, I had to ask for my dinner in Latin under threat of not getting any. I still remember the awful occasion on which, at the age of six or thereabouts, I asked for "the beef" instead of "some of the beef," and my father pushed the huge sirloin on its dish over in my direction and I dissolved into tears; and I have been told of another time when, having forgotten the Latin for sausage, I was told that if I could say "half" I might have *half* a sausage—and squealed out "dimidium!" through sobs.[82]

Cole's final words on the "direct method" would hardly have endeared her to Professor Postgate:

The direct method never "took" with me; all I retain of that early training is a few scraps of totally useless information, as that *sinapi* is the Latin for mustard. . . . [My father] was an exacting and irritable teacher, and what was perhaps more unfortunate, he did not succeed in giving me any idea that there was anything worth reading for its own sake in that horrible tongue. . . . I hated Latin, all though my childhood, as bitterly as anyone can ever have hated it; and it was not until I ceased to be his pupil that I found any beauty in it at all.[83]

Expanding on a theme of the all round inadequacy of her father, Cole listed a veritable catalogue of his failings: Postgate, we learn, was a professionally disappointed man who lost the Professorship of Latin at Cambridge to A. E. Houseman (Postgate

---

[82] Cole, *Revolution*, 5.
[83] Ibid., 5-6.

later became Professor of Latin at the University of Liverpool), as well as "almost pathologically afraid of poverty, cursed with an irritable temper which he could not control, convinced, and more convinced as the years went on, that the world was marching to political damnation, and that the working-man, whom he firmly believed to be 'in the loomp, baad,' was coming more and more to control his destiny . . . and burdened with a pack of six children whom he may have desired and loved in theory but certainly found exasperating, noisy, destructive and unfilial in practice." On the whole, Cole concludes, surely not to the reader's surprise, "I think we disliked our father."[84]

Margaret Cole may have disliked her father, yet she shared some of his personality quirks—his prickliness and his stinginess—as will be seen in my discussion below. Moreover, although Margaret Cole writes of the Postgate family that "we were of the middle class," she confesses to having enjoyed the accoutrements of "middle class" living in those late Victorian and Edwardian days, items that would increasingly seem exclusively a part of upper class life even in the Golden Age of detective fiction. Of Cambridge's professional academic class she admits, "we all had nurses and servants and seaside holidays, and all of us went to upper-class schools and had dancing and drawing classes . . . as to the poor, we read about them in moral stories." Nevertheless, she urged that none in this professional academic class "was in a position to exploit or to despise socially any of the others, and I think this early experience of an equalitarian society, even within so narrow a compass, has given me a natural bent towards equality."[85]

This "natural bent towards equality" did not inhibit Margaret Cole, however, from employing servants and enjoying the benefits of the domestic labor of others during her married life with Douglas. Margaret recalled that after she and Douglas wed in 1918, he—"a man of leisure and of possessions" who "had never had to shop or to wash dishes and could not be expected to begin to do so"—

---

[84] Ibid., 6.
[85] Ibid., 8-9.

insisted on their having a house staffed with servants. Fortunately the house the couple purchased came with a caretaker who was able to stay on as their cook-housekeeper, "inhabiting the basement with her family." Into the basement Margaret never ventured and she later was much surprised to learn that a total of seven people dwelt in her domicile's lower depths. During the decade this good woman was with the Coles, Margaret Cole gave birth to three children; there was also a nurse to help Margaret manage with child care. Regrettably, their cook-housekeeper left them after a decade and was replaced for a year by a "terrible, cretinous couple" (perhaps the model for the terrible, cretinous servant couples in *The Brothers Sackville* and *Toper's End*?). However, they in turn were thankfully replaced, by "an out-of-work miner from Barnsley and his wife," who suited the family quite well. "We were, in fact," Margaret Cole reflected, "a household on the Edwardian pattern."[86] With an ample supply of servants on hand, the busy couple always managed to find time to do that which came most naturally to them: write and write and write.

Margaret Cole's opposition to snobbery and anti-Semitism in her works has already been discussed above, and certainly her long career of political writing and activism reflects a powerful commitment on her part to the achievement through socialism of social and political equality in Britain. For example, in a 1938 pamphlet for Virginia and Leonard Woolf's Hogarth Press, *Books and the People*, Margaret Cole memorably derided dual-track education in 1930s England ("Culture for the Governing Class: No Expense Spared" and "Cheap and Nasty: for the Masses"), bitingly concluding that it "perpetuates the class-system and the inequalities that arise therefrom, with the consequence that in no country is an honest democracy or an equalitarian system so hard to imagine as it is in England."[87] Yet for all her recorded fervor for equality and social change, her detective fiction occasionally

---

[86] Ibid., 80, 81, 82, 103, 104, 133; Cole, *G. D. H. Cole*, 172-173.
[87] Margaret Cole, *Books and the People* (London: Hogarth, 1938) (Day to Pay Pamphlets 38), 12.

reflects a personality somewhat more reminiscent of that which she attributes to her formidable, conservative father. Already noted has been Cole's ambiguous treatment of snobbery in *Greek Tragedy*, where the author condemns the attitude while simultaneously indulging in it herself at times, and her sympathetic treatment of such gentrified idlers in her novels as Everard Blatchington, Sir Charles Wylie and Lydia and Tony Redfern. Snobbishness also is evident in the author's treatment of the nouveau riche in *Burglars in Bucks*. Perhaps most significant of all is Cole's contemptuous treatment of lower middle and working class characters in one of her most admired novels, *Dead Man's Watch*. I have already discussed the tale's dichotomous treatment of the working class Cockney girl, Dolly Daniells, and the white collar clerk, Percy Bittaford. Even more strikingly, when a corpse is fished out of a creek (to be identified as an uncle of Percy's), the author assures readers that "it was certainly a body belonging to the clerk or small tradesman class."[88] Note the precision here: the corpse is immediately recognizable not merely as a corpse of the tradesman class, but as one of the *small* tradesman class! Margaret Cole no doubt believed in egalitarianism, but in *Dead Man's Watch* class distinctions seem so immutable and immemorial that they follow her characters beyond the grave.

Throughout the novel one is struck by the author's rather contemptuous treatment of characters coming from the lower middle and working—or more accurately servant—class. Sir Charles Wylie, who functions as the novel's detective and author surrogate for two-thirds of its length, is a frequently charming young wastrel, but his treatment of the lower orders, the naively endearing Dolly excepted, is condescending. When Sir Charles finds the murder victim's sister-in-law (Percy's aunt) copiously shedding tears over her husband's fate he wonders if she truly is "deeply grieved" or whether she is merely indulging in "the natural response of her

---

[88] Coles, *Watch*, 15.

class to death of any sort." Later in the novel Sir Charles, a man who, according to another character does "absolutely nothing whatever," bestirs himself to perform some amateur investigating in the murder case, an endeavor that proves rather an ordeal for him. First he has to board with a landlady in a lower middle class establishment that is clearly not up to snuff:

> Mrs. Sarah Fishcote was amiable, but she was a dirty, slatternly fool; and her amiability was that of the irritating bovine quality which so often goes with imbecility. She was incapable of making a bed so that it did not come unmade at the first opportunity, or of cleaning a room so as to remove instead of scattering the dust, or of boiling an egg so that it was neither as hard as a brick nor completely liquescent; and attempts to improve the service which she provided only resulted in worse confusion.[89]

Merely being in the same room with Mrs. Fishcote is a trying experience, for it seems the woman is quite unpleasantly odiferous: "Mrs. Fishcote lumbered down the stairs to fetch a taxi. As soon as she had gone, Wylie leaped to the window and flung it wide. The morning was hot, the street stuffy, and Mrs. Fishcote fat and overclothed. Definitely, Wylie thought, he would have preferred the 'am" (Mrs. Fishcote before leaving Sir Charles had been attempting to ply him with rancid ham). In this connection, I am forcibly reminded of an exasperated observation on the psuedo-amusing Mrs. Fishcotes of British fiction made in 1933 by Roger Pippett, book review editor of the Labour organ the London *Daily Herald*, two years after the publication of *Dead Man's Watch*: "I forget how many times I have read of the boarding-house keeper

---

[89] Coles, *Watch*, 52, 58, 124.

who drops her aitches and skimps the food in the dining-room, and is so very, very unfunny all the while."[90]

Unfortunately for Margaret Cole's wilting sprig of the gentry, Sir Charles Wylie of *Dead Man's Watch*, his troubles with social inferiors continue when he transfers the seat of his investigations to the Hotel Splendide at Sands-on-Sea. On arriving in his room Sir Charles finds "no soap in the soap dish" and a bed "so unnecessarily soft as nearly to stifle him," with the result that "the chambermaid, coming in to set the room to rights" finds herself "greeted with a volley of remarks" that sends the poor young woman "flying out into the corridor again." Later Wylie has to deal with a "half-witted" library attendant. He finally damns the whole town to blazes in a letter to Dolly Daniells. The girls of Sands-on-Sea he finds "expensive, ugly, vapid," the cinema "stifling and showing continually bad American comic films" and the food "bad and expensive." Sir Charles, it seems, is not one to suffer fools gladly, and he frequently finds himself confronted with fools. Such an impatient and imperious tone on the part of the author is not entirely absent from other of her novels—in *Poison in the Garden Suburb*, for example, we learn in passing that "the maid . . . was an idiot, and could not say what she had done or not done"—but it is by far most obviously present in *Dead Man's Watch*.[91]

Members of the Detection Club described Margaret Cole in terms rather similar to those Cole applied to her own father, suggesting (more than suggesting in one case) that they found her something of a demanding and unpleasant presence. In a reminiscence of the Detection Club penned in 1979 (when she assumed, incorrectly, that Margaret Cole was dead), esteemed mystery

---

[90] Ibid., 146; *London Daily Herald*, 16 March 1933, 17. In a review of Douglas Cole's *The Great Southern Mystery*, Pippett took the Coles specifically to task for caricatures of lower class speech. "They really ought to come off that stale Cockney stuff," Pippett snorted derisively. "'William 'Ardy, with a haitch'." *London Daily Herald*, 5 March 1931, 6. In truth, both Coles are among the most egregious offenders of the Golden Age when it comes to ostensibly amusing dialect writing.

[91] Coles, *Watch*, 147, 148, 149, 150; Coles, *Suburb*, 210.

writer Christianna Brand remembered Margaret Cole "with simple resentment as rude and bullying." Though Cole and her husband were "deep in the Labour movement," recalled Brand with some rancor over thirty years later, "it wouldn't occur to her, I suppose, that I had been for years as poor and downtrodden as anyone she had ever met in the course of her political thunderings."[92]

Margaret Cole's surviving correspondence with the Detection Club suggests a prickly relationship between Cole and her fellow members (there is no direct evidence that Douglas Cole bothered to attend meetings), mainly based on her own parsimoniousness, or thriftiness as she no doubt would have seen it. In 1939, Cole wrote Dorothy L. Sayers, complaining of the state of the Club's private library, which was formed of volumes donated by members. Evidently on the hunt for books to borrow, Cole had recently been inspecting the library premises and she was not pleased with the result of her inspection. "It appears to me that recently admitted members have presented nothing whatever and old ones not for some time," she complained. "You will find, on the table by the library, a pile of books left here in order to put my record in order, but I think somebody else might oblige." Some three months later, as war engulfed Great

---

[92] For this quite disparaging assessment of Margaret Cole, see Christianna Brand's introduction to the 1979 Gregg Press reprint of the Detection Club's *The Floating Admiral*. Part of Brand's directness may be due to the fact that she believed Margaret Cole to be dead, though in fact Cole passed away the year after Brand's introduction to *The Floating Admiral* was published. Even Margaret Cole's admiring biographer, Betty D. Vernon, concedes that, in later years, after the death of Douglas Cole in 1959, Margaret Cole's "long-suppressed wilfulness, hauteur even, began to surface," with the socialist doyenne behaving "imperiously, erratically, and even on occasion with a sharpness that could be quite disconcerting." Vernon, *Margaret Cole*, 142. Evidence from Christianna Brand and other members of the Detection Club, however, indicates that imperious and sharp behavior was perceived in Margaret Cole much earlier than 1960. Writing of his first meeting with Margaret Cole, back before the Second World War, the English diplomat Rowland Kenney memorably recalled her as "a provocative elfin-tigress," smoking a large cigar. "Peddling and Politics," *Sydney Morning Herald*, 6 January 1940, 10.

Britain, Cole again wrote Sayers about the library situation, batting down Sayers' suggestion that the library, potentially in danger from German planes, might be closed and the books distributed among members. "I should *not* agree, at present," wrote Cole vociferously, "to any disbandment of the Club or distribution of the library, which was given for Club purposes. I should doubt in any event whether the Club has the right to send books away without specific permission."[93]

The Club did disband during the war, Luftwaffe bombs proving more persuasive than Margaret Cole's bombast, though the library was not dispersed. When the Club began meeting again after the war, Margaret Cole was back, just as vocally cost-conscious as ever. Of the price for tickets to a 1948 Detection Club dinner and lecture, Cole complained, in a letter to the Club Secretary, that "34/- for self and guest, apart from liquor, is much too much in these times. I must therefore forego the pleasure of listening to Mr. Hawke." Not content to let it rest with that, Cole added that "only a few days ago I attended a private dinner for Mr. Roosevelt, for which I paid 7/6d. The difference seems excessive." The Secretary of the Detection Club (Anthony Gilbert?) took time, in her response to Cole, to counter that the price quoted by Cole was not "unusually high these days for the use of two rooms and special staff and cocktail bar in a West-End restaurant for a dinner of about fifty people. . . . [L]ast year the Cafe Royal provided such an excellent dinner and service, and everybody was so well-satisfied, that the Committee preferred not to make a change." In the case of the "private dinner for Mr. Roosevelt" to which Margaret Cole had referred in her letter, the Secretary speculated that "the organizing body must have borne all the overhead charges," something that had never "been the custom of the Detection Club on any previous occasion." Clearly Margaret Cole had won for herself a Reputation, for four years later (in 1952), Dorothy L. Sayers, writing to Anthony Gilbert of an upcoming Detection Club function,

---

[93] Margaret Cole to Dorothy L. Sayers, 7 June 1939, 21 September 1939. Dorothy L. Sayers Papers, Marion E. Wade Center, Wheaton College, Wheaton, Illinois.

noted with mock wonderment that "the prospect of an inexpensive evening has lured Margaret Cole!"[94]

Servants are sometimes satirized in the detective novels of G. D. H. Cole, as in the case, for example, of the hotel employees in *The Death of a Millionaire* and *The Great Southern Mystery* or the domestics in *The Brothers Sackville* and *Toper's End* (the Arkells and the Mudges, the servant couples in the latter two novels, both likely based on actual former domestics of the Coles, are quite splendidly horrid), but one gets the feeling that in these instances what is being expressed is more a left-wing contempt on the author's part for those he sees as cravenly prostrating themselves before the ruling classes, rather than any personal petulance with poor service from the lower orders. Nor do servants stand alone as objects of satire in Douglas Cole novels—indeed, hardly so. The male Cole seems to take a rather less indulgent view of England's traditional ruling gentry than does his wife, with corrupt lords coming in for ridicule in *The Death of a Millionaire* and *Big Business Murder* as well as dotty lords in *The Blatchington Tangle* and *The Affair at Aliquid*. Additionally, Anglican bishops are targets of derision in *The Affair at Aliquid* and *Double Blackmail*, dowager philanthropists in *Double Blackmail* and, closer to home, college officials in *Disgrace to the College*. Only the manual working class goes unpricked by Douglas Cole's poisoned pen.

One lapse Douglas Cole does share in his fiction with his wife is an occasional anti-Semitic tone to his writing, though this fact seems at odds at first with the strong condemnations of anti-Semitism that can be found in the fictional works of both authors. Douglas Cole's novel *The Great Southern Mystery* has a stereotypically odious, lisping Jew character, while Margaret Cole in *Death of a Star* includes a couple of indelicate portrayals of Jews. In its blunt bigotry the depiction of Aaron Cohen in Douglas Cole's

---

[94] Margaret Cole to Dorothy L. Sayers, 15 April 1948; Anthony Gilbert to Margaret Cole, 19 April 1948; Dorothy L. Sayers to Anthony Gilbert, 22 September 1952. DLS Papers.

*The Great Southern Mystery* rivals something out the anti-Semitic thrillers of Sydney Horler. Stephanie Adam, the novel's heroine, does "not like the look of Mr. Aaron Cohen at all," we are informed; and, as Mr. Aaron Cohen, a shady nightclub owner, is described, it was surely no wonder to Cole's readers: "He was a small, fair Jew, with shifty eyes and a hand like a fish. She shivered as she shook it. She was almost certain, too, he painted his cheeks; and his greasy hair stank of oil." Naturally such a repulsive creature possesses the lisp so often associated with Jews in mystery novels of this period, giving Cole the chance to compose such "amusing" utterances for Mr. Aaron Cohen as these:

> "How do I know Thamuel Quinthy told you anything? ... If he thaid anything againtht me, it wathn't true."

> "I mutht thee my tholithiter. . . . Mither Golthtein, of Goldthtein, Goldthtein and Rothenberg."[95]

Margaret Cole's depictions of Jews in *Death of a Star* are masterpieces of subtlety compared to Douglas Cole's portrayal of Mr. Aaron Cohen, yet they are still unfortunate. One Jew is let off lightly on the grounds that he does not look very Jewish: "a tall, fair, perfectly polite young man, with only an indefinable curve of nose and nostril to remind them of his ancestry." The film producer Max Ikeman, however, suffers the full barrage of Semite-averse descriptive vocabulary. Ikeman is described as looking "large and florid and Jewish" and wearing clothes that are "florid and expensive and badly put on." When Ikeman spoke, Cole notes acidly, "his hearers noticed almost with pain the absence of a lisp."[96] Were Margaret

---

[95] G. D. H. and M. Cole, *The Great Southern Mystery* (London: Collins, 1931), 178, 226, 227. It rather boggles the mind that a great Oxford scholar actually spent time thinking up such "corking" lines for a lisping Jew as "I mutht thee my tholithiter ... Mithter Goldthtein, of Goldthtein, Goldthtein and Rothenberg," but he did indeed do so (unless these lines were stray Margaret Cole contributions to this tale—which would boggle the mind as well).

[96] Coles, *Star*, 299.

Cole's readers likewise disappointed at being cheated in this instance of the "fun" of a lisping Jew? Whatever readers' expectations were, it seems that the Coles themselves were not entirely immune to a cultural environment in which anti-Semitic stereotypes were seen as amusing bits of "local color" in popular fiction. Given the fact that the pair personally associated with Jews—indeed, their daughter Jane in 1944 married, with her parents' blessing, an American Jew, Will Abraham—the Coles' use of these crude stereotypes comes as something of a surprise. Perhaps the couple did not take the genre seriously enough to see that any harm could flow from their employing offensive, anti-Semitic stereotypes (Margaret Cole's later use of the genre to attack such stereotypes suggests a belated such realization on her part). It also is worth noting in this connection that the Jews portrayed so unfavorably in *The Great Southern Mystery* and *Death of a Star* come from nightclub and theater backgrounds, occupations for which the Coles no doubt had little respect.

Both Coles disliked painted woman almost as much as Douglas Cole abhorred the cheeks-painting Mr. Aaron Cohen. For example, in *Dead Man's Watch*, Margaret Cole's Sir Charles Wylie includes overly made-up women in his parade of horribles at Sands-on-Sea, while in *The Brooklyn Murders*, Douglas Cole primly makes mention of "a coarse-looking woman of about forty or forty-five" and "the artificial obstructions which [she] had placed in the way of those who might be minded to inspect her too closely." Christianna Brand records scathingly that Margaret Cole "clearly disapproved of young women . . . with blue on their eyelids," a reference to Brand's predilection at that time for blue eye shadow.[97] According to Brand, this fashion choice on her part served as a source of antipathy between the two women, Margaret Cole evidently making it sufficiently clear to Brand that she considered her something of

---

[97] Cole, *Brooklyn*, 112; Brand, Introduction to *The Floating Admiral*. Although Margaret supported her daughter Jane's choice of spouse from the start, Douglas initially objected—not, however, because Will Abraham was Jewish, but because he was American. See Vernon, *Margaret Cole*, 148.

a flighty floozy. While Margaret Cole tended to be more outspokenly progressive on sexual matters in her novels then many Golden Age writers, it would seem that, as with the concept of equalitarianism, her commitment was perhaps somewhat more theoretical than actual.

On the other hand, there is discernible feminist subtext in Margaret Cole's crime writing, such as, for example, her elevation of plucky young women over their weak, neurotic boyfriends (see my discussions above of *Poison in the Garden Suburb* and *Dead Man's Watch* and the one below of "The Toys of Death"). Notable in this context is "The Case of Adelaide Bartlett," an essay Cole contributed to the Detection Club book *The Anatomy of Murder* (1936), wherein she scrutinizes the intimate relationships of one of Victorian England's most notorious accused murderers. Cole likens the attitude of Edwin Bartlett toward his wife, Adelaide, to that of a master toward a favored pet dog, speculating witheringly that Edwin may have deemed the arrival of Reverend George Dyson, the third member of the triangle in the Bartlett case, "as a godsend to enable his pet dog to be kept happy and amused." Cole drew the sardonic conclusion that "It is very clear that, if you are going to get into trouble with the law, it does not pay to be odd, particularly if your oddity is in any way connected with your sexual or matrimonial relations. . . . Adelaide Bartlett . . . was very nearly hanged because in the year 1885 she had in her possession a book which discussed birth-control, and, what was worse, had actually lent it to a gentleman friend." Rejecting the contention that at the time of Edwin's death Adelaide was having an affair with Reverend Dyson, Cole writes bluntly: "She did not want to sleep with him. I myself think that, like a good many women, she did not want to sleep with anybody." Intriguingly, Margaret Cole's essay may have reflected concerns from her own life, as at this time she and Dick Mitchison—a "large, self-effacing, gentle and humorous" barrister married to the novelist Naomi Mitchison who later, with the Coles' support, was elected a Labour MP—had developed a close friendship that some people in their social circles assumed was a sexual affair carried on with the acquiescence of their compliant spouses.[98]

Though themselves in many ways socially and economically progressive individuals, the Coles, like many other Golden Age detective novelists, expressed in their works skepticism of and disdain for popular Freudianism, experimental educational methods and commercial development schemes. As they were a couple who believed in class identity as the central determinant in human behavior, the Coles' unconcealed contempt for Freudian psychiatry (which posited an alternative determinant in the human subconscious) should not come as unexpected. G. D. H. Cole memorably lampooned Freudian psychiatry in *The Affair at Alquid's* deranged Miss Perks, the spinster who finds in Freud the answer to every riddle of human behavior and insists on expounding at great length to her hapless victims upon the Master's revelations. Margaret Cole turns an amused eye as well on psychiatry's foibles in her novel *Dead Man's Watch*, when she details a criminal psychologist's convoluted case for Ron Bittaford's guilt in the murder of an uncle of his (there has been some doubt as to which of two uncles the corpse actually is):

> "[He] says he's the type who's very likely to have a phantasy, by which, I gather, he means a sudden homicidal impulse against anything or anybody who'd thwarted him in his earlier days, as his uncle undoubtedly did. Sort of revenging his own ill success in life, you see."

---

[98] Margaret Cole, "The Case of Adelaide Bartlett," in *The Anatomy of Murder* (1936; rpnt, New York: Macmillan, 1937), 89-90, 100-101, 113; Vernon, *Margaret Cole*, 69. In a February 1936 letter the great intellectual Isaiah Berlin passingly referred to Dick Mitchison as Margaret Cole's "lover." See Berlin's *Letters 1928-1946* (Cambridge and New York: Cambridge University Press, 2004), edited by Henry Hardy, 155. See also Marina Warner's introduction to the 2014 edition of Naomi Mitchison's *The Fourth Pig* (Princeton University Press), wherein Warner characterizes Margaret as Dick Mitchison's "longtime lover" (p. 12).

"For which reason, I presume," said Wilson dryly, "he tried to strangle the uncle who had *not* thwarted him, and threw him into the water. Do you really mean to tell me, Cavanagh, that he went out in a boat with the wrong uncle, and murdered him, and never discovered it was the wrong one? Do you think that makes sense?"

"It wouldn't, of course, with you or me," Cavanagh said, "because we're normal people. But Dr. Paish's whole point is that this fellow isn't...."

.... "And why does Dr. Paish . . . think that [Bittaford] shaved his uncle? And what with?"

"He thinks," said Cavanagh, "that it was symbolic, in a way. Done to make him more like his recollections of the uncle who bullied him. He was clean-shaven when he knew him, you see; so he'd got to be clean-shaven now. What he did it with I don't know. I suppose he may have had a razor on him."

"Oh, I should think so," Wilson said. "I should think, in fact, that his subconscious sent him into a shop and made him buy one, just to be on the safe side. I wouldn't produce Dr. What's-his-name in court, if I were you, Cavanagh, though there's no knowing what some juries will swallow."[99]

As discussed above, Margaret Cole in part devoted one of her best novels, *Scandal at School*, to satirizing, through Everard Blatchington's bemused eyes, what Cole saw as the follies of 'thirties progressive education (her own children at the time she was writing this novel were aged fifteen, fourteen and seven). In this same novel, Everard makes clear he dislikes modern housing as well, scornfully noting a journalist's description of Acott, Oxfordshire, the locale of Santley House School, as "a lovely old-world village." "It isn't anything of the sort," howls Everard. "It's a lot of bungalows on a sandbank. . . . It isn't an old world village

---

[99] Coles, *Watch*, 225-27.

and never was one." Margaret Cole's hostility for the rapid development of cheap suburban housing in this period also finds expression in *Poison in the Garden Suburb*, where dwellings in the titular garden suburb are condemned by the author in no uncertain terms as unbearably shoddy. Similarly in *Death of a Bride* (exact authorship unknown, but I presume Margaret Cole), we learn from narrator Cuthbert Perkins that murder victim Anna Bredon's father "was a master-builder here in Bath, and did quite a lot in his day to spoil its outskirts."[100]

Just as tasteless and crude suburban expansion is condemned in the Coles' novels, the pristine countryside is celebrated. Douglas Cole's *The Man from the River*, for example, provides a highly idealized rustic idyll for the vacationing Superintendent Wilson and his friend and sometime Watson, Dr. Michael Prendergast. In her biography of her husband, Margaret Cole recalled his intense fondness for rural England, which she believed to be grounded in his great reverence for William Morris, the nineteenth-century socialist and key figure in the arts and crafts movement. However, she insisted, Douglas Cole "was no industrial Luddite"; and, indeed, his novel *Murder at the Munition Works* displays extensive knowledge of matters of labor organization in modern factories, at times reading more like one of his non-fictional economic tomes. Yet this novel remained rather a rarity not only among Golden Age works in general, but among Cole's own works as well. Novels by both Coles generally reveal only the vaguest details about actual business operation (though acid references to stock market shenanigans abound). Additionally, in contrast with John Street, who similarly loved the countryside, Douglas Cole's ruralphilia was of the romantic sort, ungirded by practical considerations. "In fact, he knew nothing whatever about farming, and was nowise concerned to learn," his wife admitted. "He was a complete townsman as regards 'honest muck' or bulls in the field, and turned quite sick with horror the first time he laid eyes on a little white runt in a litter of pigs."[101]

---

[100] Cole, *Scandal*, 7; G. D. H. and M. Cole, *Death of a Bride* (London: Vallancey: 1945), 7.
[101] Cole, *G. D. H. Cole*, 36.

PART FIVE: THE SHORT DETECTIVE FICTION OF THE COLES
LIKE HENRY WADE, the Coles also produced a significant body of short detective fiction: thirty-five known short stories, all but two of them gathered into three book collections—*Superintendent Wilson's Holiday* (1928), *A Lesson in Crime* (1933), and *Wilson and Some Others* (1940)—and five novellas, four Mrs. Warrender tales collected, with a short story, in *Mrs. Warrender's Profession* (1938), and one, *Death of a Bride* (1945), a stand-alone. (Douglas Cole's *Disgace to the College*, is a very short novel, but longer than a novella.) The first—and most definitely the best—of the Coles' short story collections is *Superintendent Wilson's Holiday* (1928), which contains eight long stories, all with Superintendent Wilson, four of which likely were written by Douglas and four by Margaret.

The tales that Douglas likely authored are the title story, "In a Telephone Cabinet," "The Oxford Mystery," and "The Camden Town Fire." Each is first-rate, with the top honors going to "In a Telephone Cabinet," which was justly included in the classic Ellery Queen anthology *101 Years' Entertainment: The Great Detective Stories 1841-1941*; its murder is truly original. "Superintendent Wilson's Holiday" concerns a man found murdered on a beach and involves analysis of shoeprint trails (a map is included). Both these tales feature Michael Prendergast, but he is absent from the remaining two stories likely authored by Douglas, as well as all four likely authored by Margaret (the female Cole apparently never took to Wilson's best friend). The third of the likely Douglas Cole tales, "The Camden Town Fire," is a clever story that concerns what appears to be a case of arson and insurance fraud that resulted in death; while the fourth, "The Oxford Mystery," about the strangling of an Oxford student, has Cole for the first time in his crime fiction taking readers to a murder committed within an academic milieu.

"The Oxford Mystery," which revolves around the question of the reliability of eyewitness perception, has the most interesting sociopolitical content of the Douglas Cole tales in *Superintendent Wilson's Holiday*, for it delves into the matter of racial prejudice against Indians. When an Oxford student is found "strangled by means of a fine chord drawn tightly round his neck," suspicion falls on his "closest friend," a half-Indian named Laj Russell, particularly after an eyewitness places a "nigger" at the scene of the crime. Throughout the story, Cole puts the word "nigger" in quotation marks when speaking in the authorial voice or quoting non-bigoted characters who dislike the epithet. Only when those who are obviously ignorant and bigoted use the word are quotation marks deleted. Superior people like Wilson make it clear that they do not approve of such a word, even when they find it necessary to state it. "What surprised me," says Wilson to the witness, "was your saying the man was a 'nigger,' as you call him"; while the now nettled witness angrily replies, "See here, mister, what are you gettin' at? Ain't I saying he was a nigger, and ain't he a bloomin' nigger? What more d'ye want?" Even an Oxford professor of ancient history blandly observes that "half breeds" are "nearly always moral degenerates."[102] Of course the bigots are proven wrong and the murderer does not turn out to be Laj Russell, who proves for his part to be a quite decent young man.

A couple of the likely Margaret Cole stories in *Holiday* have, like Douglas' "The Oxford Mystery," strong social and political content. In "The International Socialist," about the fatal shooting of a Continental European socialist politician at a London conference, the character Tony Redfern (who also appears the next year in Margaret Cole's *Poison in the Garden Suburb*, 1929, and in her *Greek Tragedy*, 1939), twice refers to "dagoes" when speaking of attendees at a socialist conference, but he is portrayed as an ingenuous, politically unaware young man, in contrast to his informed, leftist pal, Dick Warren. Even the ideologically slumbering Tony awakens later in the story when down-on-his-luck working man J. D. Evans—"a hollow-cheeked, dark-eyed little Welshman, whose face and clothes, to Dick's more practised eye, spelt unemployment and long-continued unemployment"—is implicated in the murder. Asked by Tony whether Evans is "a decent sort of

---

[102] G. D. H. and Margaret Cole, *Superintendent Wilson's Holiday* (New York: Payson & Clarke), 1929), 187, 204, 208.

lad" (the use of the term of masculine endearment "lad" signifies that Tony already is feeling warmly disposed toward the miner), Dick describes the Welshman in terms clearly marking him as an individual deserving of reader sympathy: "[He's] a bit grumpy at times, as you saw . . . got plenty of excuse, poor chap. He's a miner from South Wales; his wife died during the lock-out and left him with a family of kids, and he's been out of work ever since. I don't know how he manages to live, but he does, and works like a nigger for the Party, too." In a Coles story, such a paragon cannot be guilty of murder; and, much to Tony's relief, Evans' lack of forthrightness about his whereabouts during the commission of the murder is easily explained away by Superintendent Wilson:

> "Evans," said Wilson, ". . . committed a crime in his own eyes, but not quite the crime of which you suspected him. He left his spot [at the conference] for a short while during the afternoon . . . and it was during his absence that [—] got in. . . . I understand," he said to Dick, "that your people's discipline is pretty strict, and he was afraid of losing his conference allowance, which, as you know, he couldn't afford to do."
> "I say, poor devil," said Tony repentantly. "And there was I thinking he'd committed murder at least. I am a rotten fool."[103]

Tony learns his lesson for doubting the integrity of a politically conscious member of Britain's working class, and all ends happily.

Another likely Margaret Cole story, "The Robbery at Bowden," is set in a north England industrial town in 1924 (before, we are pointedly informed, "the black depression of unemployment had overtaken the district"). Wilson, we learn as the story opens, "had seldom seen so wholly dismal or so dirty a place. From his window, over the roofs of the low houses opposite, was visible the

---

[103] Coles, *Holiday*, 111, 113, 122.

wheel of the nearest shaft belonging to the great colliery which practically owned the town and the lives of the few thousand inhabitants; the reek of coal dust was in the air; and the very money which changed hands in the town was blacker than any Wilson had seen elsewhere in England." When his niece's husband, who works as a cashier for the Bowden Colliery Company, is arrested and charged with theft of the payroll and assault on the manager, Wilson, a private detective in this story, is forced to prolong his visit to try and exonerate the young man, which of course he does. In the course of his investigation, Wilson learns that the manager, Mr. Franks, is a "skinflint and a nigger-driver, spiteful and a bully"; and when he fails to recover the stolen money along with the true culprit, he is untroubled: "An organization that employs Mr. Franks, and gives him carte blanche to sweat his clerks as much as he likes, should be able to look after itself—without any help from me."[104]

Of the two likely Margaret Cole stories without overt political content, by far the better one is "The Missing Baronet" ("The Disappearance of Philip Mansfield," about the search for a missing actor, is the only weak tale in *Holiday*). At thirty-nine pages the second-longest likely Margaret Cole story in the collection, "The Missing Baronet" offers ample clues and ratiocination by Wilson in the vexing case of a vanished baronet. As in Margaret's slightly earlier novel, *The Murder at Crome House*, a photograph plays a significant role in the affair.

Altogether *Superintendent Wilson's Holiday* is, with such works as Agatha Christie's *The Thirteen Problems* (1931) and Dorothy L. Sayers' *Lord Peter Views the Body* (1928), one of the better Golden Age English detective short story collections and deserves reprinting. The Coles' second book of short mystery fiction, *A Lesson in Crime* (1933), is markedly inferior, although

---

[104] Cole, Holiday, 151, 176, 186. The term "nigger-driver" seems to be peculiar to Margaret Cole, as opposed to her husband, a point leading me to conclude that "The Robbery at Bowden" was authored by Margaret Cole. See Margaret Cole's *Dead Man's Watch*, where a character, facetiously named Mrs. Cole, is referred to as "a nigger-driver and an old miser." Coles, *Watch*, 122.

the title tale is perhaps the most inspired piece of short fiction the Coles ever wrote and another story, "The Mother of the Detective," merits notice as well. Both these stories likely were written by Margaret Cole (it is my view that of the eleven tales in the collection, six—all with Wilson and Michael Prendergast—were written by Douglas Cole and five—two with Wilson, albeit solo—were written by Margaret).

The title story, "A Lesson in Crime," soars on the wings of satire, being a splendidly nasty little stiletto planted in the back of the famously best-selling and incredibly prolific English thriller writer Edgar Wallace, at this time the most popular writer in England and one of the most popular writers in the world. The story opens with Joseph Newton, an Edgar Wallace proxy, traveling in a railway carriage on his way to his "pleasant little seaside cottage with twenty-seven bedrooms." Newton is reading one of his stories in a magazine. Thinking the tale "poor stuff," he makes a mental note to ascertain which of his ghost writers actually produced it, so he can have the man sacked. Another man enters the carriage, a little, elderly fellow, eccentrically dressed. Despite his unprepossessing appearance, he is "certainly a gentleman," possibly "an exceptionally absent-minded professor." Newton pays no attention to the insignificant little person, until the man suddenly begins speaking, "in a quiet, positive voice, as of one used to telling idiots what idiots they were." "Talking of murders," the man abruptly begins, "you have really no right to be so careless." He then begins to lecture Newton about the slipshod, unrealistic quality of his thriller fiction. "Really, in your last book, you have exceeded the limit," the little man declares, before proceeding to detail Newton's manifest literary crimes:

> "You call the heroine Elinor and Gertrude on different pages. You cannot make up your mind whether her name was Robbins with two *b*'s or with one. You have killed the corpse in one place on Sunday and in another on Monday evening. The corpse was discovered twelve hours after the murder still wallowing

in a pool of wet blood. The coroner committed no fewer than seventeen irregularities in conducting the inquest; and, finally, you have introduced three gangs, a mysterious Chinaman, an unknown poison that leaves no trace and a secret society of international Jews high up in the political world."[105]

The little man explains to Newton that what is really needed is not another such volume of sensationalistic dreck, but a book with "a perfectly simple murder, followed by a perfectly simple solution." He proceeds to give Newton a personal demonstration of his lesson in crime, first offering Newton an opium-laced cigarette, then strangling the thriller writer with a rug-strap before finishing off the job by "placing a pillow firmly on [Newton's] upturned face" and sitting on it, "smiling delightedly," until Newton's death gurgles cease. "Really, Mr. Newton," the madman tells Newton's corpse, "murder is even easier than I supposed—though it is not so often, I imagine, that a lucky chance enables one to do a service to the literary craft at the same time." The rest of the story deals with Superintendent Wilson's eventual apprehension of the mad murderer, who very properly ends up in an insane asylum. There he occupies himself complaining that the authorities will not let him have any new Joseph Newton thrillers to read, in order to ascertain whether Newton "has benefited by his lesson in practical criminology."[106]

"A Lesson in Crime," a criminal fantasy in which the egregiously successful Edgar Wallace is symbolically—and nastily—murdered, gives readers a fascinating look at the aesthetic standards of the British detective fiction intelligentsia at this time. There is no doubt that the victim indeed is intended to represent Wallace, by far the best-selling mystery writer in Britain through the 1920s right up until his death in 1932 (of natural causes, one should hasten to

---

[105] G. D. H. and Margaret Cole, *A Lesson in Crime and Other Stories* (London: Collins, 1933), 10, 12, 14.
[106] Coles, *Lesson*, 15, 17, 27.

add). The reference to Newton's huge sales and palatial living (the "cottage' with twenty-seven bedrooms) and the claim that his early "Indian stories . . . were the best things he had ever done," as well as the accusations that Newton found it necessary to employ ghosts to maintain such a prolific output, that he made such slipshod errors in his books as calling a novel's heroine by two different names and that he endorsed a cigarette brand that he personally had never smoked—all these mimic details from the life of Edgar Wallace. "A Lesson in Crime" suggests the contempt and, it might be suggested as well, jealously that the higher-browed detective fiction writers had in respect to the great (and great selling) thriller writer. In 1930, the Coles, along with the other leading lights of British detective fiction, would take an oath to forego, among other things, the devices Newton stood accused of using in "A Lesson in Crime": mysterious Chinamen, international gangs and undetectable poisons. Such devices were considered unworthy of a higher detective novelist trying to appeal to the ratiocinative centers of the brain, however much they might appeal to the presumably lower-browed, sensation-seeking readers who avidly read Wallace's books. "A Lesson in Crime" crystallizes this attitude wonderfully. When the interloper in the carriage chides Newton that "if you expect intelligent people to read your stories, you might at least trouble to make them plausible," Newton thinks to himself complacently: "he had far too large a circulation among fools to bother about what intelligent people thought."[107] In teaching Newton the ultimate lesson in crime, the diminutive, professorial man strikes a blow for higher intelligence, exemplified by writers and readers of truly ratiocinative detective novels.

The other noteworthy story in the collection is "The Mother of the Detective," a tale by Margaret Cole in which a little old lady (reminiscent of Agatha Christie's Miss Marple and Patricia Wentworth's Miss Silver, though more dithery) uses her knowledge of domestic detail and the ways of servants to foil a crime that had

---

[107] Ibid., 13.

befuddled her own son, James Warrender, a well-known private detective. In the space of a mere eight pages, Margaret Cole manages to get in a bit of satire, having Mrs. Warrender demur from her son James' claim that "servants with a little more intelligence" are needed: "I don't think one really wants servants to be *too* clever, does one? They get such curious ideas."[108] The story is a stand-alone delight, though Margaret Cole later in the 'thirties expanded the conceit into a generally weak series of lengthy Mrs. Warrender tales, collected in book form under the title *Mrs. Warrender's Profession* (see below); she also, as already discussed, authored a single Mrs. Warrender detective novel, *Knife in the Dark* (1941).

The Coles' final short story collection, *Wilson and Some Others* (1940), includes thirteen short stories, seven with Wilson—two of these with Prendergast—and six non-series. (My guess is that Douglas wrote five of the Wilson tales and two of the non-series tales, Margaret two of the Wilson tales and four of the non-series tales.) Of the seven Wilson tales, three in my view have merit, two of them, the longest tales in the collection, "Death in the Tankard" and "Murder in Church," likely authored by Douglas and one, the shortish "Glass," probably written by Margaret.

"Glass" is particularly pleasing in its adept clue placement and memorable evocation—perhaps inspired by the disinheritance of Margaret Cole by her conservative father after her marriage to Douglas—of a classic situation in Golden Age novels, that of the miserly, ancient and spiteful Victorian-era relative provoking his or her long-antagonized heir to criminal thoughts:

> [The room] was high and square and ugly, papered with a yellow flock paper with a pattern of enormous, impossible brown poppies, and filled with heavy and shabby Victorian furniture which was hardly ever dusted, much less polished. It was dark, too, but darker than it need have been, for though the main

---

[108] Ibid., 226.

windows faced south-east and a brilliant April sun should have been streaming in, its passage was impeded by queer bits of glass, colored, dark, bottle-green and clouded, with which the small panes were filled. It was old James's fancy to have very little clear glass in his window.... Young James's eye followed, as it had followed many times before, the curious spots and streaks and pools of light which this window let through, to a single blood-red shaft falling upon his uncle's hands as they fondled that precious stamp collection which he knew now would never be his; and he thought, not for the first time, that old James resembled nothing so much as a miserly alchemist of the Middle Ages, gloating in semi-darkness over his evil gains. God! If he had only a little of that obscene old creature's money for his own....[109]

Also quite fine are the much longer Wilson stories "Death in the Tankard" and "Murder in Church." In the nicely-clued "Death in the Tankard," which originally appeared in *The First Class Omnibus* (Hodder & Stoughton, 1934), Wilson happens to be on the scene at the public house The Two Chairmen in the town of Bleaford, Gloucestershire, when a man dies from strychnine poisoning, after having loudly complained of his cider's bitter taste. In "Murder in Church," set in "the rustic village of Wilstone, on the Welsh border beyond Clun," Wilson and his invariable travelling companion, Michael Prendergast, encounter a spectacularly bizarre death when a Christian anarchist minister, in the midst of

---

[109] G. D. H. and Margaret Cole, *Wilson and Some Others* (London: Collins, 1940). Recalls Margaret Cole in her fascinating personal memoir, *Growing Up Into Revolution* (London: Longmans, Green, 1949): "[A]fter a single meeting [with Douglas] and an ideological correspondence in which I think he got distinctly the worse of it, [my father] severed relations, and refused to let my mother stay in our house, though he allowed me and my children into his.... [H]e also turned out his eldest son [Raymond Postgate, a socialist, World War One conscientious objector and infrequent crime novelist], and later disinherited both of us." Cole *Revolution*, 77, n. 1.

# THE SPECTRUM OF ENGLISH MURDER

delivering a fiery sermon, is crushed under a falling pulpit hood before their very eyes:

> ... there was a loud cracking sound, and then a second, following hard upon it. Even as the congregation was leaping to its feet by a common impulse, came a resounding crash, as the great metal canopy over the pulpit fell hurtling down and settled over the top of the pulpit itself like a giant candle-extinguisher. A moment before, the rector had been standing bolt upright, denouncing with outstretched arms the sin of those who would not busy themselves about the Lord's work. But now, in an instant, he had been snuffed out....[110]

The six "others" tales in *Wilson and Some Others* are, with one exception, forgettable trifles, rather tiresomely facetious. ("A Present from the Empire," it should be noted, takes place in Douglas Cole's imaginary British African colony of Malaria, once governed by a Blatchington; but it is a poor tale.) The exception is "Ye Olde Englysshe Christmasse; or, Detection in the Eighteenth Century," an acerbic crime story, very likely authored by Douglas Cole, concerning jewel theft during 1788 Christmas Eve festivities at Eslington Hall, the country mansion of the haughty Sir John Newcastle. (The story was later reprinted under the distinctly less original title "Crime at Eslington Hall.") The tale, which reflects Cole's interest in eighteenth-century English history and his scorn for aristocratic privilege (see, for example, his 1924 biography of the political reformer William Cobbett), is an early example of the historical mystery sub-genre, now of course quite common but still rarely found in crime fiction of the 1930s, as well as, of course, a Christmas mystery. One of the tale's sympathetically-treated characters is a village cobbler, a partisan of the radical English politician John Wilkes (1725-1797), as this passage indicates:

---

[110] Coles, *Wilson*, 57.

"We common folk has our rights, same like others, and we holds, if so be there should be a search, 'tis only proper the gentry should be searched as well as us."

"What!" exclaimed Sir John, in a voice of thunder. "Despicable wretch! Have you the temerity to hint that the members of my family are not above suspicion?"

"What's fair to one is fair to all," said the cobbler doggedly.

"A thoroughly immoral and subversive doctrine," said Sir John. "I never thought to have heard such villainous sentiments uttered upon my estate."[111]

Also worth noting is the final Cole crime tale collected in book form, "Birthday Gifts" (first published in May 1946 in the booklet *Birthday Gifts and Other Stories*, where it is the only piece in the collection that had not been previously published).[112] It too was likely authored by Douglas Cole. This well-written and intriguingly-plotted story sees Wilson back in the 1920s as a private detective, stopping for a couple days' relaxation at a Lake District inn after concluding a routine case and finding himself once again coincidentally in at a kill, this time the late-night bedroom coal gassing of a classically tyrannical, querulous, will-altering old man. The solution, like that of "In a Telephone Cabinet," is reminiscent of the clever works of R. Austin Freeman and John Street.

There are at least two published uncollected Coles short stories, one of which, "Bring Me an Axe and Spade," was one of the last pieces of mystery fiction that the Coles wrote. The story was published in *Lilliput* in March 1945. Its title is drawn from the last stanza of William Blake's "Song: My silks and fine array," a poem first published in Blake's *Poetical Sketches* (1783):

---

[111] Coles, *Wilson*, 236.

[112] The jacket flap blurb claims that "Birthday Gifts" was "specially written" for the booklet, but the story is rather reminiscent of 1920s Coles stories, suggesting to me that it may have been written earlier, though for some reason never previously published.

> Bring me an axe and spade,
>   Bring me a winding sheet;
> When I my grave have made,
>   Let winds and tempests beat;
> Then down I'll lie, as cold as clay.
> True love doth pass away!

Perhaps the Coles' shortest crime story, "Bring Me an Axe and Spade" details a murder that takes place in a prison convict work gang, while the gang is out on labor detail, under the supervision of a warder, John Masters. While Masters' attention is momentarily distracted, one of the convicts is savagely impaled with a pickaxe by another convict—but which one? Masters makes some quick deductions, but is only able to solve the crime due to a fortuitous circumstance. With its unique setting and ironic resolution, "Bring Me an Axe and Spade" is a worthy edition to the Coles' corpus of short crime fiction. The story may have been authored by Douglas Cole, as the next year he edited Nonesuch Press' Centenary Edition of William Blake's works. On the other hand, both Coles are credited with editing a collection of William Blake poetry back in 1927.

The Coles also published five detective novellas, the first four concerning the exploits of Margaret Cole's elderly amateur sleuth, Mrs. Warrender, and the last, *Death of a Bride*, a standalone, also likely authored by Margaret Cole. *Death of a Bride* was published in January 1945, shortly before the appearance in *Lilliput* of "Bring Me an Axe and Spade." In that issue it was stated that "because of pressure of war work [the Coles] have had very little time for some years for writing detective stories. But they have just managed a 25,000-word short novel, *Death of a Bride*, which will be out soon [in fact it actually had already appeared]."[113] Set in peacetime Bath, *Death of a Bride* concerns the mysterious poisoning death of Anna Bredon, one of those classic middle-aged spinsters of the period who rashly marries a handsome, designing younger man of indeterminate social origin. Told in three parts by a nosy, priggish bachelor neighbor, the gigolo widower's winningly self-aware first

---

[113] *Lilliput* 16 (March 1945): 252.

wife and the investigating private detective, *Death of a Bride* is one of the Coles' best tales, being both amusingly narrated and well-plotted.

Indeed, *Death of a Bride* is far superior to three of the four Mrs. Warrender novellas, all of which were collected, along with the short "The Mother of the Detective," in the book *Mrs. Warrender's Profession* (1938), the title of which alludes, for some reason, to George Bernard Shaw's once highly controversial play about prostitution. By far the best of the Mrs. Warrender novellas is "The Toys of Death," which was published separately under this same title in 1948. (Several decades later it also was included in Academy Chicago's *Women Sleuths* anthology, edited by Bill Pronzini and Martin H. Greenberg.) "The Toys of Death" takes Mrs. Warrender and her detective son, James, on a vacation to a southwestern coastal town presided over in season by an egocentric "great novelist," the marvelously named Crampton Pleydell. Mrs. Warrender, who makes acquaintance with Pleydell and his circle, soon discerns that the author is an exploitative emotional vampire, feeding off ingenuous and vulnerable admirers (female and male), draining them of what he can take and then casting them aside, like sucked oranges. When Pleydell is found dead in his study of cyanide poisoning, there are several suspects, but the ever-observant Mrs. Warrender discovers the truth. Along the way, she manages as well to set true love on its right course, mending the affair of a plucky young woman and her neurotic male friend (we have seen such couples before in Margaret Cole's *Poison in the Garden Suburb* and *Dead Man's Watch*). The means of murder proves especially intriguing and the story has, like the Mrs. Warrender detective novel *Knife in the Dark* (1941), an unexpected emotional resonance, dabbling with darker matter that we tend to associate today with such modern Crime Queens as P. D. James and Ruth Rendell.

### Conclusion

Despite occasional forays toward more realistic crime fiction, the Coles in their aesthetic views of the detective story tended towards traditionalism, as we can see from the critical commentaries on the subject by Margaret Cole. While her husband appears to have remained silent on the subject, Margaret Cole sometimes expressed in her writings—see her 1949 memoir of her life, her 1971 biography of her husband, her 1935 essay on Superintendent Wilson in the collection *Meet the Detective* and her book reviews in the *Daily Herald* in 1935 and 1936 and in the *Spectator* in 1931—what generally can be taken as the couple's opinions on the aesthetics of detective fiction. As articulated by Margaret Cole, the crime-writing couple firmly viewed detective fiction as a craft, with "a definite technique which can be learned point by point." In their view, the author's attention in a detective novel should focus first on plot. However, they deplored, as Margaret Cole put it in a review of a Freeman Wills Crofts mystery, pure puzzle novels in which the characters were no more than "simple structures provided only with name-labels and impregnable alibis." Detective novel characters, Margaret Cole insisted, "must have *verisimilitude* sufficient to hold the reader's attention." Yet the Coles drew a line at detective novels that attempted to be more straight novels than mysteries. Characters must not develop "the realism which would cause them to tear the carefully-made plot to pieces," Cole added, noting that inventing such "nicely balanced" characters—real but not too real—was a pleasing exercise for writers like herself and her husband, who both enjoyed a good tale but lacked "the creative gifts of your born novelist."[114]

Margaret Cole had made her preferences clear fourteen years earlier in "Meet Superintendent Wilson," when she cataloged the different types of detective novels or, to be more precise, the diverse types of tales lumped into that category. First there were "thrillers," stories "full of crimes and gangs and secret treaties and unknown poisons." Cole clearly did not think much of that sort of story, declaring that readers of such tales "don't mind whether the plot makes sense or not." Then there were "mathematical or scientific novels" (clearly those of R. Austin Freeman, Freeman Wills Crofts, J. J. Connington and John Rhode), "with elaborately worked out clues and no characters worth speaking of." Cole obviously did not think so much of those either. Next there was the

---

[114] Margaret Cole, *Revolution*, 179, 180; *Spectator* 146 (May 1931), 746.

"psychological novel," all about the murderer's "complexes." "Personally," avowed Cole bluntly, "I hate that sort of story." Finally, Cole listed the story type she obviously preferred, namely the "straightforward" tale, "where the interest is mainly in the plot and the characters taken together."[115]

In her detective fiction reviews, Cole never mustered enthusiasm for puzzle makers like Crofts or Street, but at the same time she was careful to note the distinction between the structure of what would today be called a crime novel and that of a detective novel. Maria Belloc Lowndes' *The Chianti Flask*, for example, Cole found to be "a good story, though there is no detection in it at all." Crime novels seeking to appeal too strenuously to the reader's emotions met with her disapproval. In her detective novel *Death in the Quarry*, Margaret Cole asserted that, presumably like herself, "the average educated reader of detective novels . . . liked a bit of excitement and a bit of a puzzle; but he did not want his imagination forcibly stirred" by such things as child murders "or the presence of insane, sadistic cruelty." As she explained in her 1935 essay, what she preferred most in her mystery fiction reading were those "straightforward" tales where a rationalistic puzzle plot and colorful character interest were evenly intertwined. By far her most enthusiastic book review went to Nicholas Blake's *A Question of Proof*, a book she found to be of this type. Cole deemed *Proof* to be "a real story" that repaid "reading twice over, which is high praise." She congratulated Blake's publisher, England's great Collins Crime Club, on finding a new writer "who can write," perhaps suggesting that in her own mind she contrasted Blake with certain other writers in Collins' vast stable, one which included at this time Agatha Christie, Freeman Wills Crofts and John Rhode (and even the Coles).[116]

Reflecting the Coles' traditionalist aesthetic view of the mystery genre, in Collins' 1953 reissue of Wilkie Collins' *The Moonstone*,

---

[115] Cole, "Wilson," 116, 117.

[116] *London Daily Herald*, 17 March 1935, 15; G.D. H. and M. Cole, *Death in the Quarry* (1934; rpnt., New York: Caxton House, 1939), 52.

famously described by T. S. Eliot as "the first, the longest and the best of modern English detective novels," there is an introduction, credited to both Coles but probably by Margaret, wherein Dorothy L. Sayers is taken to task for pronouncing that "*The Moonstone* is probably the finest detective novel ever written." The Coles dissent not from the judgment that *The Moonstone* is a fine novel, but from the judgment that *The Moonstone* is a *detective novel*:

> There are, of course, elements in *The Moonstone* which have since become classic detective-story components.... There is the very stupid policeman, in this case Superintendent Seagrave, who is a worthy ancestor of Lestrade, Inspector Japp, and of all the police officers whom Dr. Thorndyke bewildered in his day. There is the crime brought home, after suspicion has been well distributed, to "the most unlikely persons".... There are some clues, notably the paint-stained nightgown, though the paint-stained nightgown does not solve the mystery; it is, in fact, not much more use to Sergeant Cuff than a blood-stained nightgown was to that unfortunate Detective Whicher whom some suppose to have been the real model for the Sergeant (The Constance Kent case, as a matter of fact, except for the incident of the nightgown, bears practically no resemblance to the plot of *The Moonstone*.) Finally, there is the clear attempt to build up Sergeant Cuff into a "character," by stressing his peculiar physical appearance and his reiterated interest in the growing of roses. This might legitimately be regarded as a foreshadowing of the long array of detectives noted for personal idiosyncrasies....[117]

---

[117] GDH and Margaret Cole, Introduction to *The Moonstone* (1868; rpnt., London: Collins, 1953), 10, 11.

The Coles point out, however, that in *The Moonstone* "Sergeant Cuff, though doing in the course of the book, some pretty detection, was quite wrong in his conclusions, and did not solve the mystery in this, his first recorded case. . . . Poe's Dupin is a far more plausible prototype for the twentieth-century paladins [Great Detectives]. Sergeant Cuff is what his creator intended him to be, a character in his own right, a policeman playing his part in a story of real people with a mystery at its heart." In fact, there were many Victorian novels, including *The Moonstone*, that

> had a mystery (often involving a policeman) as their main or subsidiary plot. . . . But these crimes and punishments happened to real characters. . . . The characters were not subordinated and compelled to dance around the exigencies of a plot which demands a body in a country-house library, a number of residents guests and servants each with their own discreditable and penetrable motives for murder, a paraphernalia of scientific instruments of detection, and a veneer of literary erudition to cover up any lack of human interest. . . . As counterbalance, of course, the Victorian novels tend to lack the puzzle fascination. . . .[118]

As I hope this chapter has made sufficiently clear, Douglas and Margaret Cole should not be seen as members of the "Humdrum school of detection," though neither should they be viewed as innovators in the sense that were, for example, Henry Wade, Dorothy L. Sayers, Ngaio Marsh, Margery Allingham, Anthony Berkeley Cox, and Nicholas Blake. The husband and wife generally had not the Humdrums' surpassing patience and impressive technique for careful and complex plot construction (Margaret Cole's *Counterpoint Murder* is the most notable exception to this rule concerning the Coles' novels), yet they mostly shied from

---

[118] Coles, Introduction, 11, 12.

attempting detective novels that were overly "realistic," serious or psychological.[119] Margaret Cole wrote that in comparison with her and Douglas' scholarly tomes on economics, politics and history their mysteries were easy to write, because they did not necessitate undertaking any research; and, in truth, it is evident that most of the Coles' detective fiction lacks the finish and polish of the work of other prominent names of the period. In short, it is simply not as *memorable*. Certain settings from genre classics linger long in the imagination of readers: the rattling trains in *Murder on the Orient Express* and *Sir John Magill's Last Journey*; the postcard villages of Fenchurch St. Paul and St. Mary Mead in *The Nine Tailors* and *The Murder at the Vicarage*; the publishing house in *Flowers for the Judge* and the dress salon in *Death in High Heels*; the secular and convent schools in *A Question of Proof* and *St. Peter's Finger*; the haunted landscapes in *The Three Coffins* and *The Burning Court*; the London street shops in *The Murders in Praed Street* and the sophisticated flat in *Surfeit of Lampreys*; the tangled woods in *Diabolic Candelabra* and the tidal flats in *Mist on the Saltings*. The Coles' books fail to make the impression these works do, in part because the Coles only rarely achieve strong authenticity of detail.

Oddly, Margaret Cole does not highlight in her critical writings what seems to me clearly to have been the pair's greatest contribution to the genre, evident in many of their best novels, such as *The Death of a Millionaire*, *The Blachington Tangle*, *Burglars in Bucks*, *Scandal at School* and *The Brothers Sackville*: their satirical humor. As with the works of Michael Innes, the best of the Coles' books are donnish delights full of quirky situations and humor, albeit with a socialistic slant. The Coles wrote some of

---

[119] "He had only the interest of an amateur in crime and of a dilettante amateur at that," writes Margaret Cole of Everard Blatchington in *Death in the Quarry*. "He would never have gone through one-tenth of the routine labour necessary to solve an entire case. But he did enjoy, from time to time, a puzzle on a small scale." Coles, *Quarry*, 75. This description of Everard Blatchington as an amateur detective might well be applied to the Coles as detective novelists.

the most amusing mystery fiction of the British Golden Age, an accomplishment for which they deserve some remembrance.

Also deserving remembrance is a point continually stressed in this chapter, namely the unique social and political content of the Coles' detective fiction. That the detective fiction of the British Golden Age was uniformly conservative and that the Coles never dealt with "social realities" in their mystery tales simply is not true, as I hope I have demonstrated. The Coles may not have wanted their detective fiction to be strictly "realistic," but at the same time, it was hardly likely that the pair could have entirely insulated their lighter works from such an essential part of their very being as their socialist political ideology; and they clearly did not do so.

I grant that although the Coles, unlike many of their Golden Age contemporaries, evinced great empathy in their detective fiction for the industrial worker, their tales nevertheless reflect the privileged class from which they themselves came, being told and experienced almost exclusively through educated middle or upper class characters. With the partial exception of *Murder at the Munition Works*, one gets stronger depictions of members of Britain's manual laboring class in the works of John Street, no friend of socialists or communists, but someone who had direct knowledge of the working class from his time spent in the army and as an electrical engineer, as well as from the daily visits to the pub that he devoutly observed with an almost religious fidelity. Allusions are made in the Coles' novels to topical labor issues and sources of social stress in those troubled days, but we never really feel the visceral pain or anger of the working class, which likely is what Julian Symons meant when he faulted the Coles for not taking the social realities of the time *seriously*. Still, it strikes me as unjust of critics not to credit the Coles with what they did do for the genre, which was to provide readers with some witty, well-written mysteries that occasionally tartly reminded a readership perhaps tending toward social and political complacency that not all was rosy in the garden of England.

# APPENDIX I

## Crime Genre Works by Henry Lancelot Aubrey-Fletcher

Novels
1. *The Verdict of You All* (1926)
2. *The Missing Partners* (1928)
3. *The Duke of York's Steps* (1929) (John Poole)
4. *The Dying Alderman* (1930) (Herbert Lott)
5. *No Friendly Drop* (1931) (Poole)
6. *The Hanging Captain* (1932) (Lott)
7. *Mist on the Saltings* (1933)
8. *Constable, Guard Thyself!* (1934) (Poole)
9. *Heir Presumptive* (1935)
10. *Bury Him Darkly* (1936) (Poole)
11. *The High Sheriff* (1937)
12. *Released for Death* (1938)
13. *Lonely Magdalen* (1940) (Poole)
14. *New Graves at Great Norne* (1947)
15. *Diplomat's Folly* (1951)
16. *Be Kind to the Killer* (1952)
17. *Too Soon to Die* (1953) (Poole)
18. *Gold Was Our Grave* (1954) (Poole)
19. *A Dying Fall* (1955)
20. *The Litmore Snatch* (1957)

SHORT STORY COLLECTIONS
*Policeman's Lot* (1933)
1. "Duello" (Poole)
2. "The Missing Undergraduate" (Poole)
3. "Wind in the East" (Poole)
4. "The Sub-Branch" (Poole)
5. "The Real Thing" (Poole)
6. "The Baronet's Finger" (Poole)
7. "The Three Keys" (Poole)
8. "A Matter of Luck"
9. "Four to One—Bar One"
10. "Payment in Full"
11. "Jealous Gun"
12. "The Amateurs"
13. "The Tenth Round"

*Here Comes the Copper* (1938) (all John Bragg)
1. "These Artists!"
2. "The Seagull"
3. "The Ham Sandwich"
4. "Summer Meeting"
5. "Anti-Tank"
6. "A Puff of Smoke"
7. "Steam Coal"
8. "Toll of the Road"
9. "November Night"
10. "The Little Sportsman"
11. "Lodgers"
12. "One Good Turn"
13. "Smash and Grab"

UNCOLLECTED SHORT STORIES
1. "Cotton-Wool and Cutlets" (1940) (Bragg)

# APPENDIX II

## Crime Genre Works by G. D. H. and Margaret Cole

Probable authorship of each work, in my estimation, is indicated either "DC" for Douglas Cole or "MC" for Margaret Cole.

Novels

1. *The Brooklyn Murders* (DC) (1923) (Henry Wilson)
2. *The Death of a Millionaire* (DC) (1925) (Wilson)
3. *The Blatchington Tangle* (DC) (1926) (Wilson, Everard Blatchington)
4. *The Murder at Crome House* (MC) (1927) (non-series)
5. *The Man from the River* (DC) (1928) (Wilson, Michael Prendergast)
6. *Poison in the Garden Suburb* (MC) (1929) (Wilson, Tony and Lydia Redford)
7. *Burglars in Bucks* (MC) (1930) (Wilson, Blatchington)
8. *Corpse in Canonicals* (DC) (1930) (Hubert and Emily Welsh)
9. *The Great Southern Mystery* (DC) (1931) (Wilson)
10. *Dead Man's Watch* (1931) (MC) (Wilson, Sir Charles Wylie)
11. *Death of a Star* (1932) (MC) (Inspector Walling, Blatchington)
12. *The Affair at Aliquid* (1933) (DC) (non-series)
13. *End of an Ancient Mariner* (1933) (DC) (Wilson, Welshes)
14. *Death in the Quarry* (1934) (MC) (Wilson, Blatchington)
15. *Big Business Murder* (1935) (DC) (Wilson)
16. *Dr. Tancred Begins* (1935) (DC) (Wilson, Dr. Benjamin Tancred)

17. *Scandal at School* (1935) (MC) (Blatchington)
18. *Last Will and Testament* (1936) (DC) (Wilson, Tancred)
19. *The Brothers Sackville* (1936) (DC) (Wilson, Tom Fairford)
20. *Disgrace to the College* (1937) (DC) (Blatchington)
21. *The Missing Aunt* (1937) (DC) (Wilson, Prendergast)
22. *Off with Her Head!* (1938) (DC) (Wilson, Fairford)
23. *Double Blackmail* (1939) (DC) (Wilson)
24. *Greek Tragedy* (1939) (MC) (Wilson, Redfords)
25. *Murder at the Munition Works* (1940) (DC) (Wilson)
26. *Counterpoint Murder* (1940) (MC) (Wilson)
27. *Knife in the Dark* (1941) (MC) (Mrs. Warrender)
28. *Toper's End* (1942) (DC) (Wilson, Prendergast, Welshes)

SHORT STORY COLLECTIONS
*Superintendent Wilson's Holiday* (1928)
1. "In a Telephone Cabinet" (DC) (Wilson, Prendergast)
2. "Superintendent Wilson's Holiday" (DC) (Wilson, Prendergast)
3. "The International Socialist" (MC) (Wilson, Tony Redford)
4. "The Disappearance of Philip Mansfield" (MC) (Wilson)
4. "The Robbery at Bowden" (MC) (Wilson)
6. "The Oxford Mystery" (DC) (Wilson)
7. "The Camden Town Fire" (DC) (Wilson, Prendergast)
8. "The Missing Baronet" (MC) (Wilson)

*A Lesson in Crime* (1933)
1. "A Lesson in Crime" (Wilson) (MC)
2. "A Question of Coincidence" (DC) (Wilson, Prendergast)
3. "Mr. Stevens's Insurance Policy" (MC) (Wilson)
4. "Blackmail in the Village" (DC) (Wilson, Prendergast)
5. "The Cliff Path Ghost" (DC) (Wilson, Prendergast)
6. "Sixteen Years' Run" (DC) (Wilson, Prendergast)
7. "Wilson Calling" (DC) (Wilson, Prendergast)
8. "The Brentwardine Mystery" (DC) (Wilson, Prendergast)
9. "The Mother of the Detective" (MC) (Mrs. Warrender)
10. "A Dose of Cyanide" (MC)
11. "Superintendent Wakley's Mistake" (MC)

*Mrs. Warrender's Profession* (1938)
1. "Death in the Sun" (MC) (Warrender)
2. "The Toys of Death" (MC) (Warrender)
3. "Fatal Beauty" (MC) (Warrender)
4. "In Peril of His Life" (MC) (Warrender)

Also includes "The Mother of the Detective" (see *A Lesson in Crime*).

*Detection Medley* (1939) (collection of short pieces by the Detection Club)
1. "Too Clever by Half" (DC) (Tancred) (originally serialized in 1936, and expanded into the short novel *Disgrace to the College* the next year)

*Wilson and Some Others* (1940)
1. "Death in the Tankard" (DC) (Wilson)
2. "Murder in Church" (DC) (Wilson, Prendergast)
3. "The Bone of the Dinosaur" (MC) (Wilson)
4. "A Tale of Two Suitcases" (DC) (Wilson, Prendergast)
5. "The Motive" (MC) (Wilson)
6. "Glass" (MC) (Wilson)
7. "Murder in Broad Daylight" (DC) (Wilson)
8. "A Present from the Empire" (MC)
9. "Strychnine Tonic" (MC)
10. "The Letters" (DC)
11. "The Partner" (MC)
12. "The Strange Adventures of a Chocolate Box" (MC)
13. "Ye Olde Englysshe Christmasse; or, Detection in the Eighteenth Century" (DC)

*Birthday Gifts and Other Stories* (1946)
1. Birthday Gifts (DC) (Wilson)

Uncollected Short Stories
1. "Mr. Smith and the Co-op" (*The Christmas Cracker*, 1933) (not currently known whether this is crime fiction)

2. "Bring Me an Axe and Spade" (DC) (*Lilliput*, March 1945)

Novella
1. *Death of a Bride* (1945) (MC)

Essays on True Crime and Crime Fiction
1. "The Case of Adelaide Bartlett" (MC) (in *The Anatomy of Murder*, 1936)
2. "The Trial of Oscar Slater" (MC) (in *Great Unsolved Crimes*, 1938)
3. Introduction to *The Moonstone*, by Wilkie Collins (MC) (Collins reprint edition, 1953)

# BIBLIOGRAPHY

PRIMARY SOURCES

BOOKS, ARTICLES AND ESSAYS BY G. D. H. AND MARGARET COLE AND HENRY WADE (HENRY LANCELOT AUBREY-FLETCHER)

Cole, G. D. H. *The Brooklyn Murders*. 1923. Reprint. London: Collins, n.d.

Cole, G. D. H. and Margaret Cole. *The Affair at Aliquid*. London: Collins, 1933.

—. *Big Business Murder*. New York: Doubleday, Doran, 1935.

—. *The Blatchington Tangle*. New York: Macmillan, 1926.

—. *The Brothers Sackville*. New York: Macmillan, 1937.

—. *Burglars in Bucks*. London: Collins, 1930.

—. *Corpse in Canonicals*. 1930. Reprint. London: Collins, 1933.

—. *Counterpoint Murder*. London: Collins, 1940.

—. *Death in the Quarry*. 1934. Reprint. New York: Caxton House, 1939.

—. *Dead Man's Watch*. New York: Doubleday, Doran, 1931.

—. *Death of a Bride*. London: Vallancey: 1945.

—. *The Death of a Millionaire*. 1925. Reprint. London: Penguin, 1950.

—. *Death of a Star*. New York: Doubleday, Doran, 1932.

—. *Disgrace to the College*. London: Hodder and Stoughton, 1937.

—. *End of an Ancient Mariner*. London: Collins, 1933.

—. *The Great Southern Mystery*. London: Collins, 1931.

—. *Greek Tragedy*. New York: Macmillan, 1939.

—. Introduction to *The Moonstone* (1868). London: Collins, 1953.
—. *Knife in the Dark*. London: Collins, 1941.
—. *A Lesson in Crime and Other Stories*. London: Collins, 1933.
—. *The Missing Aunt*. New York: Macmillan, 1938.
—. *The Murder at Crome House*. New York, Macmillan, 1927.
—. *Murder at the Munition Works*. New York: Macmillan, 1940.
—. *Poison in the Garden Suburb*. London: Collins, 1929.
—. *Scandal at School*. London: Collins, 1935.
—. *Superintendent Wilson's Holiday*. New York: Payson & Clarke, 1929.
—. *Wilson and Some Others*. London: Collins, 1940.
Cole, Margaret. *Books and the People*. Day to Pay Pamphlets 38. London: Hogarth, 1938.
—. "The Case of Adelaide Bartlett." *The Anatomy of Murder*. 1936. American edition. New York: Macmillan, 1937.
—. *Growing up into Revolution*. London and New York: Longmans, 1949.
—. *The Life of G. D. H. Cole*. London: Macmillan, 1971.
—. "Meet Superintendent Wilson." *Meet the Detective*. Harrisburg, PA: Telegraph Press, 1935.
Wade, Henry. *Be Kind to the Killer*. 1952. Reprint. London: Howard Baker, 1970.
—. *Bury Him Darkly*. London: Constable, 1936.
—. *Constable, Guard Thyself!* 1934. Reprint. London: Hutchinson, 1971.
—. *Diplomat's Folly*. London: Constable, 1951.
—. *The Duke of York's Steps*. New York: Payson & Clarke, 1929.
—. *The Dying Alderman*. New York: Payson & Clarke, 1930.
—. *A Dying Fall*. London: Constable, 1955).
—. *Gold Was Our Grave*. New York: Macmillan, 1954.
—. *The Hanging Captain*. New York: Harcourt, Brace, 1933.
—. *Heir Presumptive*. London: Constable, 1935.
—. *Here Comes the Copper*. 1939. Reprint. London: Hutchinson, 1972
—. *The High Sheriff*. 1937. Reprint. London: Howard Baker, 1972.

—. *Lonely Magdalen*. 1940. Revised edition. London: Constable, 1946.

—. *The Litmore Snatch*. London: Constable, 1957.

—. *The Missing Partners*. London: Constable, 1928.

—. *Mist on the Saltings*. London: Constable, 1933.

—. *New Graves at Great Norne*. London: Constable, 1947.

—. *No Friendly Drop*. London: Constable, 1931.

—. *Policeman's Lot*. London: Constable, 1933.

—. *Released for Death*. 1938. Reprint. London: Howard Baker, 1970.

—. *Too Soon to Die*. 1953. Reprint. London: Howard Baker, 1970.

—. *The Verdict of You All*. 1926. American edition. New York: Payson & Clarke, 1927.

Articles, Books, Essays, Reviews and
Short Stories by Other Authors

Brand, Christianna. Introduction to *The Floating Admiral*. Boston: Gregg Press, 1979.

Crofts, Freeman Wills. "The Case of the Avaricious Moneylender." *Murderers Make Mistakes*. 1947. Reprint. London and New York: House of Stratus, 2000.

Hicklin, Susan. "Behind the Whodunits." *Picture Post* (9 August 1952). Pp. 40

Kaye, J. W. *Lives of Indian Officers*. Voulme I. London: W. H. Allen, 1889.

"Parishes, Chilton." *A History of the County of Buckinghamshire*. Volume 4. Edited by William Page. London: St. Catherine Press, 1927. Pp. 22-27.

Read, Herbert. "Blood Wet and Dry." *Night and Day* (23 December 1937). In *Pursuits and Verdicts*. Edinburgh: Tragara Press, 1983.

von Mises, Ludwig. "Laissez Faire or Dictatorship." *Plain Talk* 3 (January1949).

—. "Remarks about the Detective Stories." *The Anti-capitalist Mentality*. 1956. Reprint. Indianapolis: The Liberty Fund, 2006.

Williams, Charles. "Passionate Policemen!" *Westminster Gazette* (3 August 1934). In *The Detective Fiction Reviews of Charles Williams, 1930-1935*. Edited by Jared C. Lobdell. Jefferson, NC and London: McFarland, 2003.

—. "Crime: The Real Thing and the Romantic." *Westminster Gazette* (4 June 1930). In *The Detective Fiction Reviews of Charles Williams, 1930-1935*. Edited by Jared C. Lobdell. Jefferson, NC and London: McFarland, 2003.

Census

1891 English Census. Class RG12. Piece 583. Folio 80. Page 13. GSU roll 6095693.

Letters

Anthony Gilbert to Margaret Cole, 19 April 1948. Dorothy L. Sayers Papers. Marion E. Wade Center. Wheaton College. Wheaton, Illinois.

Dorothy L. Sayers to Anthony Gilbert, 22 September 1952. Dorothy L. Sayers Papers. Marion E. Wade Center. Wheaton College. Wheaton, Illinois.

Edward Aubrey-Fletcher to Curtis J. Evans, 28 November 2004. Email in possession of author.

Henry Wade to Dorothy L. Sayers, 4 May 1932, 5 March 1940, 31 October 1949, 16 March 1950. Dorothy L. Sayers Papers. Marion E. Wade Center. Wheaton College. Wheaton, Illinois.

Margaret Cole to Dorothy L. Sayers, 7 June 1939, 21 September 1939, 15 April 1948. Dorothy L. Sayers Papers. Marion E. Wade Center. Wheaton College. Wheaton, Illinois.

Catalogue, Newspapers and Journals

*The Book Collector's Quarterly* 5 (Jan.-Mar. 1935)

*Catalogue of Printed Books and a Few Manuscripts*. London: Sotheby, 1935

*Land & Liberty* 44 (February 1937)

*Lilliput* 16 (March 1945)

*New Statesman and Nation* 1 June 1935, 14 December 1935, 9 January 1937, 29 January 1938, 23 December 1939, 10 August 1940

(London) *Independent*, 31 July 1994

(London) *Daily Herald*, 5 March 1931, 16 March 1933, 17 March 1935

*Manchester Guardian*, 13 August 1940

*Saturday Review*, 12 June 1937

*Spectator* 146 (May 1931)

*Sunday Times*, 17 September 1933, 5 November 1933, 22 July 1934, 3 November 1935, 1 December 1935, 7 November 1937, 6 December 1937

*Sydney Morning Herald*, 6 January 1940

*Times Literary Supplement*, 3 August 1933, 26 October 1933, 7 December 1940

## SECONDARY SOURCES

### Books and Articles

Barzun, Jacques and Wendell Hertig Taylor. *A Catalogue of Crime*. New York: Harper & Row, 1971.

—. *A Catalogue of Crime*. New York: Harper & Row, 1989.

Beckett, Francis. *Stalin's British Victims*. Stroud, Gloucestershire, UK: Sutton, 2004.

Berlin, Isaiah. *Letters 1928-1946*. Edited by Henry Hardy. Cambridge and New York: Cambridge University Press, 2004.

Cannadine, David. *The Decline and Fall of the British Aristocracy*. 1990. Reprint. New York: Vintage, 1999.

Cooper, John. "Henry Wade's Police Constable John Bragg." *CADS Crime and Detective Stories* 69 (January 2015), 17-20.

Craig, Patricia and Mary Cadogan. *The Lady Investigates: Women Detectives and Spies in Fiction*. New York: St. Martin's Press, 1981.

Evans, Curtis. "By G. D. H *AND* Margaret Cole? Who Wrote What in the Coles' Crime Fiction Corpus." *CADS Crime and Detective Stories* 63 (July 2012): 19-22.

—. *Masters of the Humdrum Mystery: Cecil John Charles Street, Freeman Wills Crofts, Alfred Walter Stewart and the British Detective Novel, 1920-1961*. Jefferson, NC and London: McFarland, 2012.

Gilbert, Michael. Introduction to Henry Wade, *Lonely Magdalen* (1940). London: Hodder and Stoughton, 1965.

Gindin, James and Joan Gindin. "Henry Wade (Henry Lancelot Aubrey-Fletcher)." In *Dictionary of Literary Biography*. Volume 77. *British Mystery Writers, 1920-1939*. Edited by Bernard Benstock and Thomas F. Staley. Farmington Hills, MI: Cengage Gale, 1988.

Keating, H. R. F. *The Bedside Companion Book to Crime*. New York and London: Mysterious Press, 1989.

Knight, Stephen. *Crime Fiction, 1800-2000: Detection, Death, Diversity*. New York: Palgrave Macmillan, 2004.

McDorman, Kathryne S. "Roderick Alleyn and the New Professionals." In *Ngaio Marsh: The Woman and Her Work*. Edited by B. J. Rahn. Metuchen, N. J. and London: Scarecrow Press, 1995.

Morgan, Kevin and Gidon Cohen. "Rose Cohen." *Dictionary of Labour Biography*. Volume 11. London: Palgrave, 2003.

Panayi, Panikos. "The Destruction of the German Communities in Britain during the First World War." In *Germans in Britain since 1500*. Edited by Panikos Panayi. London and Rio Grande, OH: The Hambledon Press, 1996.

Ritchie, J. M. "German Refugees from Nazism." In *Germans in Britain since 1500*. Edited by Panikos Panayi. London and Rio Grande, OH: Hambledon Press, 1996.

Shibuk, Charles. "Henry Wade." In *The Mystery Writer's Art*. Edited by Francis M. Nevins, Jr. Bowling Green, OH: Popular Press, 1970.

Strong, Leah A. "Henry Wade's John Poole." In *Cops and Constables: American and British Fictional Policemen*. Edited by George N. Dove and Earl F. Bargainnier. Bowling Green, OH: Popular Press, 1986.

Symons, Julian. *Bloody Murder: From the Detective Story to the Crime Novel*. 1972. Third Revised Edition. New York and Tokyo: Mysterious Press, 1992.

Thomson, H. Douglas. *Masters of Mystery: A Study of the Detective Story*. London: Collins, 1931.
Vernon, Betty D. *Margaret Cole 1893-1980: A Political Biography*. London: Croom Helm, 1986.
Warner, Marina. Introduction to Naomi Mitchison's *The Fourth Pig* (1936). Princeton, NJ: Princeton University Press, 2014.

WEBSITES

"Buckinghamshire Lieutenancy, Permanent Lieutenants for Buckinghamshire, Major Sir Henry Lancelot Aubrey-Fletcher Bt. CVO DSO (1887-1969), Lieutenant 1954-1961." At: www.buckscc.gov.uk/lieutenancy/permanent_ lieutenants/major_sir_henry_lancelot.html.

"Buckinghamshire Town & Village Photos." At: www.countyviews.com/bucks/index.htm
www.chiltonhouse.co.uk

Edwards, Martin. "Harcourt and Henry Wade" (10 January 2008). *Do You Write under Your Own Name?* At: doyouwriteunderyourownname.blogspot.com/2008/01/harcourt-and-henry wade.html

"George Wade." *Draw Paint Sculpt*. At: www.drawpaintsculpt.com/artist-biographies/george-wade

*The Peerage: A Genealogical Survey of the Peerage of Britain as well as the Royal Families of Europe* (www.thepeerage.com).

*R. C. Singleton's Diary (1847): Diary of a Victorian Education Reformer*. At: singletonsdiary.wordpress.com/2009/03/04/nugent-wade

# INDEX

Abraham, Nancy (Cole) 199, 199n97
Abraham, Will 199, 199n97
*The Affair at Aliquid* 125, 144-147, 159, 197
Alleyn, Roderick 41-42
Allingham, Margery 57, 148, 220
*Arandora Star* 182, 184
*At Bertram's Hotel* 128
Aubrey-Fletcher, Edward 19, 21, 94
Aubrey-Fletcher, Henry (4th Baronet of Clea) 15
Aubrey-Fletcher, Henry Egerton (8th Baronet of Clea) 20, 113
Aubrey-Fletcher, Henry Lancelot (6th Baronet of Clea) (Henry Wade): and Chilton House 17, 20, 21, 103; and crime novel 8, 9, 15, 34, 52, 56, 61-63, 83-84, 92; and development of genteel police detective 57-58; and Eton/Oxford 17, 17n5; and hunting 19-20; and inverted mystery 69-70; and military service 18; and *noblesse oblige* 105-110; and police procedural 8, 9, 15, 22, 70-76, 100; and social realism 84-88; civic service of 18; correspondence with Dorothy L. Sayers 101-104; critical praise for 21, 22, 44-45, 61-62, 66-67, 69, 83, 98, 109; critique of conservatism 39-40, 78-79, 86, 88; critique of modernity 21, 34, 41; distinguished from "Humdrum" detective novelists 8, 14, 21, 103, 112; family background and family life of 13, 15-21; on abrogation of death penalty 92-93; on anti-Semitism 9, 24, 34-37, 36-37n29, 38-39, 38-39n31; on British Labour party 9, 18, 92-97 passim, 104; on civic and police corruption 9, 30-32, 50-51, 67-69, 76, 84, 86-87, 87n91; on decline of gentry 9, 20, 47-50, 50n43, 51-53, 56, 59-60, 65-66, 75-83, 88-92, 90n95, 97-98, 100, 105-107, 112-113; on impact of WW1 on English life 9, 35, 37n29, 40, 49-50, 56, 63-64, 75-

76, 106, 109; on impact of WW2 on English life 9, 89-92, 95, 107; on taxes and austerity 18, 20, 92-94, 96-97; portrayal of women in his fiction 28-30, 56-57; post-WW2 conservatism of 93; sardonic edge in his fiction 25-26, 87n91, 98, 112; sexuality in his fiction 101, 111-112 *see also* individual book and story titles

Aubrey-Fletcher, Lancelot (5th Baronet of Clea) 15, 16

Aubrey-Fletcher, Mary Augusta (Chilton) 18

Baldwin, Stanley 176, 176n65

Barnes, Ronald Gorell (3rd Baron Gorell) 13-14n1

Bartlett, Adelaide 200

Bartlett, Edwin 200

Barzun, Jacques 14, 22, 44, 63, 73, 98, 99, 168

*Be Kind to the Killer* 92-93

Bentley, E. C. 130

Bevan, Aneurin "Nye" 104n114

Bicester Hunt 19

*Big Business Murder* 125, 148

Blake, Nicholas 218, 220

Blake, William 214, 215

Blatchington, Everard 124, 126n12, 127, 141-142, 154-155, 166, 168, 170-175, 173n63, 192, 202, 221n119

*The Blatchington Tangle* 124, 139-141, 155, 168, 170, 197, 221

*Bloody Murder* 7, 10

Boucher, Anthony 14, 21, 66, 96 98, 99

Bragg, John 71, 71n67, 85-87 passim

Brand, Christianna 14n1; conflicts with Margaret Cole in Detection Club 194, 195, 195n92, 199

"Bring Me an Axe and Spade" 214-215

*The Brooklyn Murders* 10, 117, 119-121, 124, 127, 199

*The Brothers Sackville* 125, 147, 148-153, 155, 162, 179n70, 180, 191, 197, 221

*Burglars in Bucks* 125, 155, 163-164, 166-168, 170, 173, 192, 221

*The Burning Court* 221

*Bury Him Darkly* 70-71, 72n68

*Busman's Honeymoon* 103

Cambridge 53, 55, 154, 166, 179, 180, 188, 190

"The Camden Town Fire" 204

Cannadine, David 47-48, 50n43, 90n95

"The Case of Adelaide Bartlett" 200

*A Catalogue of Crime* 22, 27, 30, 44, 61, 63, 73, 83, 119, 149, 168, 185

Chesterton, G. K. 8n2, 68, 118, 181

*The Chianti Flask* 218

Chilton, Reverend Robert William 18

Christie, Agatha 8n2, 14n1, 47, 92, 112, 118, 128n13, 139, 168, 181, 207, 210, 218

Crispin, Edmund 104

Cobbett, William 213
Cohen, Rose 184n78
Cole, G. D. H. (Douglas) and Margaret: and anti-Semitism 133, 142, 172, 175, 177-178, 187, 197-199, 198n95; and commercial development and modern housing 187, 202-203; and cosmetics use 187, 199; and Detection Club 118, 194-197, 211; and development of police sleuths and the police procedural novel 120-123, 156, 163, 169, 172; and Oxford 115, 135, 137, 153-154, 179-180, 185, 186n79, 187, 198n95, 204-205; and Rose Cohen 184n78; and social realism 169-172; as farceurs 10, 116, 139-141, 143-147, 150-152, 161-162, 221-222; attitude toward landladies and servants 10, 164, 191, 193-194; critical praise for 149, 167, 176, 180-181; condemnation of Red Scare and English xenophobia 130-133, 182n75, 182-184, 187; criticism of conservatism of English detective fiction and reviewers 186-187; disdain for bourgeoisie 169, 176-180, 192-193; disdain for thriller fiction typified by Edgar Wallace 208-211; distinguished from "Humdrum" detective novelists 8-10, 10n4, 220; Douglas Cole's ruralphilia 203; Douglas Cole's sexism, 138, 159; Douglas Cole's Trollopian narration 127-128, 186n79; family background and family life 187-191, 212n109; homosociality/homosexuality concerning Douglas Cole and his fiction 136-139; indifference to Stalin's purges 184n78; individual authorship of novels 123-127, 125-126n12; influence of Freeman Wills Crofts 119-120; Margaret Cole's alleged affair with Dick Mitchison 200-201, 201n98; Margaret Cole's dislike of father 188-190, 212n109; Margaret Cole's portrayal of weak male characters and strong female characters 165-166, 168-169, 200; Margaret Cole's imperiousness and snobbishness 179-180, 192, 194-197; Margaret Cole on Adelaide Bartlett murder case 200; negative portrayal of capitalism 128-130, 134-135, 141, 148, 152-153, 156-161, 164-165, 167, 170-171, 206-207; negative portrayal of Freudian psychology 145, 187, 201-202; negative portrayal of religion 144-145, 147, 150, 155, 187, 197; political bias in detective fiction 185-186, 186n79; portrayal of racism 204-205; portrayal of sexuality 146, 159, 165, 174, 199-200; sympathy toward working class 164-165, 170-171, 185-186, 186n79, 205-207; view

of Americans 142, 199n97; view of aristocracy and gentry 141-142, 147-148, 167-168, 177, 197, 213-214; view of Cockneys 169; view of colonialism 142, 144-145, 187; view of detective fiction 117-118, 217-220; view of progressive and working class education 172-174, 187, 191, 202 *see also* individual book and story titles

Cole, Humphrey 124

Connington, J. J. *see* Stewart, Alfred Walter

*Constable, Guard Thyself!* 66-69

Constance Kent murder case 219

Cooper, John 71n67, 88

*Corpse in Canonicals* 125, 143, 162

"Cotton Wool and Cutlets" 71n67

*Counterpoint Murder* 10, 10n4, 125, 163, 180-182, 220

country houses and country house mystery 13, 20, 24, 53, 63, 73, 74, 75, 90n95, 108, 139-140, 142, 155, 161, 166-168

Cox, Anthony Berkeley (Anthony Berkeley/Francis Iles) 14, 66-69 passim, 148, 220

Creasey, John 101

Crime Queens 42n34, 58, 112, 216

crime novel 8, 9, 14, 15, 61, 83, 84, 103, 112, 122, 180, 218

Crofts, Freeman Wills 7, 8n2, 10, 14, 21, 24-28 passim, 38n31, 39n31, 42, 76, 92, 100, 112, 119, 121, 122, 127, 133n20, 156, 160, 181, 217, 218

Cuff, Sergeant 219-220

Curran, John 118n4

Dalgliesh, Adam 41

*Dead Man's Watch* 125, 126n12, 127, 168-169, 192, 193, 194, 199, 200, 201, 207n104, 216

*Death in High Heels* 221

*Death in the Quarry* 125, 147n37, 155, 172, 218, 221n19

"Death in the Tankard" 211, 212

*Death of a Bride* 118, 126n12, 127, 203, 215-216

*The Death of a Millionaire* 117, 119, 124, 127-137, 139, 140, 142, 148, 162, 186n79, 197, 221

*Death of a Star* 125, 155, 163, 169-172, 197, 198, 199

*Death of an Expert Witness* 174

*The Departed* 68

Detection Club 8n2, 14n1, 45, 101, 104, 118, 194, 195, 195n92, 196, 200

*Diabolic Candelabra* 221

Dickens, Charles 127, 188

*Diplomat's Folly* 20-21, 89-92, 94, 96, 104, 112

"The Disappearance of Philip Mansfield" 207

*Disgrace to the College* 125, 147, 153-155, 163, 197

*Dr. Tancred Begins* 125, 126n12, 148

# THE SPECTRUM OF ENGLISH MURDER 241

Domesday Book 20
*Double Blackmail* 125, 155, 197
Doyle, Arthur Conan 104
*The Duke of York's Steps* 34-36, 39, 40-41, 43, 45, 96, 98, 111
"Duello" 40
Dupin, C. Auguste 220
*A Dying Fall* 98-100, 111, 112

Edwards, Martin 14, 61
Elphinstone, Mountstuart 16
*End of an Ancient Mariner* 125, 139, 143, 148, 162
*The End of the House of Alard* 65
Eton 21
*The Eustace Diamonds* 167

Faide, Chief Constable 53, 80-83, 107-108
Fairford, Tom 125, 152-153, 155, 162
First Editions Club 19
Fletcher, Henry 15
*The Floating Admiral* 195n92
*Flowers for the Judge* 221
Foot, Michael 139
Freeman, R. Austin 217
French, Emily 122
French, Joseph 38n31, 42, 121, 122, 160
Freudianism 145, 187, 201

Gable, Clark 103
Gilbert, Anthony 196
Gilbert, Michael 14, 22, 71, 73, 104
"Glass" 211-212

*Gold Was Our Grave* 98
Gould, Gerald 45
"The Grand Old Duke of York" 111n122
*The Great Southern Mystery* 125, 148, 194n90, 197-198, 198n95, 199
Greenberg, Martin H. 216
*Greek Tragedy* 125, 126n12, 163, 172, 176-180, 182, 185, 192, 205
*Growing up into Revolution* 115, 117-118, 124, 126n12, 188, 212n109
Guinness, Alec 69
Gulliver, George 156, 160-161

*The Hanging Captain* 44, 60-61, 106
Hardy, Thomas 65
Hare, Cyril 104
*Have His Carcase* 101-104
Haycraft, Howard 163
*Heir Presumptive* 19, 21, 69-70, 112
Hendon Police College 160
*Here Comes the Copper* 70, 85, 87
*The High Sheriff* 18, 19, 22, 53, 77-83, 84, 105, 107, 112
Hill, Reginald 63
Hitler, Adolf 89, 172, 175, 183
Hogarth Press 191
Holmes, Sherlock 42
Houseman, A. E. 190
Humdrum School of Detective Fiction 7-11, 14, 21, 103, 112, 116, 119, 120, 121, 130, 220

Iles, Francis *see* Cox, Anthony Berkeley
"In a Telephone Cabinet" 204, 214
Innes, Michael 17n5, 116, 119n5, 221
"The International Socialist" 165, 205
"The Invisible Man" 68

James, Henry 42
James, P. D. 7, 41, 57, 63, 112, 174, 216
Japp, Inspector 219
"Jealous Gun" 107-108
Johnson, Samuel 185

Kaye-Smith, Shelia 65
Kennedy, Milward 69, 149, 176
Kenney, Rowland 195n92
*Kind Hearts and Coronets* 69
*Knife in the Dark* 125, 126n12, 163, 172, 182-184, 184n78, 211, 216
Knight, Stephen 70
Knox, Ronald 10, 84, 112, 119n5

*Last Will and Testament* 125, 148
Laval, Pierre 90
Lawrence, D. H. 75
"A Lesson in Crime" (short story) 143n32, 208-210
*A Lesson in Crime* (short story collection) 126n12, 204, 208,
Lestrade, Inspector 219
*The Life of G. D. H Cole* 115, 124, 126n12
*The Litmore Snatch* 22, 98, 100-101
*Lonely Magdalen* 11, 22, 70-77, 88, 95, 111, 112

*Lord Peter Views the Body* 207
Lott, Inspector Herbert 43, 44, 47, 49-51 passim, 60-61 passim
Lowndes, Marie Belloc 218

MacDonald, Ramsay 132
*Malice Aforethought* 69
*The Man from the River* 125, 139, 142-143, 162
Marple, Jane 210
Marsh, Ngaio 41-42, 42n34, 57, 220
*Masters of the "Humdrum" Mystery* 7, 7n1, 11,
*Masters of Mystery* 122
"A Matter of Luck" 35, 37-38, 38n31
*The Mayor of Casterbridge* 65
*The Missing Aunt* 125, 139n27, 155, 162, 185, 186n79
"The Missing Baronet" 207
*The Missing Partners* 26-33, 41, 45, 111
"The Missing Undergraduate" 17n5
*Mist on the Saltings* 16, 18, 39, 61-66, 73, 103, 111, 112, 221
Mitchell, Gladys 119n5
Mitchison, Baron Gilbert Richard ("Dick") 200, 201n98
Mitchison, Naomi 200
*The Moonstone* 218-220
Morris, William 203
"The Mother of the Detective" 208, 210-211, 216
*Mrs. Warrender's Profession* 126n12, 204, 211, 216
*The Murder at Crome House* 125, 138, 164, 207

*Murder at the Munition Works* 125, 155-161, 163, 176, 185, 203, 222
*The Murder at the Vicarage* 221
"Murder in Church" 123n10, 187, 211-212
*Murder on the Orient Express* 221
*The Murders in Praed Street* 221

*New Graves at Great Norne* 18, 88-89
*The Nine Tailors* 221
*No Friendly Drop* 8, 21, 22, 53-60, 63, 73, 80, 87n91, 96, 103, 107, 111, 112

*Off with Her Head!* 125, 155, 162
*Oliver Twist* 188
Orde-Powlett, Nigel Amyas (6th Baron Bolton) 13-14n1
Oxford 17, 17n5, 18, 21, 27, 42, 43, 115, 124, 135, 137, 153, 179, 180, 185, 186n79, 187, 198n95, 204-205
Oxford Movement 16
"The Oxford Mystery" 204-205
Oxford University Dramatic Society 17, 43

Partridge, Ralph 148, 149, 176, 185
"Payment in Full" 110
Pippett, Roger 193, 194n90
Poe, Edgar Allan 220
police procedural novel 8, 9, 15, 22, 70, 71, 86, 98, 100, 112, 156, 163, 169, 172, 181
*Policeman's Lot* 17n5, 70, 107

*Poison in the Garden Suburb* 125, 126n12, 165-166, 200, 203, 205, 216
Poole, Inspector John 17n5, 34, 37, 39-44 passim, 53-55 passim, 57-61 passim, 67-68, 71, 74-76 passim, 80, 95, 96, 98
Postgate, John Percival 188-190, 211, 212n109
Postgate, Raymond 184n78, 187, 212n109
Prendergast, Michael 124-125, 139, 142, 155, 162, 203-204, 208, 211-212
"A Present from the Empire" 213
Pronzini, Bill 216
Proust, Marcel 143
Punshon, E. R. 185

Queen, Ellery (author) 46, 204
Queen, Ellery (detective) 120n6
*A Question of Proof* 218, 221

Read, Herbert 83
*Released for Death* 77, 84-88, 93, 111
Rendell, Ruth 32n24, 63, 163, 216
"The Robbery at Bowden" 206-207, 207n104
*Romeo and Juliet* 56
Rooney, Mickey 103

*St. Peter's Finger* 221
Sayers, Dorothy L. 8n2, 9, 14, 17, 17n5, 57, 61, 66, 67, 69, 105, 111, 112, 118, 148, 167, 181, 207, 219, 220; correspondence with

Henry Lancelot Aubrey-Fletcher 101-104, 104n115; conflicts with Margaret Cole in Detection Club 195-197; criticism of the Coles' *The Affair at Alquid* 147, 147n37

*Scandal at School* 125, 155, 163, 172, 174-176, 174n64, 180, 202, 221

Scorsese, Martin 68

*The Secret of Chimneys* 139, 168

Shakespeare, William 17, 29, 30n19, 56

Shibuk, Charles 22, 44, 61, 62n57, 83, 96, 99, 108

*Shroud for a Nightingale* 174

Silver, Maud 210

*Sir John Magill's Last Journey* 221

*The Six Queer Things* 119n5

*Snobbery with Violence* 7

"Song: My silks and fine array" 214-215

Spanish Civil War 119n5, 179

Sprigg, Christopher St. John 118-119n5

Stalin, Josef 119n5, 176n65, 184n78

Stewart, Alfred Walter (J. J. Connington) 7, 8n2, 120, 217

Street, Cecil John Charles (John Rhode/Miles Burton) 7, 8n2, 18, 21, 73, 100, 112, 120, 148, 160, 203, 214, 217, 218, 222

Strong, Leah A. 105

"Superintendent Wilson's Holiday" (short story) 204

*Superintendent Wilson's Holiday* (short story collection) 126n12, 204-207

*Surfeit of Lampreys* 221

Symons, A. J. A. 19

Symons, Julian 7, 10, 14, 19, 30, 51, 88, 115, 116, 222

*Talking about Detective Fiction* 7

Taylor, Wendell Hertig 22, 63, 73, 168

Tennyson, Alfred Lord 30n19

"The Tenth Round" 108-110

"These Artists!" 16, 87

Third Reform Act 48

*The Thirteen Problems* 207

Thomson, Sir Basil 130-131, 133, 133n20

Thomson, H. Douglas 122

Thorndyke, Dr. John 219

*The Three Coffins* 221

"The Three Keys" 35, 37

"Too Clever by Half" 153

*Too Soon to Die* 18, 20, 92-98, 12

*Toper's End* 124, 125, 139n27, 143, 155, 161-162, 182, 191, 197

"The Toys of Death" 200, 216

*Trent's Last Case* 130

Trollope, Anthony 128, 147, 167, 186n79

Van Dine, S. S. 84, 112

Vane, Harriet 102, 103

*The Verdict of You All* 22-26, 34, 41, 45, 98

Vernon, Betty 124

*A Very British Murder* 7

von Mises, Ludwig 115, 116n1

Wade, Edward 16
Wade, Henry *see* Aubrey-Fletcher, Henry Lancelot
Wade, Nugent 16
Wallace, Edgar 143, 143n32, 208-210
Warrender, James 211
Warrender, Mrs. 125, 126n12, 163, 183, 211, 215, 216
Watson, Colin 7, 88
Watson, John H. 142, 203
Webb, Mary 42
Weizmann, Chaim Azriel 175, 176n65
Wentworth, Patricia 210
Wilkes, John 213
William the Conqueror 20
Williams, Charles 68, 163, 167
Wilson, Henry 119, 124-127 129-131, 133, 139-140, 139n27, 142-143, 155-162, 165-166, 168-169, 172, 181-182, 202-209, 211-214, 217; and Joseph French 121-123
Wilson, Mrs. Henry 121-122
*Wilson and Some Others* 126n12, 204, 211, 213
Wimsey, Lord Peter 102
*The Winter's Tale* 43
Wodehouse, P. G. 144, 186n79
Woolf, Leonard 191
Woolf, Virginia 191
Worsley, Lucy 7
Wycombe Abbey 179

"Ye Olde Englysshe Christmasse; or, Detection in the Eighteenth Century" ("Crime at Eslington Hall") 213-214
*The Yeoman of the Guard* 65

## ABOUT THE AUTHOR

CURTIS EVANS, PH.D. is the author of *The Conquest of Labor: Daniel Pratt and Southern Industrialization* (LSU Press, 2001), winner of the Bennett H. Wall Award from the Southern Historical Association, *Masters of the "Humdrum" Mystery: Cecil John Charles Street, Freeman Wills Crofts, Alfred Walter Stewart and the British Detective Novel, 1920-1961* (McFarland, 2012) and *Clues and Corpses: The Detective Fiction and Mystery Criticism of Todd Downing* (Coachwhip, 2013), as well as the editor of and a contributor to *Mysteries Unlocked: Essays in Honor of Douglas G. Greene* (McFarland, 2014). He has written extensively about crime and mystery fiction for *CADS: Crime and Detective Stories*, *Mystery*File* and at his own blog, *The Passing Tramp* (thepassingtramp.blogspot.com), which Michael Dirda in the *Washington Post* has deemed a "valuable critical guide" for anyone interested in classic detective fiction and author Sarah Weinman at her Tumblr site *Off on a Tangent* has called one of the "great blogs for vintage crime fiction."

# Coachwhip Publications
## Coachwhipbooks.com

**CLUES AND CORPSES**
The Detective Fiction and
Mystery Criticism of Todd Downing
CURTIS EVANS

*Clues and Corpses*, by Curtis Evans
ISBN 978-1-61646-145-4

# COACHWHIP PUBLICATIONS
## NOW AVAILABLE

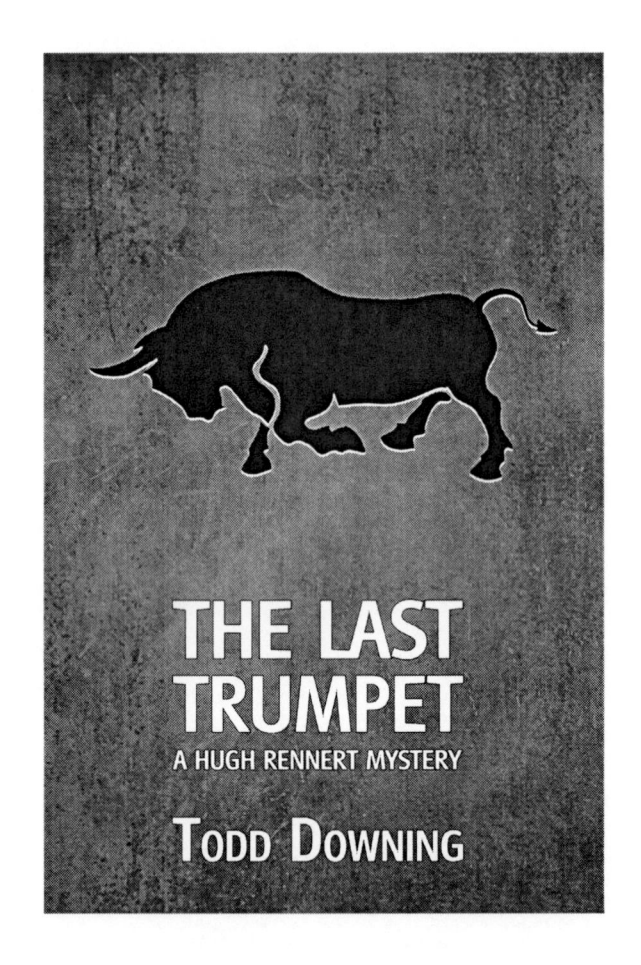

*The Last Trumpet*, by Todd Downing
Introduction by Curtis Evans
ISBN 978-1-61646-152-2

## Coachwhip Publications
### CoachwhipBooks.com

**VULTURES IN THE SKY**
A HUGH RENNERT MYSTERY
**TODD DOWNING**

*Vultures in the Sky,* by Todd Downing
Introduction by Curtis Evans
ISBN 978-1-61646-149-2

## Coachwhip Publications

### Now Available

*Murder in Style*, by Emma Lou Fetta
Introduction by Curtis Evans
ISBN 978-1-61646-232-1

# Coachwhip Publications
## CoachwhipBooks.com

### MURDER OF
### THE HONEST BROKER

### WILLOUGHBY SHARP

*Murder of the Honest Broker,* by Willoughby Sharp
Introduction by Curtis Evans
ISBN 978-1-61646-211-6

## Coachwhip Publications

### Now Available

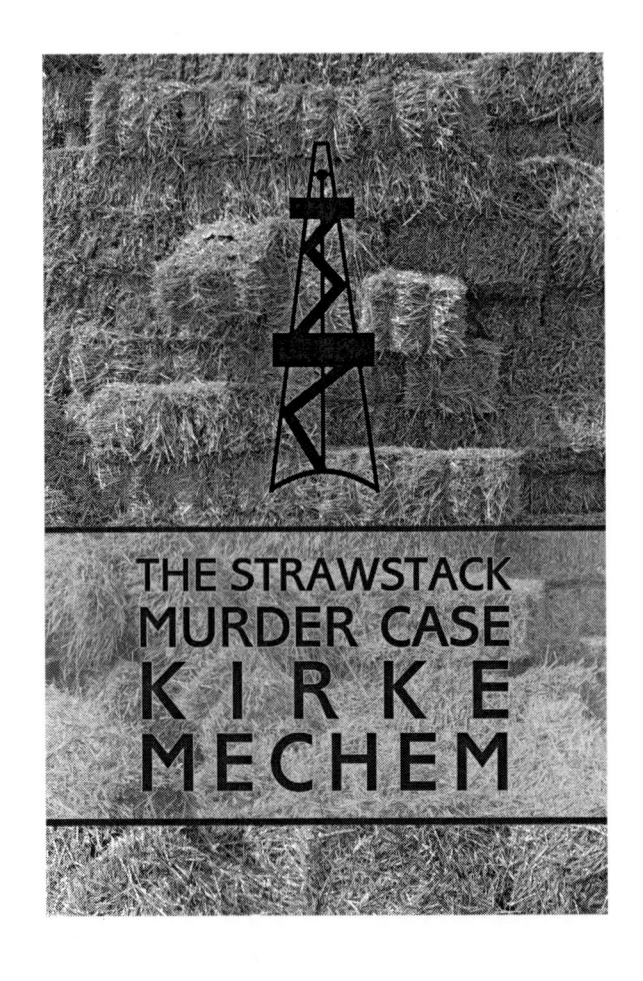

*The Strawstack Murder Case*, by Kirke Mechem
Introduction by Curtis Evans
ISBN 978-1-61646-179-9

# Coachwhip Publications
## CoachwhipBooks.com

**THERE IS NO RETURN**
THE ADELAIDE ADAMS MYSTERIES
ANITA BLACKMON

*There is No Return*, by Anita Blackmon
Introduction by Curtis Evans
ISBN 978-1-61646-223-9